Store Wars

Store Wars

The Battle for Mindspace and Shelfspace

JUDITH CORSTJENS
ARROW

and

MARCEL CORSTJENS
INSEAD

JOHN WILEY & SONS
Chichester · New York · Brisbane · Toronto · Singapore

Baffins Lane, Chichester,
West Sussex PO19 1UD, England

Telephone (+44) 1243 779777

Reprinted March 1995

Other Wiley Editorial Offices

John Wiley & Sons, Inc., 605 Third Avenue,
New York, NY 10158-0012, USA

Jacaranda Wiley Ltd, 33 Park Road, Milton,
Queensland 4064, Australia

John Wiley & Sons (Canada) Ltd, 22 Worcester Road,
Rexdale, Ontario M9W 1L1, Canada

John Wiley & Sons (SEA) Pte Ltd, 37 Jalan Pemimpin #05-04,
Block B, Union Industrial Building, Singapore 2057

Library of Congress Cataloging-in-Publication Data

Corstjens, Judy.
Store wars : the battle for mindspace and shelfspace / Judith
Corstjens and Marcel Corstjens.
p. cm.
Includes bibliographical references and index.
ISBN 0-471-95081-5
1. Marketing. 2. Consumer goods—Marketing. I. Corstjens,
Marcel. II. Title.
HF5415.122.C67 1995 94–22413
658.8—dc20 CIP

British Library Cataloguing in Publication Data

A catalogue record for this book is available from the British Library

ISBN 0-471-95081-5

Typeset in 11/13pt Palatino by Dobbie Typesetting Ltd, Tavistock, Devon
Printed and bound in Great Britain by
Biddles Ltd, Guildford and King's Lynn

To: Olivier and Thomas

Contents

Acknowledgements

Many people, mostly our students, course participants and consulting clients, have contributed directly or indirectly to the ideas pulled together in this book. We have met with considerable openness, and willingness to invest time and effort simply for the satisfaction of kicking around ideas. In particular we benefited from stimulating discussions with Bob Albrecht, Dick Bell, Christian Couvreux, Colin James, Les Pugh, Paul Stoneham, and John Taylor. We would also like to thank Norma Boultwood and Isabelle Rodriguez for their practical help.

Our ambition has been to give a coherent and thought-provoking explanation of the observed behaviour in the industry. We have tried to see the issues from both retailer and manufacturer perspectives and we hope our hypotheses will mesh with the reader's own experiences to suggest new approaches in their jobs or studies. Where possible our views are documented by real-world examples and published research, but much is speculative and offered as a contribution to furthering understanding.

Introduction

Consumer goods companies virtually invented modern marketing with their brands, their advertising and their consumer research. Fast moving consumer goods (FMCG) marketing is probably still the most sophisticated practised by any industry, with companies such as Procter & Gamble and Unilever often held to be 'universities of marketing'. When industrial, retail or service companies want to reinforce their marketing orientation, they often recruit from FMCG manufacturers.

The downside of being in the vanguard of a movement means continually having to invent the next step. FMCG manufacturers are finding that even as classic marketing practice is being adopted by other industries it is becoming less effective in their own, particularly for smaller brands and new products.

It is clear that major changes are taking place in the selling of FMCGs. This book is about taking the next step to evolve FMCG marketing in face of the changes and challenges that are currently buffeting consumer goods companies.

Marketing orientation originally meant understanding the varied wants of consumers (segmentation) and directing company resources to producing what they wanted (see Fig. I.1).

Consumers were grouped into market 'segments'. These segments suggested more appropriate brand offerings, proposed at a variety of price levels. Advertising (where possible, on TV) allowed manufacturers to build a bridge to the consumer, and so dictate to retailers what products to stock.

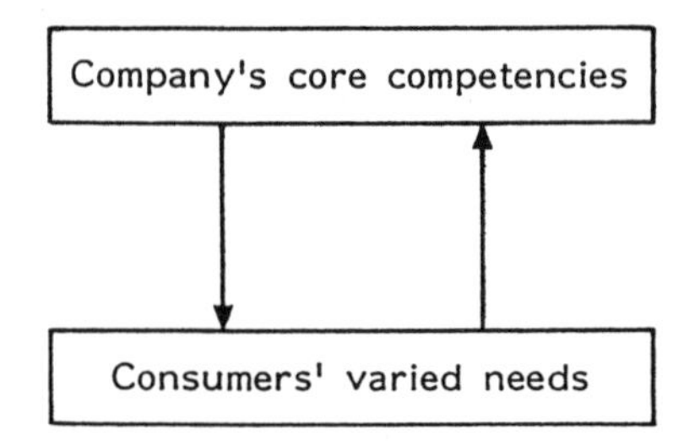

Figure I.1 *The marketing concept*

Brands satisfying varied wants were a brilliant idea for profitable business. Unfortunately, good brands attracted imitators and when similar brands were marketed side by side, profits eroded. The marketing concept went through its first rebirth to emerge as strategic marketing. Simply 'serving consumer needs' was no longer enough, the firm needed to create differential advantage. Strategic marketers focus on the way consumers perceive and evaluate competing brands. They look at their competitors (competitive analysis and benchmarking) and ask how their firm can satisfy (some) consumer needs *better* than the competitors. Differential advantage means finding a benefit based on some unique company resource (core competence) that is difficult for competitors to copy (see Fig I.2).

In strategic marketing, a manufacturer's competitors are other manufacturers. Strategies focus on differentiating brands from each other. 'Niche', 'fighting' and 'flanking' brands, brand equity and brand extensions are typical strategic marketing concepts.

But strategic marketing is no more a blueprint for perpetual growth and profits than the original marketing concept. Segmenting, sub-segmenting, brand building and brand

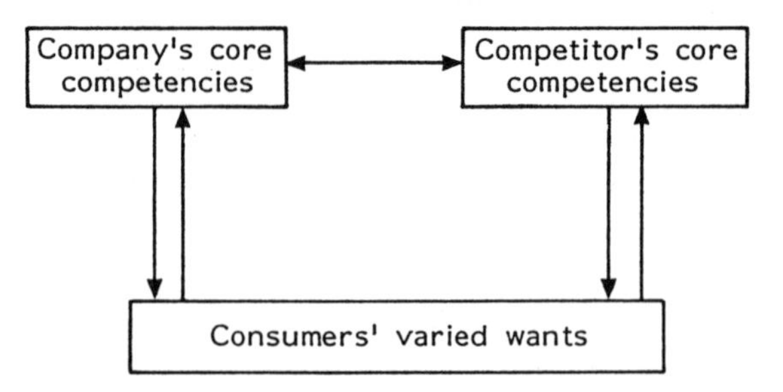

Figure I.2 *Stage 2: Strategic marketing*

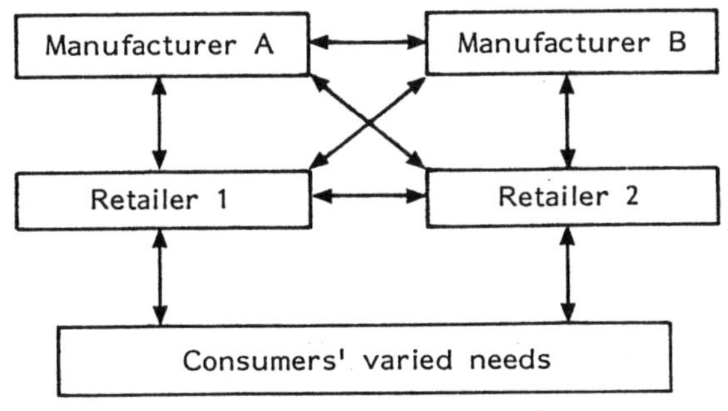

Figure I.3 *Stage 3: Matrix marketing*

proliferation are processes with limits. The process has to stop somewhere, before each consumer has his own ideal brand with his own name on it. In the mid 1980s the Persil brand covered three lines; ten years on the range (UK) has 41 products and varieties: will there be 80 a decade further on?[1]

At the same time, retailers have stepped into the relationship between producer and consumer, and have started to offer an alternative source of reassurance for the consumer. In this situation, any marketing theory based on the idea of a direct relationship between manufacturer and consumer via brands is under attack. FMCG marketing has to be rethought on the basis that retailers are players with objectives and strategies that interfere with those of manufacturers. The marketing appropriate to this changed situation is called matrix marketing (see Fig. I.3).

The rise in distributor power is pushing consumer marketing into another phase of turbulence, destined to re-shape marketing a second time. Marketing meant understanding the desires of consumers. Strategic marketing meant also understanding the strategies of competitors, and one's own core competencies. Matrix marketing adds to these skills the need for the manufacturer to understand the operations of retailers.

The book is divided into three parts. The first looks at the way marketing of FMCG goods has evolved from the point of view of manufacturers. Readers familiar with current FMCG marketing might wish to skim read Part I and concentrate their attention on Parts II and III. The second part takes the perspective of the retail side of the industry and explores the present and future aspiration and business strategies of the retailer. The last part of the book shows how manufacturers and retailers compete for profits in the industry. We look at the areas of co-operation and conflict, and discuss competitive and co-operative opportunities.

At the risk of oversimplifying and anticipating the arguments presented in the rest of the book, we summarise our key ideas and tentative conclusions below. Squashing a couple of hundred pages into just a few provides clarity and crudity in equal measure—we hope that the reader will be interested enough by these 'sound-bites' to read further.

KEY IDEAS IN THIS BOOK

The central theme of this book is that FMCG marketing has become a struggle between manufacturers and retailers for control of *mindspace* and *shelfspace*; and that in the final analysis, mindspace will be the decisive resource. Where once the manufacturer dominated on both, the retailer is now grabbing back shelfspace and making inroads in mindspace. Co-operation between retailers and manufacturers is possible in some areas, but fundamentally their interests conflict. Both are seeking to control the same scarce resources: mindspace and shelfspace. Partnership, if it is to be called that, needs to be sought from a position of strength: affecting the balance of power is a major aim of marketing strategy, for both retailers and manufacturers.

Part I: Reaching the Limits of Market Orientation

By applying the notions of strategic marketing—segmentation, differentiation and brand proliferation—manufacturers have ended up in a spiral of hypersegmentation, brand extensions and umbrella branding. Driven by short-term performance pressure and hyper-segmentation, manufacturers have taken to stretching their brand names over numerous extensions, flankers and new products.

We try to determine whether strong brands are like rice fields (perpetually self-renewing resources) or like rain forests (providing magnificent returns while being depleted). To answer this question we examine the differences between umbrella brands, and eponymous brands, and observe that while retailers have trouble creating the latter, they develop umbrella branding rather well.

Manufacturers are currently exploring four routes to escape from the hypersegmentation and market saturation in industrialised countries. These are:

(1) research and development (R&D) and innovation
(2) increasing scope, geographically or by product field
(3) producing for retailer own brands
(4) a swing back to value brands or 'counter segmentation'.

Part I closes with a discussion on new thinking of these four options.

Part II: The Rising Retailer

Strategic marketing for manufacturers assumes that retailers pass back the consumer market to the manufacturer in a true, undistorted form. Modern retailers are not at all transparent to the manufacturer and they are making efforts to become even more opaque. They have woken up to the value of their contact with the consumer and the importance of the marketing variables (price, display, promotions) under their control. As they begin to manipulate these marketing variables to further their own objectives, they construct an obstacle between the manufacturers and the end consumer, about as welcome as a row of high-rise hotels between the manufacturer's villa and the beach.

As efficient retailers expand in each country, location—once *the* crucial differential advantage—no longer provides protection and differentiation for stores. We ask whether retailers can apply the marketing concept in a similar way to manufacturers, in order to make their shoppers loyal. There are many differences between the two industries: one is a service, the other a producer, any retailer handles a much larger assortment than any manufacturer, and so on. We concentrate on four major differences which we believe have a direct bearing on a retailer's ability to apply the ideas of segmentation, differentiation and brand proliferation. These are that:

(1) Retailers are physically tied to a heterogeneous set of locations, which defines both their target market and their retail competition.

(2) There are fundamental differences in cost structure: manufacturers enjoy much greater synergy across brands.
(3) There are marked differences in the financial structures of retail companies, compared to those of manufacturers. Modern retailing is a particularly hard business under competitive conditions because of its high fixed costs and low margins. This can result in sensitivity to volume, and a penchant for price wars.
(4) Price and price perceptions play a different and more critical part in the choice of a shop than they do in the choice of a brand. Since it is more complex to compare price competitiveness across retail outlets, consumer price perceptions are also more open to influence; quality and price are less closely correlated than for product brands (a 'good' retailer can sell cheaply); 'cherry picking' has no direct product brand equivalent.

These differences imply that the marketing approach that was so successful for manufacturers (i.e. segmentation, differentiation and brand proliferation), cannot be pursued in the same way by retailers. Rather:

(1) Retailers must adopt broad, bland positionings: in contrast to manufacturers, retailers cannot de-select important consumer segments. Shopper segments exist, but they must be targeted *within the store*. The only pointed positioning with sufficiently wide appeal is that of the hard discounter.
(2) Retail formula proliferation cannot fulfil the same role as brand proliferation: it can be effective only in extremely limited circumstances.
(3) Price is a cornerstone of retail marketing. *All* mass retailers have to manage the perception of their prices to convince shoppers that they are price competitive.
(4) We dismiss services as a sustainable source of differential advantage for retailers. If they work they can usually be copied, negating their competitive effect but not their effects on costs.

We conclude that retailers in a mature retail market have three options for long-term profitability: location, low cost, or quality own label and fresh products. These three possible strategies lead to three retail formulas that can be successful and can coexist: convenience stores, hard discounters and large value-quality retailers. The losers will be those players who wander about between these three poles.

Market orientation leads 'value-quality' chains to develop their own consumer brands and their own philosophy of consumer reassurance. At the other extreme, hard discounters often handle very few national brands. In between are other stores who still rely on their location and manufacturers' brands to attract shoppers, but the market growth is not in their sector. No retailer can ignore the advantages of developing own labels: as well as being directly profitable they make the selling of national brands more profitable. When retailers implement strategies which involve ousting manufacturer brands, they must compete directly with the traditional owners of 'mindspace'.

Part III: Matrix Marketing

Ownership of the retail outlets gives retailers three important advantages in the battle for mindspace:

(1) communication with the consumer: retailers can use all types of in-store media to speak to the consumer at the time of purchase
(2) retailers control the in-store marketing mix variables: shelf position, price, promotions, merchandising, sampling
(3) retailers have access to detailed information on shopping and brand choice behaviour. Linked up with easy communication, such information will be a powerful tool in the future, if under-used today.

Manufacturers have mindspace advantages too. In comparison to the vast assortment handled by a retailer, manufacturers specialise in just a few product categories, and produce and sell huge volumes. Critical mass and specialisation give manufacturers the unquestionable lead in technology, media advertising and consumer understanding. These advantages are critical in product fields where technology, image, innovation, variety seeking or impulse buying are important, though they are less crucial in other areas.

The battle for shelfspace is about the relative costs to the consumer of switching brands compared to switching stores. For example, store saturation reduces the physical cost of switching stores, while technological parity reduces the cost of switching brands. Examining the components of these costs suggests strategies for both retailers and manufacturers aiming to modify the ratio in their favour, and highlights the importance of shopping behaviour to FMCG marketing.

Trade marketing has grown in importance and must change in nature. Trade marketing means managing a strategic triangle: balancing customer value with customer profitability while avoiding customer dependence. Trade marketing has to leave behind the traditional sales volume targets. It requires new ways of thinking, new organisational structures and, most critically, new skills.

These are the times that try companies' brands. A distinction has to be made between four different categories of brands, namely: premium brands, value brands, second-tier brands and industrial products. Premium brands are those which both operate in areas where manufacturers have mindspace advantages, and are in leading positions in their market. Even these brands have to take note of the 'Marlboro Friday' message: to keep their premium moderate compared to the retailer competition. In addition to their traditional value-adding activity, they must practise brand management via the retailer, through category planning, direct product profitability planning and trade incentives earmarked for mindspace-building activities.

For brand players who are willing to make the commitment, re-focusing single-mindedly on value may be an opportunity both to beat the retailer at their own game, and to steal a march on competitor premium brands. A 'value philosophy' goes well beyond the compulsory efficiency hunt which applies to all FMCG companies. It implies reassessing all activities to deliver a maximal value/cost ratio to users: pruning product ranges, omitting features which are not justified by value, economising on advertising and innovation on the basis that superior value is the key selling point, building up maximal economies of scale in each product field serviced. By definition, there is only one successful value positioning in each market, which is targeted by retailers in some countries.

Some manufacturers who have always operated under the brand paradigm will have to consider whether the paradigm will continue to hold for their weaker brands. It may become necessary to treat premium brands and secondary brands differently. The marketing of goods previously considered to be FMCGs, may change towards a hybrid of industrial and consumer marketing or even something more radically different. If retailers favour special retail brands, novel temporary brands, quality private label and so on, these are opportunities for some FMCG companies, especially those incapable of competing for mindspace against larger competitors. Manufacturers have to discover how their production capacity, technical know-how and even brand management expertise can best be exploited. Retailers can provide an efficient route to market.

A major avenue for manufacturers in maintaining their power is to exploit retail competition, i.e. divide and rule. This is possible by actively influencing retail structure and consumer shopping behaviour inside and outside the store. In most of the world, retailers are far behind their US and northern European counterparts; manufacturers can perhaps influence how they develop—for example, by promoting value brands as well as premium brands.

In a climate where retailers want to influence consumer choice and gain mindspace, marketing theory concentrating exclusively on the relationship between manufacturer and consumer is just plain wrong. Manufacturers now have to treat the retailer as a player with objectives and preferences, as important as, sometimes more important than, the end consumer. From now on, marketing in FMCG companies has dual responsibilities: to the end consumers and the distribution. Traditional strategic marketing asked why the consumer should choose this manufacturer's brand. Matrix marketing asks, in addition, why the distribution should stock it.

Manufacturers have to make efforts to see the market from the retailer's point of view, taking a *category based* perspective, and through this to offer retailers brands which they really wish to stock. Each category must have a role within the store, and each brand must have a role within the category. The manufacturer must show how its brands can help develop category sales to the benefit of the retailer, bearing in mind the different objectives of different types of retailer. The idea is not to sell (to retailers) what you can produce, but to produce what you can sell (to retailers).

Note

(1) Alan Mitchell, 'Asda does a Novon with brand assault', *Marketing Magazine,* Haymarket, London, 23 September 1993, p. 3.

Part I

REACHING THE LIMITS OF MARKET ORIENTATION

1
The Evolution of Marketing Orientation

1.1 PRODUCT ORIENTATION

A company usually starts up with a superior product that satisfies a clear need better than the existing competition. As profits flow from its superior product or unique resource, management's priority is to improve production efficiency and expand capacity. This focus on the company's ability to supply is known as product orientation. The agricultural sector is often product oriented: productivity and efficiency is often the farmer's only strategy. Whenever productivity leads to oversupply, prices tumble: a familiar scenario in agriculture.

Generally, industries thrive and grow for long periods by improving their fundamental operations. Demand increases as new buyers enter the market and existing buyers trade up. As long as demand remains strong, a good proportion of suppliers can grow and be profitable.

But industries lose their youth as surely as men. Over-capacity is the industrial equivalent to middle-aged spread. Humans lose their beauty and industries lose competitive advantages. There comes a time for any company, in whatever industry, when existing demand is satisfied and technological progress plateaus. From an inward focus on product and productivity, competitors have to refocus on the market: their competitors and consumers. In a mature industry competitors have to fight each other to win sales.

1.1.1 Mature Markets

Two phenomena characterise a mature market:

(1) *Overcapacity* During periods of growth, expanding capacity ahead of the competition is a winning strategy. When demand begins to plateau, this expansion cannot be halted in time to avoid excess capacity. Thus the overcapacity beast is born, destined to become a profit-destroying monster.
(2) *Product parity* Technological development plateaus and the leads given by technology lessen and shorten. Often several competitors produce goods of almost identical quality—from washing-up liquid to computers to lipstick, as far as most users can judge, brands are indistinguishable one from another. This leads to substitutability, another bête noire for any industry, twin brother to the overcapacity beast. Once consumers can swap indifferently from one product to its competitor, hopes for profits fly out the window.

During the growth period of a market players can grow without taking sales from each other. Investment in technology and capacity is the key to growth, so competitors all try to maintain good margins. When the market matures and growth slows or even stops, companies must compete directly with each other to grow. Each competitor has the capacity if only demand can be found—the battle is on to *sell*.

1.1.2 The War Spectrum of Mature Markets

Slow or no growth means sales have to be won directly from competitors. In some mature markets, *selling-oriented* producers all but destroy each other with endless price wars. At the other extreme, there are *controlled* or *protected* markets, where governments (or some other authority) control competition.

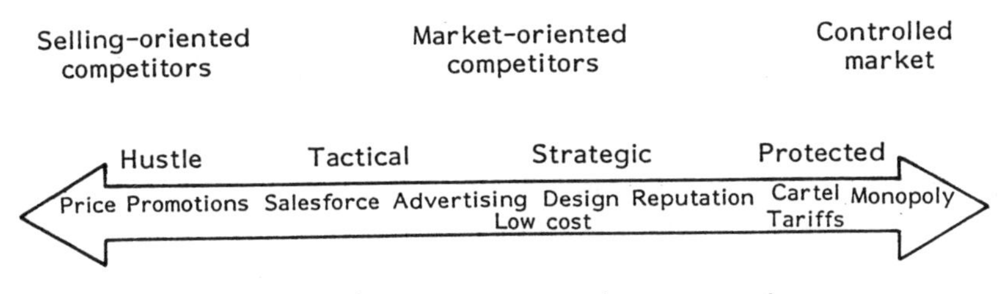

Figure 1.1 *The war spectrum of mature markets*

Between these extremes lie *market-oriented* industries where competitors have learnt to co-exist and create an orderly market responsive to customer needs and profitable to the players (see Fig. 1.1).

Fig. 1.1 visualises the idea that strategies in mature markets fall on a spectrum from the most kamikaze (on the left), to those which provide long-term benefits. The variable determining the spectrum is the time taken by competitors to copy their rival's strategy. On the extreme left of the spectrum lie the *hustle* strategies used by selling-oriented companies. Hustle strategies give only the most ephemeral advantages. Price cutting is an example of an advantage that is fast to initiate and easy to match quickly. Towards the right lie techniques which *differentiate* product offerings one from another. For example, design modifications have longer lead times. They create the more defensible positions sought by market-oriented companies.

1.2 SELLING ORIENTATION AND HUSTLE STRATEGIES

Selling orientation is often a panic reaction when a company recognises that its products are no longer superior and are losing market share. The result is sharply reduced profits. In the early 1980s, Gillette wobbled towards a price/selling orientation when it suffered an onslaught from Bic disposable razors. Conscious that their technological advantage had diminished both objectively and in the minds of consumers, the majority of Gillette's management felt that price competitiveness and other hustle strategies (ten for the price of eight, free dispenser, win a holiday) were their only alternative.

Hustle actions increase consumers' willingness to buy without adding value to the product offering. They are the brash face of selling which pressurises the buyer: price cutting, incentives, aggressive salesforce. Initially, and for the first competitors to use them, selling-oriented strategies work. The snag is that they elicit a mirror response from the competition, and so hustle strategies spiral.

Newspapers are an example of a mature industry where fixed costs are high, and volume the key to profit (through ad revenue). Typical hustle strategies include free gifts and competitions, which give an incentive to buy the paper without adding value to the newspaper itself. At one point hustle strategies got so out of hand for the UK tabloid press that the *Daily Mirror* stooped to rigging their football-based incentive competition. Their rival the *Sun*, had brought out a £5m prize 'spot the ball' competition which the *Mirror* felt obliged to match. Unable to afford the insurance to cover the risk of a winner, the *Mirror*'s boss, Robert Maxwell, economised by fixing the judges' decision.[1] The point is that the cost of the promotions quickly escalated out of control and beyond a reasonable level: the expected gains from extra sales were nowhere near the expected cost of the promotion. Hustle strategies can increase total market sales, but each action is escalated past its limit of profitability so that most or all competitors do not achieve a compensating rise in volume. This lesson is easy to forget. A couple of years later, the owner of the *Sun*, News International, slashed the price of *The Times* from 45p to 30p. *The Times*' circulation rose by over 40% as a consequence, which, remembering the ad revenues, probably meant that the price cut 'worked'. Worked, that is, until the *Daily Telegraph* felt forced to match the 30p cover price. *The Times* then dropped its price to 20p . . . .[2]

When overcapacity occurs in industries with high fixed costs, price cutting by one or two competitors often leads to a price war. Price wars are bloodiest in markets where volume is key to competitiveness and high fixed costs are involved (e.g. the auto industry, televisions, airlines, personal computers) or where barriers to exit (e.g. redundancy payments, write-offs) are high. These conditions often apply to retailing these days, as the fixed investment in retailing has risen to a point where a superstore costs as much as a sizeable factory. High fixed costs mean that high volumes are the only viable objective. Each is motivated by the dream that losses will force some competitors into submission and the less meek will inherit a profitable market.

1.3 MARKET ORIENTATION—ORDERLY COMPETITION

The key to profitability is to make products non-substitutable in the eyes of their consumers. A market divided 50:50 between two suppliers who compete primarily on price will be less profitable than a market divided 50:50 where the competitors compete for the consumer's mind, with, say, heavyweight advertising.

Achieving an orderly market where competitors can make more than survival returns, is a primary business aim. Industries need to find the road from free-for-all, gloves-off war to sustainable competition. Market orientation is one such road—an uphill road with segmentation as its destination.

Market orientation can lead to a competitive co-existence which serves both the needs of consumers and the expectations of shareholders. For this to happen the major players must implicitly agree to compete *by tailoring their offers to the different wants of different consumers*. If the main competitors follow such a policy, the total value of the market will increase—while delivering to buyers more exactly what they want.

Market orientation means focusing on the variation in customers' preferences and asking which groups of customers (segments) the company can serve particularly well. More neatly, market orientation means: producing what you can sell, rather than selling what you can produce. The aim of a market-oriented firm is to create a product-offering distinct from competitive offerings that is difficult for the competition to copy, and which provides greater value to some identified segment of the market. New products, brands extensions or improvements rarely hope to take the whole market; they target some group of people or some buying occasions.

A market-oriented producer is not jealous of the segments satisfied better by its competitors. The producer is pleased to have competitors who follow market-oriented strategies similar to its own, while despising competitors who want to copy its products and then compete on price.

Many industrial markets are still dominated by product-oriented companies. Many businesses have travelled from product orientation to selling orientation, for instance the pharmaceutical, banking and insurance industries. Few have made it through to a true market orientation. The most successful examples can be found in consumer markets.

The key to a competitive edge in a market-oriented industry it is to understand consumers, and their buying decisions, better than the competition.

1.3.1 An Industry's Position on the Spectrum

The behaviour of the industry influences its customers. For motorcycles, design and innovation is the key battlefield, thanks to the excitement created by the big four (Honda, Yamaha, Suzuki and Kawasaki) with their continual new-model programmes. When Yamaha increased its motorbike production capacity dramatically in 1981, Honda responded by introducing 113 new models in one year. Yamaha was forced to back down and cut its capacity again. Just as price promotions increase consumer attention to price, promoting motorbikes through 'tests' reported in the motorcycle press encourages consumer interest in novelty and design, which is much more profitable to the producers.

In the US cola market, Coca-Cola and Pepsi wage a permanent advertising and public relations war. This has encouraged consumers to develop emotional loyalty for one or other supplier. Meanwhile, regular price promotions (often alternating between the two of them) tend to reduce the scope for smaller brands (and own label) trying to attract promiscuous buyers willing to switch on the basis of low price. In fact, alternating price promotions between major competitors can defend their joint market share against smaller brands (or retailer's own brand) who have fewer loyal purchasers. This arrangement can even be profitable, if the big brands have a group of loyal buyers who still buy at the normal price outside promotions.[3]

The need for speed of response often dictates the types of action in a market. For example, if management is under pressure to deliver profits in the very short term, quick-response promotions will be a more attractive investment than, say, design improvements. Short-term actions are also favoured in industries very sensitive to changes in volume sales. Retailers' profits tend to be sensitive to small changes in volume. Shoppers tend to react quickly to price promotions, and this leads to price wars between stores.

The financial resources of the competitors also constrain the choice of weapon. A price war can be initiated without out-of-pocket investments; a salesforce war can be initiated only by rich competitors. In the 1980s in the ethical (as against over-the-counter) pharmaceutical industry, where those prescribing drugs tended to be fairly insensitive to price, wars were waged with larger and larger salesforces, who battled for market share for their often very similar drugs. Only where profitability is high can companies afford expensive tools such as large salesforces.

The more competitors focus on different consumer wants, and on differentiating their products one from another, the more orderly the market, and the greater the opportunities for individual competitors to be profitable. It is hard for a single competitor to move its offering over to the right of the spectrum (see Fig. 1.1). There comes a point where competitors are all so sick of ongoing selling wars that they find ways of moving, as an industry, towards the right.

There are three ways to escape from the selling end of the war spectrum: collusion, concentration and signalling.

(1) Collusion

Cartels such as OPEC (Organisation of Petroleum Exporting Countries), are often formed in an attempt to end price wars. When OPEC discovered collusion in 1973 it more than quadrupled the price of a barrel of oil, and its members' incomes. Protectionism to reduce the competition from abroad is similarly attractive. Producers have long been convinced of the benefits of these methods; governments generally disapprove.

Beyond possible legal problems, there is the ever-present risk of falling back into selling strategies if the cartel breaks, or once protection is withdrawn. In a cartel, there is a permanent temptation for each member to break ranks, and sell more or cheaper than agreed with the other members. This is not a matter of being short-sighted and selfish—the temptation is logical. Each member organisation of the cartel recognises that it is better off if everyone sticks to the agreement, which is why it agreed to the cartel in the first place. However, after signing, each signee becomes painfully aware that it will be worse off than ever if it sticks to the agreement but its co-signees renege. If they *are* going to renege, the company risks being a complete sucker by holding faith. Conversely, it is as aware as its co-signees of the possibility of extremely high short-term profits if it is the *first* to renege! The more producers involved, the more realistic it is to believe that someone will crack, and thus the greater the temptation to be that one (the reasoning can get more complex). Cartels have this inherent fragility, and this fragility grows dramatically with the number of parties involved. Witness OPEC in the 1980s.

Beyond this, high profits make an industry attractive to potential new entrants. When oil prices are high companies appear with proposals to turn guano into burnable fuel; when profits in the UK grocery industry soared in the 1980s, most of the hard discounters in Europe tabled plans to expand into the UK.

(2) Concentration

An important side-effect of selling strategies is that they tend to drive weaker competitors out of the market. They either go bankrupt or are bought by stronger competitors (or both). A market in the throws of a price war is hard on management and shareholders. Concentration, however, can benefit the survivors.

Mergers and acquisitions are motivated by many different objectives, but one important consideration is that fewer competitors are left afterwards. In a situation where competition is reducing profits, one solution is to buy up competitors until there are few enough left that each can see real hope in co-operating with the others. This can, of course, like cartels, be against the consumers' interests and most governments have some monopoly and mergers legislation. However, effects are progressive, and some oligopoly/monopoly influence is helpful to a group of competitors wishing to move towards a market orientation. Concentration, coupled with a desire among the survivors to restore normal profit levels, helps to usher in an era of 'orderly competition', based on serving the variety of wants.

(3) Signalling and 'Rules'
Firms can signal to one another their willingness, or unwillingness, to abide by certain 'healthy competition' rules. By making the right signals, they can sometimes collectively withdraw from unwinnable battlegrounds and create a competitive, but orderly, market.

Agreeing to compete under an implicit set of rules is like fighting under a Geneva convention: still war, but a more polite one. Implicit rules (if made explicit) would include:

- avoiding hustle strategies or operating at a loss (predatory pricing)
- not copying the products of competitors (me-tooing)
- searching for and investing in non-price differences to promote products: invest in adding value (e.g. advertising) rather than selling pressure (e.g. promotions).

A retailer announcing that it will match a competitor's low prices can be a signal to stop fighting on price. In a real-world experiment in the USA a grocery retailer promised to match a competitor's prices exactly on 100 specified product lines.[4] After two years the prices for the matched products had risen significantly in both stores, compared to the prices on the unmatched lines. The trick is in the promise to match and not to 'beat'. Announcements promising consumers the most competitive prices is an aggressive invitation for the industry to start a price war. Switching tactics loudly from price to quality, is an offer to a competitor to follow suit.

It is always the consumer's willingness to substitute that kills profitability, and loyalty, based on whatever reason, that allows higher margins.

1.3.2 Swinging Back to Hustle Strategies

A successful shift towards market orientation does not eliminate the risk of a future swing back to the left. This is not surprising when one considers the following five mechanisms, each capable of producing a price war:

(1) A price war can re-occur because competitors get too 'good' to each other. If profitability makes the market unusually attractive, new operations are bound to enter. Usually they enter at the bottom of the market, serving price-sensitive segments with lower quality offerings. In retailing this process has been observed so frequently that it has been named the 'wheel of retailing'.

(2) If competitors (existing or entering) are determined to grow in a static market, they may start to break some of the orderly market rules. Producing copies of rivals' products is tempting because in the short term it 'steals' share and makes money. Competitors with strong technological and marketing skills are unlikely to launch exact copies of rival brands, but me-toos common in mature markets where innovation is slowing down. Once me-too strategies get a hold in an industry, there is an inevitable downward pressure on prices. The price cutting tactics of Rupert Murdoch's *Times* in 1994, tugging mirror response from the *Telegraph*, being a clear example.

(3) Another risk comes from changes in the market. If the variation in wants, or the consumers' willingness to pay, reduces for some reason, marketers may find price competition unavoidable. For example, the relatively high inflation levels in the 1970s and 1980s gave way to simultaneous recession and low inflation in the 1990s. This gave producers less scope to increase prices, and the long periods of relatively fixed price points gave consumers more chance to memorise and compare prices. This climate tended to push FMCG manufacturers towards the left. In early 1993, most analysts would have classified the Philip Morris tobacco company as the epitome of a market-oriented company. Marlboro, one of the largest cigarette brands in the world, was achieving up to 40% premiums over own label and cheap branded competition in its home market. In April 1993, however, Philip Morris reacted against 'budget brands' by price cuts on all its main brands, citing slipping market share against value brands as the main reason.

(4) Price wars may be engaged intentionally by an aggressive competitor out to 'steal' share. This strategy is tempting to a competitor who has a more efficient cost structure. By fighting a war of attrition on price, a competitor may be able to drive other competitors to the wall. The survivor(s) can hope for profitable

years to come. Some industry analysts saw Philip Morris's price cuts as an aggressive action focused on removing RJR Nabisco from the cigarette market. RJR's domestic tobacco sales, and that division's operating profit were indeed dramatically affected—down 72% by the end of the year.[5]

It is easy, however, to miscalculate the staying power of the adversary. Price wars drag on long and painfully especially when the players have backers with deep pockets, for example PepsiCo's Frito Lay versus Anheuser-Busch's Eagle Snacks in the US snacks market.[6]

(5) Lastly, a weak competitor may resort to dropping prices because it is the only available action for increasing its sagging volume in the short term. Tesco achieved this reversal in the late 1970s. Tesco had been suffering because of its legacy of small, town-centre sites but succeeded in taking the industry by storm with its 'check-out' campaign. The whole UK retail market became price driven for several years, before it swung once again towards a market orientation.

The damage done by a new price war is twofold: everybody loses money but, worse, price wars actually destroy the brand differences built up during the period of orderly competition. Communications focused on slashed prices push out the messages focused on quality and functions. Quality has to be trimmed to ensure price competitiveness: advertising, R & D and other brand differentiating investments are reduced in the drive to cut costs. This encourages the buyer to believe that all products are similar and increases the salience of price. Consumers are made more price sensitive, destroying the added value of the whole market.

An orderly market is not a particularly stable state of affairs, it is just one of a series of phases that a market can pass through. Even during phases of marketing orientation, markets are dynamic. A marketing orientation is a permanent uphill struggle, like trying to stay at the same level on a descending escalator. Competitive initiatives are continually eroding competitive advantages. When companies feel themselves losing their position on the escalator, they panic and turn to selling strategies. It is easier to devalue the products and return to a selling orientation than it is to create sustainable advantages.

1.4 SEGMENTATION AND DIFFERENTIAL ADVANTAGE

Market orientation means exploiting the variation in the needs or desires of a market and only if there is variation in needs can a marketing orientation pay off. Product fields that really show little variation in needs or wants are called 'commodity markets'. In commodity markets price is the main determinant choice, all suppliers must accept the same price, and that price simply reflects the laws of supply and demand.

FMCG manufacturers go out of their way to ensure that their markets do not become 'commodity'. As most consumers have considerable appetites for novelty, convenience and prestige, suppliers have many opportunities for adding value. For example, white granulated sugar is a commodity and difficult to differentiate, but sugar suppliers create added value by mixing white sugar with artificial sweeteners or brown colouring to create novel forms with extra functions. Thus the value of the sugar market can be increased by satisfying the variety of wants of less price-sensitive consumers. Aspirin and paracetamol are commodity drugs, but some consumers will pay more for mixtures promising extra strength, fewer side effects, less stomach problems or specific action against hang-overs, period pains, backache, and so on. Since the buyer and user of FMCGs are often either the same person or a close relative, emotional values such as confidence and caring also play a major role in brand choice. Using a full range of functional and emotional propositions, brands such as Anacin, Excedrin, Bufferin, Tylenol, etc., all find their groups of customers, and add value to what could be a commodity market. In some countries toilet paper operates like a commodity, while in the UK, thanks to Scott's consistent marketing efforts (involving, among other techniques, a Labrador puppy), Andrex is one of the biggest retail brands in the country.

Marketing is sometimes defined as finding appealing and legally acceptable ways to discriminate between consumers with different price sensitivities. A segmentation scheme divides the buyers in a market into groups with common priorities, different from those in the other groups.

Segmentation is the market-oriented company's creed. By segmenting consumers, manufacturers reduce the complexity of

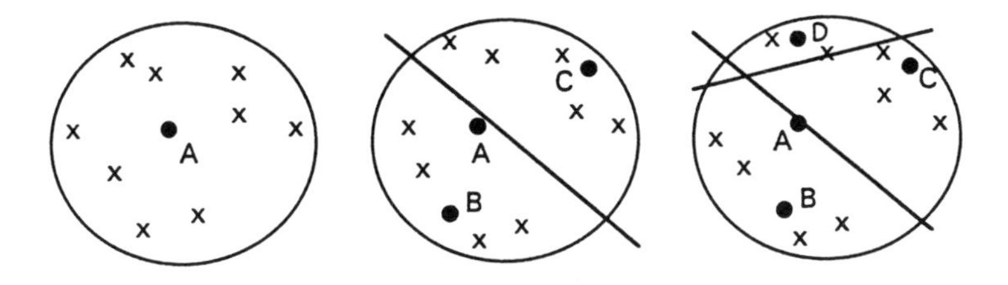

Figure 1.2 *The market developed by brand A is attacked by brands B and C and, finally D*

their customer base to manageable proportions, yet separate out the differences hidden in the averages. These differences then direct the design of the product, its channel of distribution and its positioning (in terms of price, image, advertising, etc.) to create a differential advantage with respect to this segment.

The idea of segmentation can be visualised by the diagrams in Fig. 1.2. The left-hand circle in the figure represents a market with the Xs representing groups of buyers. The distances between the Xs represent the differences in the product offerings they would ideally prefer. Initially, the majority of consumers buy brand A as it satisfies them all fairly well and is the only option available.

Suppose a competitor wishes to enter. The competitor company investigates the market and decides to consider it as two segments. Its 'segmentation' is represented on the second circle as a line, cutting the market roughly into two halves. The company then launches brands B and C, designed to appeal to the two segments identified. Brand A will be likely to hold on to a good share of the market. Loyalty, familiarity and habit will favour A, and A will still offer a package of benefits preferred by some buyers. The third circle shows how another segment might be sliced off by a fourth brand (D), which particularly attacks brand C.

Segmentation inspires the company to create product offerings which are intrinsically more appealing to its target segments. The segments will prefer this offering without being hustled.

It is especially important for new products to appeal strongly to some definite segment of buyers. It is not enough to be rated well in some average or aggregate for a cross sample of a market: by aiming for everyone you will end up convincing no one. What is important is that a certain segment of consumers think the new product is clearly superior to what they buy currently.

The advantage of focusing is also particularly crucial for smaller competitors. Segmentation provides the opportunity to be more efficient with resources, for example by having more focused R&D and reduced ranges to simplify production. In a one-segment market, with undifferentiated products, the largest brand would have a great advantage, through economies of scale and muscle in negotiation with suppliers/partners. In a segmented market, where differentiated products are targeted at distinct groups, a smaller competitor can face down a larger one. Thus, Clarins—small compared to competitors such as L'Oréal—manages to hold their own in premium skin-care products. Their chosen segment is attracted by a brand image angled towards health and nature ('anti-pollution' make-up) rather than glamour, supported with product quality and customer service via selective distribution. Price points reflect the 'practical, health' positioning and offer good value compared to luxury brands such as Lancôme found in the same outlets.

Segmentation reduces competitive pressure because it makes competitive products less substitutable. Differentiation can be the start of a virtuous circle, the higher profitability being channelled back into reinforcing differentiation, through further investments in R&D or communication.

1.4.1 The Dynamics of Segmentation

Marketing orientation is not a state of grace attained and then peacefully enjoyed. Companies following a market orientation are constantly being driven towards new and more subtle segmentation by competitive pressure.

The price–quality axis usually provides the first segmentation scheme in any market. Manufacturers guarantee a certain quality with a 'brand', often simply their own company name. Once competitors match the pioneer on quality, substitutability re-emerges and prices will drop unless some new method for segmenting consumers is found.

The competitors need to find new ways to segment their markets, on a new range of benefits. In FMCG markets there are two basic approaches to segmentation superimposed on the original price–quality spectrum. The first is based on looking at the different functional benefits sought from the products or the different uses made of the products by different groups of consumers. The second is based on understanding the differing emotions and aspirations which motivate consumers, so that the company can provide products which reflect their emotional and 'image' needs.

(1) Functional Segmentation

Functional segmentation is probably the most abundant source of segments in the FMCG area. The idea is to group consumers into segments according to the functional benefits they seek from the product. The different functions depend on usage, occasion, attitudes and price sensitivity. For example, in washing powders, some consumers are particularly motivated by cleaning power, some are interested in keeping their clothes looking bright and new, some are largely motivated by economy, others have environmental concerns in mind.

Companies bundle together groups of benefits into brands to satisfy the priorities of the different segments. Some consumers buy milk as a source of nutrition for children: offer them milk reinforced with vitamins. Some consumers restrict their intake of milk because of the calories: offer them fat-free milk. Some weight watchers can't bear the taste of totally skimmed: offer them half fat.

Functional segmentation does not necessarily mean that the products themselves are functionally different. In many FMCG markets the objectively measurable differences between the competitors are small, and difficult for the consumer to assess accurately. For example, the cleaning power of detergents or the strength of coffee or an analgesic. In these situations, perceptions will be influenced by communication and packaging and functional differential advantages can exist strongly in perceptions of the users.

Usually, quality and functional segments are the first segments to be targeted by companies becoming market oriented. In industrial markets, the services and conditions attached to the product are often the next focus of segmentation. One of the characteristics of consumer marketing is the wide and intangible range of emotional needs satisfied by consumer products. Professional buyers acting for companies tend to be rational and consistent in their decisions. Consumers, being both buyers and users, and not having to justify their decisions to others, are more emotional and whimsical in their buying decisions. A consumer making an FMCG purchase may seek variety for no rational reason, and may derive pleasure from the purchase and use of certain brands because of associations attached to the brand.

(2) Psychological Segmentation

We all get emotional satisfaction as well as functional satisfaction from certain FMCG products. None of us is completely immune to the images of products. For example, people may see themselves as being family centred, or trendy, or canny, or traditional, or sophisticated, and so on, and these self perceptions will be reflected in all their choices—the music they listen to, the clothes they wear and the products they buy. It surprised some researchers to find an upmarket profile in the buyers of 'generic' brands, when they were in vogue. From a functional point of view, generics (cheap, no-frills versions of consumer branded goods) should have appealed to financially disadvantaged groups. Emotionally, however, upmarket consumers wanted to believe that they were not exploited by manipulative advertising. The emotional logic won the day.

While functional segmentation will give toothpaste for fresh breath, white teeth, no caries or good taste, psychographic segmentation will give shampoo for people who are sensual, health conscious, 'green' or glamorous. Advertising and supporting communication (packaging, point of sale, etc.) are an intrinsic part of the product-offering for such segments. There are many FMCG areas where quality differences between the products are small and choice largely depends on the 'emotional' connotations of the brand. In some product fields (e.g. whisky), prestige and symbol have value—the ability of the product to 'communicate' to third parties is an important vector for choice. An example would be Heineken beer in the USA. When rival Kronenbourg ran a campaign based on the premise of French good taste and brewing tradition, Heineken replied with advertising saying 'Kronenbourg is the reason that the French drink wine'. Such cheek and verve, independent of traditional product claims, creates a personality for the brand that is its differential advantage. Perrier, in the UK, have followed a consistent theme with their witty, French accented communications, exemplified by lines such as 'Eau lá lá'. Moët and Chandon (champagne) have created associations with celebrations and success by supplying their product to winners at the end of prestigious races. Success depends not on the creativity of the communication per se, but on the understanding of the target market and the emotional benefits they derive from the brand, followed consistently over time.

For a further group of products—treats such as bath additives and cosmetics, or children's products, such as breakfast cereals—the 'personality' of the product is important. In more banal product fields, habit and familiarity (also emotional values) for their own sake are often decisive. Thus, in a whole series of FMCG markets, associations in the minds of consumers is the main source of sustainable differential advantage.

Many sophisticated FMCG companies, recognise that it is only by answering psychological as well as functional needs that they can create genuine differential advantages, and they have to deal with segmentation on this basis.

Psychological differential advantages may seem insubstantial, but in terms of sustainability, they are often more resilient than functional differential advantages. Intangible emotional associations are difficult to copy: once an emotional territory is occupied by a well-known brand, it is more difficult to displace than a brand with a functional claim that can be beaten. Thus advantages built on emotional values and brand image (e.g. Levi jeans) can turn out to be the most durable.

1.5 SUSTAINABILITY

Many markets have moved through product orientation to selling orientation. A few markets have then achieved an orderly market via market orientation (segmentation and differentiation) or some other means—e.g. cartel, government control. Unfortunately, an orderly market is not achieved once and for all, it can dissolve for various reasons into selling strategies and price wars once more.

Segmentation in consumer markets has become more subtle over time. Most FMCG manufacturers are now adept at providing not just functional benefits but also satisfying the emotional requirements of their 'psychographically' defined targets. Segmentation has gone much further in consumer markets than in other markets both because consumer companies have been market oriented for longer, and because the range of needs satisfied by FMCG products is so wide and complex. The ideas of segmentation and differential advantage have diffused to even the smallest FMCG companies.

By definition, the idea of a differential advantage is, first, that some quality, attached to the product, is perceived to be unique. Only then is the product differentiated. The second axiomatic characteristic of a differential advantage is that it is motivating to the target segment, i.e. that it does indeed confer an advantage in the race to be bought. To be of any real value, a differential advantage needs a third characteristic: it must be sustainable against the competition.

This last demand, sustainability, is often the most challenging. Finding a segment and providing a product-offering to satisfy it uniquely requires information and imagination, but once the product-offering is out in the market, how is that information and imagination to be protected from competitors? Lack of sustainability in the long term will destroy an orderly market.

The next chapter looks at this issue of sustainability, in the case of consumer products.

Notes

(1) Roy Greenslade, *Maxwell's Fall*, Simon & Schuster, 1992, p. 114.

(2) Tony Jackson, 'Ruthless killers or paper tigers?', *Financial Times*, weekend 2–3 July 1994, p. 9.

(3) Rajiv Lal, 'Price promotions: limiting competitive encroachment', *Marketing Science*, Vol. 9, No. 3, Summer 1990.

(4) J.D. Hess and E. Gerstner, 'Price matching policies: an empirical case', *Managerial and Decision Economics*, August 1991, pp. 305–16.

(5) Richard Tomkins, 'RJR Nabisco slumps to $496 m net deficit', *Financial Times*, 2 February 1994, p. 25.

(6) Bill Saporito, 'Price wars, why they will never end', *Fortune International*, 23 March 1992, pp. 26–9.

2
Creating Sustainable Advantage in Consumer Markets

If a company has found a profitable segment and created a product-offering to serve it, it will attract imitators. Thus, to be sustainable, a differential advantage must be based on some resource that is difficult for competitors to copy. R&D sometimes provides inimitable company resources—such as Polaroid's Instant Photography patents. In FMCGs this is pretty rare, and the most valuable resources of an FMCG company are often those which are built up incrementally over time. A lead in a particular advantage that can only be built up over time can be sustainable, if the company commits to it and continues to invest enough to stay ahead. The advantage is even more valuable and sustainable if the resource in question is zero-sum, i.e. more for one competitor means less for another.

Resources which take a long time to build, and increase incrementally over time, are usually the more intangible assets: first, the knowledge and experience accumulated within the company, and second, the knowledge and experience built up among the company's customers (consumers and distributors). In FMCGs it is generally these two sets of intangible assets which competitors find the hardest to replicate.

2.1 THE COMPANY LEARNING CURVE: EFFICIENCY

The company learning curve is a concept used to capture the intangible advantages that a company builds up internally, over time. Long experience builds up know-how. This know-how exists within the company's employees, but also in the systems, traditions and culture evolved in the company.

The development in manufactured goods such as cars, radios and videos since, say, the early 1970s, is clearly astounding, but it is probably equalled by developments in disposable nappies, adhesives, razors or chilled foods. Developments are so incremental that they go unnoticed, but each mundane consumer product is the pinnacle of some zone of human achievement. Products continually improve so that if a company is out of the swim for several years its products become significantly inferior. Such is the case of consumer goods produced in eastern Europe. The ability of a company to produce frozen meals with excellent texture and taste qualities at a high level of consistency and hygiene is not due to one well-kept secret or one well-paid employee. It is due to a huge combination of factors difficult to replicate in another plant or company. The only way to keep abreast—to 'stay on the learning curve'—is by continually innovating, improving and investing.

This idea of a company learning curve is widely accepted and used. For example, it forms the basis of the BCG (Boston Consultancy Group) 'portfolio matrix' analysis, and is one of the fundamental assumptions justifying market share strategies (i.e. aiming to gain share as a way of gaining competitive advantage). The theory behind the BCG matrix is that pushing ahead of competitors in volume production and thus on the learning curve, in some area, gives economies and efficiencies which can be exploited in the market. Thus firms should commit themselves to the markets and product areas where they will be able to get ahead on the learning curve and be able to deliver better value more profitably than their competitors.

A company's learning and experience can take different forms. It may involve a better understanding of what the consumer seeks so that only the most valued features are offered. It may mean efficient, large-scale production, which reduces unit cost. It may

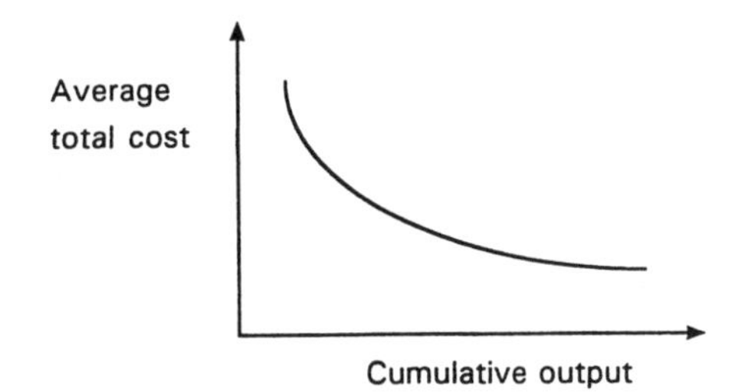

Figure 2.1 *A company experience curve—as cumulative production increases, the company becomes more efficient at producing 'value'*

mean more R&D that leads to better technology: technological know-how that improves the functional delivery of the product.

The learning curve (see Fig. 2.1) is not simply a cost curve, but the cost involved in creating a certain amount of value. Thus to move down the learning curve, the company must either produce the same products more efficiently, or produce products which give greater satisfaction, but at the same cost.

Travelling down the company learning curve is not inevitable or automatic. In this sense, Fig. 2.1 represents the optimal curve. Companies can find themselves shooting off the curve through complacency, or by being undercut by the faster development of a competitor (see Fig. 2.2).

Many of the business decisions a company makes are concerned with exploiting its assets to move on down its curve. Each company has a heritage of strategies and assets (the company's 'strategic heritage') which can become a hindrance as the market evolves. For example, Adidas and Puma invested in large-scale European manufacturing capacity, to give them economies of scale. Then fleet-footed marketing organisations Nike and Reebok introduced a new element into the learning curve: the ability to bring out new designs and 'visual' shoe technologies in rapid succession. They did this by sourcing their designs from subcontractors based in the Far East, gaining both low costs and flexibility. Adidas and Puma by contrast suffered from high fixed costs and from time to time huge excesses of out-of-date designs.

In many FMCG industries products have reached such a state of perfection that the scope for 'serving consumer desires ever more closely' has diminished. This means that the slope of the

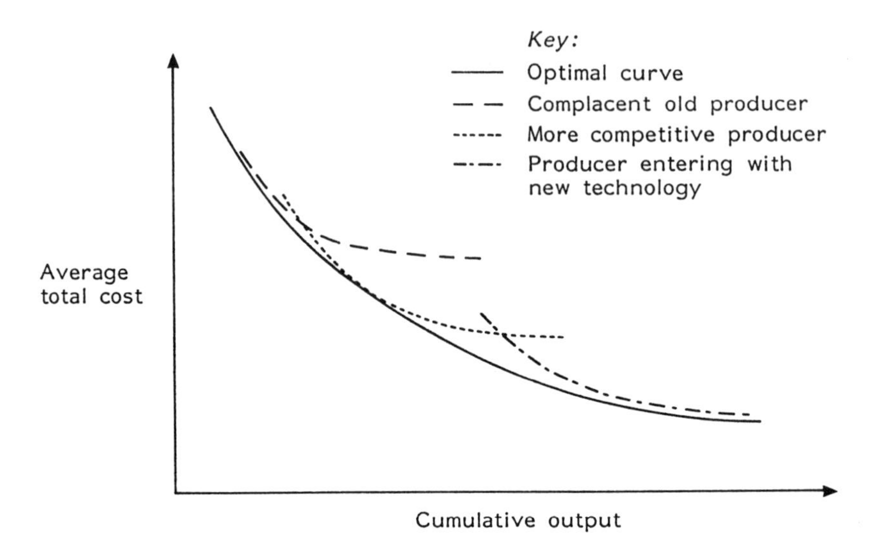

Figure 2.2 *Optimal and sub-optimal learning curves*

curve now depends more on productivity than increasing the value of the product. In other words, because many companies can produce excellent products, the only way to gain an advantage on the basis of the learning curve is via productivity. The emphasis thus thrown on productivity has been highly visible in the last few years (see Fig. 2.3).

2.1.1 Limits of the Technical Learning Curve in FMCGs

The ability to produce better goods or cheaper goods (sometimes protected by patent) is a traditional source of protection from imitators. This type of technological lead is a necessary and sufficient condition for market success in many industrial markets. Markets such as agro-chemicals (pesticides, herbicides, etc.) are driven by the market's knowledgeable and rational assessment of the product's economic worth and the cost of using it, compared to competitive substitutes. Once an agro-chemical product loses its economic advantages, its days of high profitability are numbered: the only solution for an

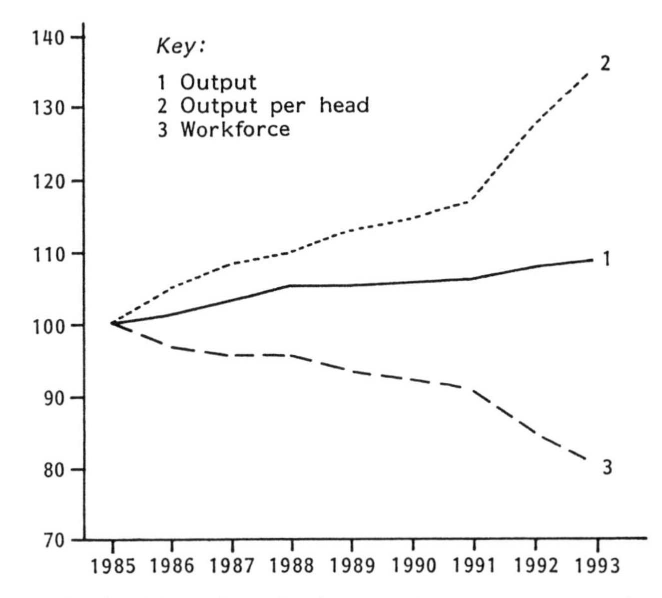

Figure 2.3 *Productivity at large food companies, 1985–93. Reproduced, with permission, from Henderson Crosthwaite,* Consumer Brief, *Vol. 16, 9 November 1993*

agro-chemicals producer is to have profitable new products coming on stream.

Not so in FMCG markets. In FMCG markets, a certain degree of technological excellence and value are necessary for success, but they are often not the only, or even major determinants of success. For example, consider that, prior to launch, most new products are tested objectively for functional superiority and competitive value relative to the existing competition. Notwithstanding this, many fail. This means to say that a product can be ahead on a technical learning curve and yet be beaten by a technically inferior competitor once put out in the marketplace. New products which offer technically better value frequently fail to oust familiar but less advanced products. Conversely, many brand leaders—for example, Wrigley's chewing gum—hold on for decades without significant technological leads.

The longevity of product-brands, despite little technological advantage, is a striking characteristic of FMCG markets (see Table 2.1).

Table 2.1 *Examples of the many FMCG brands that have held leadership positions over most of this century*

US	UK
Swift Premium, bacon	Hovis, bread
Eastman Kodak, cameras	Stork margarine
Del Monte canned fruit	Kellogg's corn flakes
Wrigley chewing gum	Cadbury's chocolate
Nabisco biscuits	Rowntrees Pastilles
Ever Ready batteries	Schweppes mixers
Gold Medal flour	Brooke Bond tea
Gillette razors	Colgate toothpaste
Coca-Cola soft drinks	Johnson's floor polish
Campbell's soup	Kodak film
Ivory soap	Ever Ready batteries
Lipton tea	Gillette razors
Goodyear tyres	Hoover vacuum cleaners

Source: Adapted from *Advertising Age*, 19 September 1983, p. 32—based on current market surveys, and 1933 advertising expenditures.

This is because, for a consumer brand to succeed it needs not just technical excellence and value but also 'mindspace' and 'shelfspace', as explained below.

2.2 THE CUSTOMER LEARNING CURVE: MINDSPACE AND SHELFSPACE

Some industrial companies survive with very few customers—for example, a supplier of brake pads to car manufacturers. Consumer markets are fundamentally different in that any successful FMCG brand needs to attract literally millions of consumers to make it successful. These millions of consumers are hidden among millions of other consumers who reject the brand. Car manufacturers have a tendency to cluster together; consumers are scattered in towns and villages over whole continents. To get products to consumers usually demands the support of another industry—the distribution channel. For FMCG products, the investment and time required to build awareness, trust and distribution is enormous and is as essential to success in FMCGs as technical and production skills.

Thus, for consumer goods companies there is a parallel achievement to the internal learning curve which takes place outside the company. All the customers, retailers and consumers, have to learn about the product—its name and its qualities. All these millions of people have to be pushed along a 'customer learning curve'.

Over the long term, a successful consumer product will build up a web of experiences, associations and buying habits simultaneously among both end consumers and the distribution. These are intangible resources that the company holds outside the company, in the heads of consumers and the decision makers in the distribution industry. We call these assets mindspace and shelfspace. An idiosyncrasy of FMCG markets is that the assets mindspace and shelfspace are crucial sources of sustainable advantage. They are important sources of sustainable advantage because both take a long time to build and both are finite: zero-sum: more for you means less for your competitor.

The consumer's mind and the retailer's shelf both have limited capacity. If a competitor takes over mindspace, some other competitor must correspondingly be edged aside. If a competitor dominates the supermarket shelves, another is less noticeable.

The total amount of mindspace and shelfspace available to a product field varies by nations. It seems that French consumers, on average, are willing to expend greater mental effort remembering the names of shampoo brands, compared to citizens of the USA. The latter concentrate better when it comes to toothpaste. These national biases are also reflected in the amount of shelfspace devoted by French and US retailers to these categories. Collectively, over a period of time, producers can to some extent increase the amount of mindspace/shelfspace devoted to an area, by creating interest through new products and advertising. However, for both consumer mindspace and retail shelfspace, there is a ceiling. What there is has to be fought over by the competitors.

Shelfspace and mindspace are linked and complementary. If a product has achieved considerable mindspace—it is present and liked in many consumer minds—this in itself will be a powerful incentive for the distribution to stock it. On the other hand, shelfspace is a powerful generator of mindspace. Seeing a product regularly helps increase its presence in the consumer's mind, and improves its image by suggesting it is popular. Both come into play at the point of purchase (see Fig. 2.4).

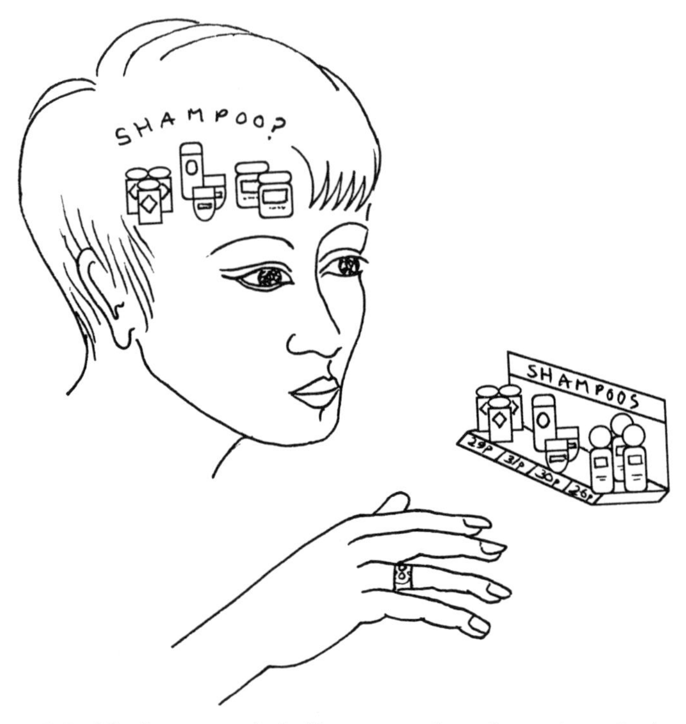

Figure 2.4 *Mindspace and shelfspace are interdependent. Both are finite commodities*

2.2.1 Controlling Shelfspace

Control of shelfspace is necessarily a preoccupation of FMCG manufacturers because for low-value purchases, presence in-store is often a critical influence. Many FMCG companies have invested for years to provide themselves with a good distribution network. In the case of brewers this has often meant tied pubs and cafés. For impulse purchase goods (e.g. confectionery) manufacturers have developed extensive sales and delivery forces, and developed business via a whole range of outlets even beyond the traditional retail trade—vending machines and at leisure activity centres (cinemas, swimming pools, sports events). Dairies have organised home deliveries of milk and other dairy produce. Dried grocery manufacturers have invested in powerful salesforces and developed many incentives and aids for retailers willing to help them reach their consumers.

Shelfspace has many qualitative aspects. Shelfspace at eye level or hand level is worth more than shelfspace at foot level. The number of facings, depth of inventory, position compared to flow of traffic, and the position within the store, all affect the amount of notice and purchase for the product. Shelfspace can be augmented further by special displays, end-of-aisle features, or flagging information ('Star Buy', '30% off this week'). And all these aspects are competitive: more for us means less for the competition.

For many years, large manufacturers had very good control over shelfspace, not just quantity but also quality. Shelfspace could be planned and bought, rather like advertising or promotions, by high rolling FMCG companies. Small retailers were the willing agents of the large manufacturers, and allowed them to advise on the optimal management of shelfspace. Independent stores have declined dramatically in the face of competition from major chains, and producers' control over shelfspace has declined with them. The methods and skills needed to gain and hold good-quality shelfspace are undergoing fundamental changes as a result.

With the concentration in the retail trade, sophisticated retailers are imposing their own objectives, and taking back control of 'their' shelfspace. Since shelfspace is such an important marketing influence, sophisticated retailers want to direct it towards their own business objectives. In particular, retailers who are actively marketing their own brands in competition with manufacturers will use shelfspace to promote their own brands.

As a result of this change in power, gaining shelfspace has become a much more strategic challenge for manufacturers. Shelfspace has to be won by planning product-offerings to satisfy both trade and consumer needs. The distribution wants to increase its category sales, to improve average margins, to provide a good range to shoppers, perhaps to offer products exclusively. Often working in conflict with these objectives is the retailer's continual need to increase operational efficiency and reduce inventory costs by minimising the number of lines stocked. Manufacturers now have to win shelfspace by working through these needs of the retailer.

Gaining and holding shelfspace has become an enormously important strategic challenge for FMCG companies, and is treated in detail in the last three chapters of this book.

2.2.2 Creating Mindspace

Just imagine trying to do a week's shopping in a supermarket where all the names and labels changed each week. Each decision would take twice as long, half the purchases would be a disappointment and not being able to repeat the successful buys of the previous week would be a constant aggravation. Shopping would be a nightmare. It is quite clear that consumers do not want, for the most part, to buy a different product each week. Purchase decisions have to be made, and most shoppers believe that they can make these decisions well or badly. Picking randomly or even purely on price (without trying to trade off for quality) is not acceptable, rational, or comfortable behaviour for most people. Thus, most shoppers come to the shop shelf with biases which help them to make their hundred little decisions. Consumers find it well worth their while to remember the name and characteristics of satisfactory products. We call this information, stored in consumers' heads, mindspace.

The most obvious and direct route for creating mindspace for a new product is by communicating about it to the consumer. The traditional tools for creating mindspace are advertising, sampling, PR, sponsoring and endorsement, all carefully orchestrated to deliver a consistent, coherent message. As more and more consumers become aware of the product, try it, experience satisfaction with it, and fit it into usage habits, the product accumulates a nice piece of territory in consumers' minds. The process is slow and incremental, and thus it is hard for a later competitor to catch up.

Mindspace is often easier to win in higher interest areas where consumers are interested in learning about the product. Consumers pay more attention to advertising, opinion leaders, word of mouth, and so on, in the higher interest segments such as cars, perfume or hair colouring (higher cost, higher visibility, higher risk, etc.). Similarly, a genuinely innovative product, or new category of products is of greater interest to consumers than established categories and thus, until the area becomes banal, there are greater opportunities for winning mindspace. The downside is that communication from new competitors also attracts more attention and consideration.

Many FMCG areas can be characterised as relatively trivial purchases which excite minimal interest. Trying to win mindspace off established brands in low-interest product fields (such as mustard or salt), simply by communicating to the consumer, is tough if not impossible. This is to the advantage of the brands that already have mindspace and is the reason why these markets often show considerable inertia. If a new brand does wish to build mindspace in a low interest area it is now usually necessary to take a more aggressive or indirect approach: by forcing use, borrowing or buying mindspace as described below.

2.2.2.1 Forcing Use via Tactical Marketing

In low-interest areas managing tactical activities which influence consumers at the level of behaviour are very important for developing mindspace.

Promotions such as free gifts and competitions can create impulse purchases. The act of purchase, however prompted, and the usage which naturally follows, will translate into mindspace. Intelligent management of impulse buying for low-interest products can in this way be a source of differential advantage. Thus breakfast cereals run a series of promotions and attractions: plastic toys in the packet, cut-out cardboard novelties printed on the box, competitions on the back of the box, coupon-collecting offers, as well as price promotions. Procter & Gamble use massive sampling at the launch of an FMCG product: sampling leads to use which leads to mindspace. Amora won its lead in the French mustard market when it introduced the idea of mustard packed in 'free' glasses. The 'habit' of buying Amora, was spawned from the impulsive decision to acquire the 'free' glass. Amora continues to nurture its mindspace differential advantage, in the face of up to 50% premiums over own label, with attractive packaging promotions.

Many FMCG markets are mature and with such small differences between the products that creating sustainable differential advantages based on functional delivery is almost impossible. On the other hand, since the decisions are so routine they are often made for the most trivial of reasons. Where this is the case, tactical marketing can have a vital (and sometimes underestimated) role. Over the longer term, creating usage and thus familiarity and loyalty can build a strategic advantage for brands which are bought largely through habit. In this way marketing activities which appear to be purely tactical can in fact build a critical strategic advantage: mindspace.

When consumers are attracted to a new brand, the new brand will gain in mindspace, pushing the previous brand to the 'back of their mind'. If a high price on one occasion forces a buyer to choose a different brand, this may not alter their *perceptions* of the two brands. However, the act of choosing and possibly being satisfied by the new brand increases mindspace for the bought brand. More mindspace for one brand means less for the other. If price lures consumers to cheaper brands, these brands will have a good chance of permanently gaining mindspace. This can be particularly brutal in a market hit by recession, or when competitors are making a special play on price to increase price sensitivity.

2.2.2.2 Buying and Selling Mindspace

A short-cut to owning mindspace is to buy the rights to a brand, or to buy a company which owns established brands. The value that a brand represents is often reflected in the high prices paid for companies which own brands. In this way, money can buy time, for a specific company. Money does not substitute for time in the sense that it does not *create* mindspace, it merely transfers the ownership.

Mindspace is about getting consumers (and distributors) to learn and remember, and it is this that takes a long time. Another way of buying time is to rent or buy information and names that are already in consumer minds. Well-known names can be licensed and attached to products: most haute couture houses rent their names out these days, as do many film and sports stars.

It is possible to own mindspace without being able to make a physical product. Franchise operations develop mindspace and then sell it to people (franchisees) who are able to attach it to their physical output. If you want to open a car exhaust replacement outfit, you can build up awareness and trust through local advertising and word of mouth, but this will take time. You can kick off much faster by buying mindspace from Midas.

2.2.2.3 *Shelfspace plus Packaging plus Quality*

Mindspace can be created spontaneously, via shelfspace and packaging. For example, assuming the shopper can read, a plain box marked 'Salt' will identify the product contents, and the packaging, whether a plain white box or a glossy cylinder with closing plastic spout, will set up certain expectations about price and quality. Similarly, an end-of-gondola display of glossy boxes of chocolate, will spontaneously create mindspace. Such mindspace will usually be relatively light on specific imagery and perhaps also on quality reassurance. However, in certain product fields, this kind of weak mindspace may be adequate for trial. Once the consumer has direct product experience, mindspace will include knowledge about quality, which could be very positive.

In times when paid-for media are more expensive and fragmented the shelfspace–packaging–quality route is an economic source of mindspace.

2.2.2.4 *Losing Mindspace*

A brand that has been marketed to a population over many years has enviable mindspace. Many US and European children now recognise the yellow double arch of McDonald's before they can read. When children become buyers some brands are already firmly established in their minds. Once a brand has achieved this level of mindspace, it is in a strong position to defend it.

However, it is a big mistake to think that mindspace is not volatile. Staying on the technical learning curve demands commitment and investment, and similarly, customers will fall off their learning curve if they are not continually coaxed and pushed. Every dominant brand (such as those listed in Table 2.1) has had to reinvest in mindspace every year to keep its position. Being dominant in a market usually means that the brand *can* afford to defend its position. Large brands can finance the R&D needed to keep their technical performance abreast or ahead of the market, and similarly a dominant brand can usually afford the greatest share of voice in advertising, can offer competitive service to the distribution and can attract the best brand management to co-ordinate all these activities. However, things can go wrong. Mindspace is hard to earn off diligent leaders, but easy to throw away through complacency or mistakes. Managers can observe that mindspace appears to be rather stable and shows little sensitivity to small changes in marketing inputs (such as advertising). In fact, like the altitude of an aeroplane, mindspace depends at each point on the 'thrust' provided by the company.

The loss of repeat sales through reducing the quality of the product is a classic failure brought on through management cost-cutting and complacency: taking consumer faith as a given. American brewer Schlitz was a highly successful brand of beer in the USA, but it saw its sales tumble from 18 million barrels in 1974 to one million barrels in 1988, through sheer mismanagement.[1] The American brewer underestimated the effect of reducing quality to gain cost savings. It accelerated its fermentation process, substituted corn syrup for the traditional barley malt and changed stabiliser. The consumer spotted these cost savings, and their perceptions of the brand's quality fell. Heavy advertising expenditures and a return to the previous quality were in vain. The mindspace had been taken by competitors Miller and Anheuser-Busch, and could not easily be retaken.

Cadbury's 'Dairy Milk' chocolate bars once held a dominant position in the British chocolate eater's mind. However, under competitive pressure from cheaper 'filled' bars (filled with cheap ingredients such as caramel, wafer and rice) Cadbury's shaved their bars thinner and thinner. Rowntree's research picked up the consumer frustration with the decreasing thickness of the Cadbury bars. They launched the Yorkie bar, so thick that some women found it difficult to bite through. A powerful advertising campaign featured a hunky truck driver who had no problem pulverising the thick chunks. Rowntree were able to take a large slice of this enormous market. And in mindspace terms Cadbury's have never been able to recover the 'chunky' attribute lost to Rowntree.

Reducing levels of communication can have similarly disastrous and asymmetric (easy to lose, hard to regain) effects. This can happen because marketing investments are channelled towards the trade rather than the consumer or because of financial or political pressures inside the firm. Cristal Alken beer lost mindspace in its native Belgium when French BSN bought it up and then channelled resources into building up the French brand Kronenbourg. When Mars cut back on their UK advertising budgets in order to invest more in western Europe, they saw some lag in consumer response, but then a definite drop in market share.

Mindspace can be lost, and is never permanently won.

2.3 PRODUCTIVITY, MINDSPACE AND SHELFSPACE

In modern FMCG markets, a better functioning product on its own is unlikely to succeed. There are too many eager competitors waiting to imitate any innovation. Technological expertise must be backed up with the communication skills and marketing muscle to win mindspace and shelfspace.

Procter & Gamble consciously prefer to stick to functional benefits, feeling that if they switch to more emotional benefits they will be less likely to have a clear advantage over their competition (see Section 1.4). However, this does *not* mean that their technological prowess is more important than their ability to create mindspace. Procter & Gamble's major entry into the hair care market with their 'Wash and Go' brand was a clear example of technological know-how. Buying the famous Vidal Sassoon name was a short-cut for gaining mindspace, backed up with tremendous marketing muscle in terms of TV advertising, sampling and continuous promotions. A functional benefit established in consumer minds *is* mindspace, and mindspace, i.e. awareness and the belief in the functional benefit, is as essential to functional positioning as it is to emotional ones. (See Fig. 2.5.)

It is difficult to have a sustainable differential advantage based on the technical delivery of the product. In many cases there are hardly any discernible differences between competitors, because if one competitor introduces an improvement it is quickly copied. By looking at the extended product—extended to include mindspace and shelfspace assets—a company has a wider competitive base giving more opportunities for creating a sustainable differential advantage.

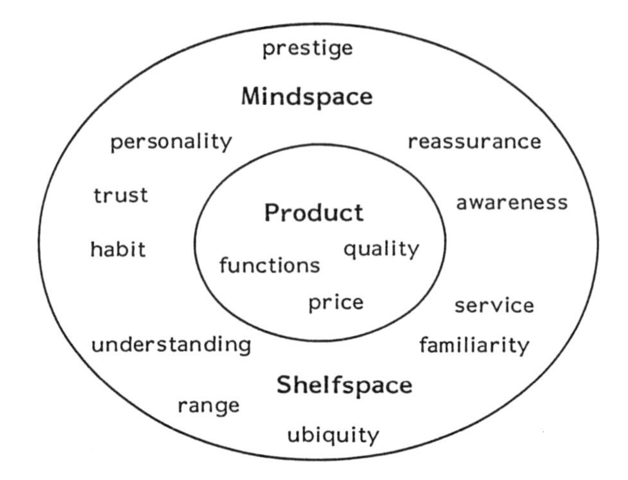

Figure 2.5 *Extended product versus core product*

To provide a sustainable advantage in FMCG markets a technological benefit has to be both:

- costly (or time-consuming) to imitate, and
- backed up by immediate and intensive mindspace and shelfspace building.

The innovator must develop the new segment as fast as possible so that any would-be competitor finds it impossible to achieve sufficient market share to amortise an investment. The ability to develop a large market quickly is also essential for the innovator to ensure a rapid payback as, by definition, the technology must be costly. If the technology is sufficiently expensive, and the pioneer's marketing efforts gain it rapid market penetration, the company reaches a point where a competitor's me-too type strategy is unlikely to be profitable. A later entrant will attract fewer users (because it is more difficult to convert customers to an equivalent product), and will suffer a more price-sensitive market (because there are at least two substitutable competitors). The second company will hesitate before investing as it knows it would struggle to break-even on the expensive technology.

When Gillette launched the Sensor razor the marketing roll out was extremely fast—production could not keep pace with demand in the early stages. It is also worth noting how keen Gillette were to emphasise in the marketing press how expensive the production technology was ('costing $200 million to develop and protected by 22 patents') and how much further investment ('$110m in 1990') they were allocating for a world-wide consumer communication campaign.[2] These actions reinforce the power of the technological lead more surely than the 22 patents. Warner Lambert (owners of the Schick brand) have patents for laser technology similar to that used to produce Gillette's Sensor, but they cannot justify the investment needed to exploit the patents.

Mindspace *protects* technology, and greater facility for creating mindspace can even be an effective weapon against technological innovators. Procter & Gamble's Pampers took the lead from Mölnlycke's Peaudouce, the pioneers in the European disposable nappy market, largely through their ability to create mindspace. Innovation dates only from the consumer's first use or awareness.

Often products which begin life with a technological lead rely in their maturity on the mindspace/shelfspace built up during the years of functional superiority. They stay ahead by converting their technological superiority into mindspace, before it is matched. The mindspace survives long after the functional benefit has ceased to exist in reality.

Apart from sustainability, the other key difference between technology know-how and mindspace/shelfspace is that the latter are finite. The typical supermarket has doubled, trebled and quadrupled its shelfspace in 30 years to stock the vastly increased number of lines, but still cannot keep up with the number of products waiting to be crammed in. It seems unlikely that consumer brain capacity devoted to FMCGs has even doubled.

Technological expertise, by contrast, tends to diffuse and increase. Alternative sources of know-how can often be purchased, and purchase increases the overall supply. Mindspace/shelfspace can be purchased (as when a brand is bought) but the sale does not increase the overall supply of either. New brands often gain sales through launch promotion, but find that repeat purchases dwindle, not through technical failure, but through lack of mindspace/shelfspace. Mindspace and shelfspace are the bottlenecks. Ownership of mindspace and shelfspace is often the only critical resource of a brand.

For most FMCG companies, in most product fields, technological know-how (efficiency, quality and value) is a necessary condition for a brand's success. Know-how, mindspace and shelfspace together form the necessary and sufficient condition for success.

Retailers are becoming competitors to manufacturers in many fields. They have some advantages and some disadvantages when it comes to creating mindspace—but they have mostly advantages when it comes to controlling shelfspace. Much of this book is devoted to the battles for mindspace and shelfspace.

Notes

(1) David Aaker, *Managing Brand Equity: Capitalising on the Value of a Brand Name*, New York, Free Press, 1991, pp. 78–84.
(2) Keith Hammonds, 'How a $4 razor ends up costing £300', *Business Week*, 29 January 1990, p. 62.

3
Brand Proliferation

Many large consumer companies see themselves as 'brand machines'. They organise themselves around their brands, they value their brands separately from, and sometimes above, their physical assets. Creating powerful brands is their key goal.

3.1 THE ROLES OF BRAND PROLIFERATION

As shown in Chapter 1, marketing orientation leads companies to create a set of differentiated brands to cater for the varying needs (segments) in their markets. That is to say, brand proliferation is a method for applying the marketing concept: differentiating products from those of competitors, and from each other, while fitting as closely as possible to the needs of a heterogeneous market.

Aside from this original impetus, there are three other important reasons why brand proliferation is appropriate in many FMCG markets. These are the consumer's desire for variety; as a barrier to keep out small or new competitors; and lastly, as a source of leverage with the distribution. We now look at the four roles of brand proliferation in detail.

3.1.1 Implementing Segmentation

For most large companies, implementing a market orientation means targeting a range of different segments with brands tailored to their respective needs.

Table 3.1 *Nestlé's brands in the UK instant coffee market. Typically, large companies dominate markets by 'proliferating' brands to serve all segments*

Segment	Brand
Mainstream value, spray-dried granules	Nescafé
Premium, freeze dried	Gold Blend
	Blend 37
Super premium, freeze dried, pure arabica	Alta Rica
	Cap Colombie
Decaffeinated	Nescafé Decaffeinated
	Gold Blend Decaffeinated
	Alta Rica Decaffeinated
Price, old fashioned, spray-dried powder	Fine Blend
Speciality, convenience (sachets) and novelty	Nescafé Cappuccino
	Unsweetened Cappuccino
	Espresso

Segmentation leads most large FMCG companies to design a series of brands, within one product category, which between them cover a large proportion of the market. Nestlé services all the main segments of the UK instant coffee market with appropriate brands (see Table 3.1). This brand portfolio enables Nestlé to hold on to *over half* of the UK's £500m instant coffee market.

A company proliferates brands in relation to the segments in the market, trying to minimise competition between its own brands while maximising the impact on its competitors. In some cases a company is driven to cannibalise its own brand, rather than leave it juicy prey to a competitor. Thus Gillette launched a disposable razor in the US, ahead of French company Bic. New brands can be used to protect a brand whose segment is being sub-segmented by a competitive brand. The new brand will do this by positioning itself more pointedly for the sub-segment than the competitor (see Fig. 3.1).

This pattern of brand proliferation will be familiar to most readers. The interesting point to note is that, as segmentation progresses in an industry, the company needs to cover a greater number of segments. It often has the technical know-how to serve them, or will invest in the R&D and production facilities to do so. The crunch comes in finding economical ways to generate mindspace and shelfspace for all the little sub-segmenting brands.

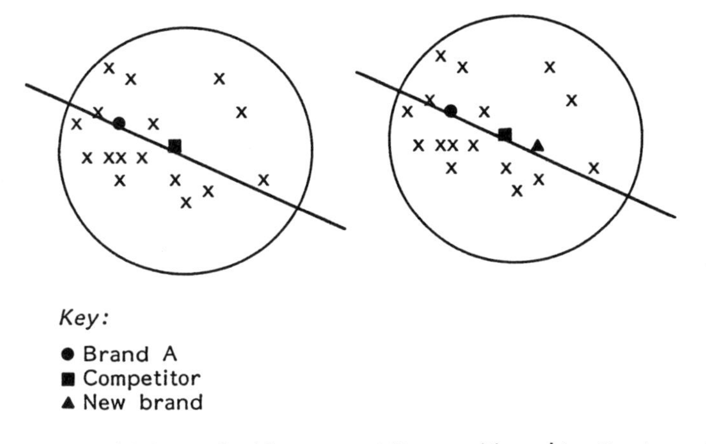

Figure 3.1 *Brand A is attacked by a competitor, positioned to attract a certain type of consumer. The owners of brand A launch a new brand positioned further from the original brand, on the dimension offered by the competitor*

3.1.2 Variety Seeking

Unlike industrial buyers, FMCG consumers seek variety and novelty, even when they are satisfied with their favourite brand. The need for variety and change can outweigh a preference for one brand (imagine a car manufacturer getting *bored* with its brake pads).

In markets such as breakfast cereals or chocolate bars this 'desire for variety' is a major market dynamic. The effect is often known as repertoire buying and consumers are said to have an 'evoked set' of brands, from which they will buy on any buying occasion with a certain probability. A large manufacturer, such as Kellogg's in breakfast cereals, can win a larger share of one homogenous segment by brand proliferating. For example, many sweetened children's cereals are positioned identically to each other to satisfy a segment best characterised as 'fun'. 'Fun' is created and communicated by a troop of anthropomorphic characters: bee, frog, tiger, monkey, bear, etc. In a promiscuous, variety-seeking market, being able to proliferate brands gives a significant advantage to the supplier most able to do this: a larger number of brands and a stream of new brands, means a better chance of being bought on each buying occasion, even as the *average* chance of being bought goes down for each brand.

3.1.3 Deterrence of Entry

Brand proliferation helps large firms to dominate their product markets. In most FMCG markets any small company finding a viable niche will either be profitably bought up by a larger competitor (Unilever buys companies more frequently than a typical household buys shampoo), or unprofitably squeezed out of its niche. The costs to a multi-brand company of producing an extra brand are usually less than the costs to a small company producing a similar brand. This is because many of the costs associated with new brands can be shared with established brands.

These 'economies of scope' nearly always apply to production facilities, R&D and distribution; often they apply to media buying and promotional spend. There is synergy across brands, and this is one of the reasons that brand proliferation is such a successful strategy for large manufacturers. Even if a new brand adds nothing to overall profits, it makes it more and more difficult for new entrants to compete—there are no profitable segments left to take. Kellogg's help to sustain their dominant position in breakfast cereals by promoting a series of brands (All Bran, Bran Flakes, Crunchy Nut Corn Flakes, Frosties, Fruit 'n Fibre, Coco Pops, Muesli, Crunchy Muesli, Smacks, Loops, Trios, etc.) positioned strategically on the different psychological and health/taste dimensions important to the market.

When Post's Banana Nut Crunch showed promise in the US, Kellogg's rushed out Banana Nut Muslix in Canada. This indefinitely postponed Post's BNC launch in Canada. Kellogg's BNM itself achieved little more than half a percentage point of market share, but it was a success for Kellogg's in that it blocked a gap in the market. When General Mills launched Fiber 1 in Canada, Kellogg's came out simultaneously with Fiber Up. The opportunity turned out to be about the same size as that for Banana Nut Crunch and not big enough for two brands. Both were withdrawn: a satisfactory outcome to Kellogg's.

3.1.4 Leverage with Distribution, Category Management

Increasingly, brand proliferation is seen as a variable in the struggle for power with the retailer. The idea is that by becoming more important in a category (having brands which serve all significant segments) a manufacturer can better influence the retailer's approach to the whole category. Retailers will look to one of the major players to form the basis of their category layout. The manufacturer who dominates such a layout can often justify better presentation of its brands. For example, the producer's niche brands will be taken in preference to those from other suppliers, and the opportunities for merchandising and promoting will be enhanced. Since shelfspace is one of the most powerful sources of mindspace and shelfspace is another zero-sum resource, any gains of this type are won from competitors and are doubly valuable. Thus, category thinking, and the desire to provide a comprehensive 'category', will suggest adding (i.e. proliferating) brands to serve category roles.

The increasing importance of shelfspace as a resource (partly due to the pressure on shelfspace from retailers' own brands) means that the 'leverage' argument for catering to as many segments as possible is now a major incentive to brand proliferate. Even if category management as such does not come into play, gaining presence on shelf is frequently an argument for increasing the number of lines. It seems evident that a manufacturer only offering a small and patchy range is disadvantaged in the race to gain presence in store compared to one with a comprehensive range.

3.2 THE EFFECTS OF BRAND PROLIFERATION

Three of the four motivations listed above for proliferating brands are not about serving segments with different needs. As a result, the will to create genuinely differentiated brands has eroded markedly. Brand proliferating simply to complete a range, or to keep out niche players has had two important effects on brand marketing. The first is that companies have become increasingly willing to launch copies of competitors' brands (colloquially known as 'me-toos'). The second is that many of the new products launched are not expected to become large-volume sellers, and thus cannot be adequately financed.

3.2.1 Me-toos

It is a familiar spectacle: one manufacturer comes out with a modest innovation, only to be followed by a cascade of me-toos, most of which hardly break even. This strategic emphasis on me-toos is equally apparent in the USA and Europe. To pick an example at random, a regional French company called Saint-Hubert hit on the idea (already established in Japan) of a yoghurt-like product using the bifidus bacteria. The concept was that a booster dose of this bacterium, normally present in the human gut, would have beneficial health effects: doctors sometimes recommend yoghurt alongside a course of antibiotics to replace the 'flora' in the digestive tract. In April 1986 Saint-Hubert launched B'A (Bifidus Active) as a more active, organic, yoghurt compared to the deadish yoghurts sold on taste and child platforms. The implied benefit was that B'A made your body firmer, skin younger, hair thicker etc. Gervais (Danone/BSN) were the first to react, in October 1987, with a bifidus product called Bio, with advertising that featured smooth young bodies that had clearly benefited from Bio's action. 'What it does on the inside, shows on the outside' (a fairly non-committal line, when you think about it), said the Bio advertising. The floodgates were then open, and progress is best viewed as a chart: see Table 3.2. The first own label came out in October 1988. By this stage, dark blue and green had become the calling card of the bifidobacterium, so later entrants dispensed with advertising by

Table 3.2 *An example of the phenomenon of me-toos in the French yoghurt market*[1]

Date	Brand	Manufacturer/Retailer
April 1986	B'A	Saint-Hubert
October 1987	Bio	Gervais-Danone
January 1988	O'filus	Yoplait/Sodiaal (took over Saint-Hubert Jan. 1990)
March 1988	Zen	Lactel
September 1988	Bifidou	Senoble
October 1988	La Forme	Monoprix (Retailer)
December 1988	Lactus	Carrefour (Retailer)
May 1989	Oh! Chambourcy	Nestlé
1989	Fob	Casino (Retailer)
1989	Actifidus	Leclerc (Retailer)
1989	Doufidus	Intermarché (Retailer)
1989	Biac	Cora (Retailer)
1989	Bifidus Forza	Prisunic (Retailer)
1990	Nat Plus	Sodim (Retailer)

following the packaging codes. By 1990, the bifidus sector of the market had reached about 12% in yoghurt and 3% of fromage frais.

For each individual player, the arguments for bringing out me-toos are valid, even compelling. Aside from the hope of making money, the me-too brand will complete the range offered to the distributor, and in particular make the innovator superfluous to the distributor. The me-too will reduce the profits made by the innovator. Unchecked these profits could provide greater competitive strength to attack other segments. When a new brand attacks the segment belonging to an established brand, a me-too can be used defensively, to limit the damage and preserve mindspace (see below).

At the product category level, however, bringing out me-toos is a sure way to move a market back towards price competition. Me-toos are like weeds that grow up in the marketing garden, throttling the flowering plants. Many FMCG markets are beginning to look like a garden belonging to a vacant house.

In a market where other manufacturers are willing to bring out me-toos, being an innovator and marketer in the traditional mould begins to look like a sucker's strategy. Such a sad example is Heudebert, a biscuit maker owned by French food giant Danone. Heudebert launched a Swedish 'crisp brod', with a strong emphasis on the Swedishness—personified in their advertising by a sexy, blonde Swedish girl. The product was good, the advertising gripping, and competitors (including retailers) had but to say 'Swedish' on their me-toos to cash in on the communication paid for by Heudebert.

Imitation is *not* a market-oriented strategy, and the manufacturers who use it know that they are moving their markets to the left on the war spectrum. When companies wilfully copy the successful differentiation of their competitors, they destroy the market for all. Out-of-control brand proliferation is bringing the brand system to the point of bankruptcy.

3.2.2 Brand Extensions and Umbrella Branding

Creating mindspace for an entirely new brand name is now an extremely ambitious objective. Reaching consumers has become more expensive in real terms as more organisations (health authorities and many other governmental agencies, charities, political parties, insurance companies, direct mail outfits, retailers, lotteries, etc.) have learnt to use the media as effectively and avidly as FMCG marketing companies.

Even once a name is learnt, it has to gain credibility and meaning. The ultimate source of quality reassurance is satisfaction, and particularly satisfaction extended over time. Credibility tends to increase with familiarity, other things being equal, and the longer a name has been around, the more reassuring it seems to become. The amount of investment necessary to achieve all this in our media-saturated societies is now so great, that this route cannot be contemplated unless the expected return from the product is correspondingly enormous. In mature FMCG markets, most companies recognise that very few of their new products have this much potential.

The alternative solution for creating mindspace for a new brand is to *borrow* some of the mindspace from some established product. The mindspace already built for other brands can be stretched to give presence, quality reassurance and image to a new product. All that is left to do is to identify the new product, by explaining its particular function. If the function is already familiar, e.g. orange juice, no additional communication is necessary. Thus, in 1993, Nestlé launched 120 new lines in France. Five aimed to establish new brand names, the other 115 borrowed their brand names from previously established products.

This is the most dramatic change in brand management in recent years: from a mission to create new brands for new technologies and new segments to an increasing reliance on brand extensions.

Even in the early 1980s, brand extensions were anathema to many big FMCG companies. For decades, Mars' official company philosophy was that names such as Twix, Bounty or Mars should identify unique, inviolable and indivisible products. Now Mars are well into the process of extending virtually all the brands they own: into drinks, ice-creams, spreads for bread and flavour variants. Other famous chocolate brands adorn everything vaguely chocolate flavoured from chilled desserts and biscuits to liqueurs.

Similarly, for about five decades Persil identified one washing powder with one proposition (even if the actual product was regularly reformulated). Persil now signs a range of washing products (about 40 in the UK), and even when Lever Brothers wants to launch a new generation of detergent it feels obliged to stretch the Persil name ('Persil Power') rather than establish a new brand. When Procter & Gamble bought Oil of Ulay from Richardson Vicks it was simply a beauty fluid. Its mindspace has since been harnessed to sign a bath bar, shower lotion, foaming wash and, ironically, a new *oil-free* moisturiser, called Hydro Gel. The other skin-care products of yesteryear, Nivea (now Nivea Visage) from Smith & Nephew (Beiersdorf in Europe), Pond's cream (Pond UK, Unilever in Europe) and even Savlon (Zyma healthcare) are all doing the same thing.

The conventional wisdom on brand building has been dramatically reformulated. In the past manufacturers built a series of power brands like a series of independent forts. The modern approach is to buttress existing brand castles with extensions and formats and varieties, like rings of defensive earthworks, moats and look-out towers. New product development now means marrying up the reputation and renown of established brands with the endless permutations coming out of R&D. The reasons for this change are quite clear. We now try to look at the implications.

3.2.2.1 What's in a Brand Name?

The idea of one name being used on a number of products is familiar. Company names such as Cadbury or Kellogg have long been used in this way. Companies have also long been in the habit of using an 'umbrella' or 'family' name to sign a range of products having certain qualities in common. For example, Nestlé uses its company name to sign coffees, chocolate and (now) cereal products, 'Findus' and 'Lean Cuisine' for frozen food, and Chambourcy for yoghurt and other chilled dairy products. Mars uses 'Dolmio' for tomato products, 'Pedigree' for petfood.

At the other end of the spectrum companies also invent (or co-opt) names to identify specific products. These brand names act like nouns in the consumer's vocabulary. We can call such brand names 'eponymous' because they give their name to a 'thing'.

'Wispa' is an eponymous brand name—if you ask for a 'Wispa' in a confectionery shop, you will be handed a delicious chocolate bar. Cadbury, by contrast, is an umbrella brand name—if you ask for 'a Cadbury', you will not be making sense. Nobody would argue that one type of branding is good and the other bad, but most people would agree that umbrella branding and eponymous branding serve rather different roles. Brand names in general serve three essential roles:

(1) Identification
At the simplest level, consumers have to know what it is they are buying. Once a product is uniquely identified it can be selected quickly and without effort. Identification is an essential first step which allows a consumer to repeat a positive buying experience and to attach positive imagery.

(2) Trust
That is, reassurance of quality and safety. Many FMCG products are eaten, and others we smear on our bodies. We use them in, on and around our nearest and dearest, so we need to feel they are safe. In industrialised societies these cares can slip into the subconscious, but we still don't want to be landed with a product of inferior quality. Buying tasteless biscuits that the kids reject or a cosmetic to which we are allergic is a waste of money. We want to avoid wasting our money; we want quality reassurance.

(3) Images or associations
An important part of mindspace consists of the associations and images attached to the brand, usually via advertising. This aspect is less tangible but often of great importance in choice and in satisfaction. In many FMCG purchases, such as cigarettes, choice may be overwhelming (about 150 brands of cigarettes are available in the USA). Image can help a consumer come to some decision, where rational reasons for choice are vague, though the decision may still be important to the shopper.

Whenever a company brands a product it aims to satisfy each of these three roles, but there are several different ways that brand names help perform the three functions.

The first option is to establish a single, eponymous brand name to perform all three functions on its own. 'Kit-Kat' is an example of a brand that works in all three ways, identifying one familiar biscuit for its loyal buyers, guaranteeing quality through its own long reputation (few know which company makes it, or that this company has changed), and rich in connotations of 'taking a break'.

The second option is to combine an umbrella brand with an eponymous brand name in order to achieve the three goals. For example, 'Kellogg's Frosties' uses Kellogg's to provide feelings of quality reassurance, but the tiger imagery and specific identification are carried out by Frosties.

A third option is to combine one or two umbrella brands with a product description. Lever's call a brand of washing-up liquid 'Persil Washing Up Liquid'—Persil reassures and adds some imagery. 'L'Oréal's Studioline Hair Mousse' is an example of two umbrellas: L'Oréal provides the reassuring pedigree, Studioline associates the right image, and product identification is effected prosaically (see Fig. 3.2).

Other constructions are possible. L'Oréal's merging of their 'Rayonnance' and 'Energance' hair care ranges under the 'Performance' umbrella has given them some monster product designations such as 'L'Oréal, Performance, Rayonnance, Mild Shampoo'. Unilever and Danone have jointly launched a frozen yoghurt brand, 'Yolka', using two umbrellas 'Motta' (for ice cream heritage) and 'Danone' (for yoghurt values). Coke/Coca-Cola is the only brand we know of with two eponymous brand names, written alternately around the can. Anomalies exist, but it's fair to say that most brand naming follows one of the three patterns described above.

Umbrella branding works differently from eponymous branding. The main value of umbrella brands is to offer non-specific quality reassurance. This is an important role and umbrella brand names are often extremely valuable. Sony, Renault and Nikon are all umbrella names, operating in market segments where it would be, in effect, impossible to introduce new models without the assurance of a reputed name. The same is true for high-risk products such as pharmaceuticals or products for babies and prestige products such as watches or perfumes. Sometimes being part of a range is a positive help. This can give a sense of authority (Black & Decker), more control over presence in store (L'Oréal) or the opportunity for the consumer to buy into a set of complementary products (washing machine/tumble drier). Thus umbrella names have a vital role. Eponymous names have a different role. Eponymous or nearly eponymous names identify rapidly and associate very specific imagery (see Fig. 3.3).

Branding is expensive as it involves building up mindspace in millions of minds. Umbrella branding often appears more

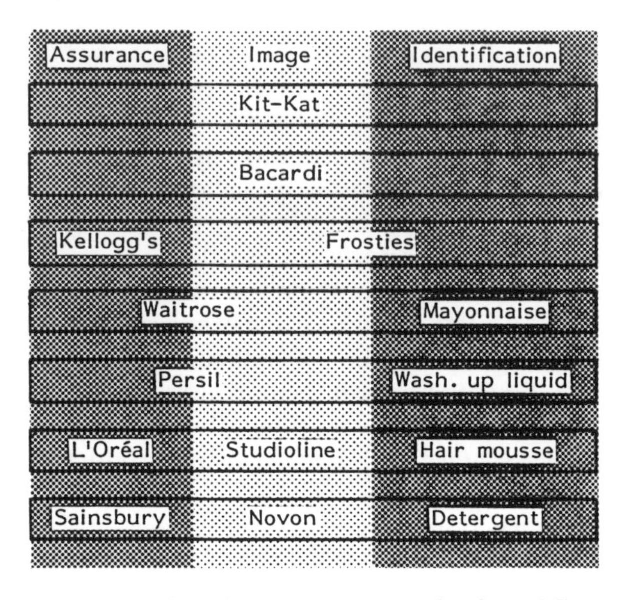

Figure 3.2 *Constructing brand names to support the three different aspects of mindspace*

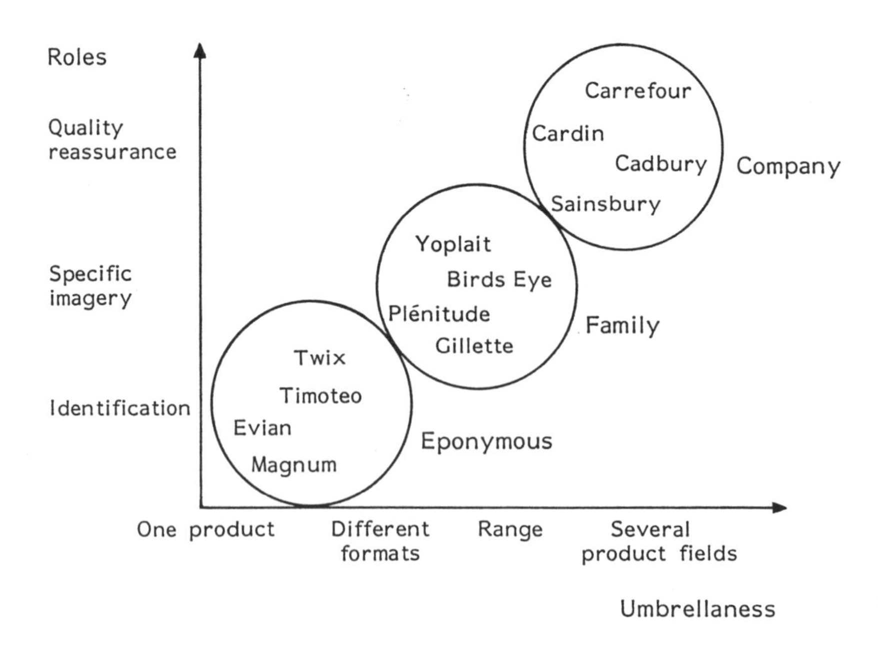

Figure 3.3 *Company, family and eponymous brand names fulfil different roles*

economical than eponymous branding. The latter can always be replaced by using descriptions. For example, instead of Cadbury's Wispa, Cadbury's could substitute Cadbury's Micro Bubble chocolate and save some advertising costs. Thus, economy suggests brand extension—pushing brands towards wider umbrellaness, and substituting at the eponymous end with prosaic descriptions.

Brand extension means a movement from specific to umbrellaness. The more a brand name is extended to different products and the more diverse these products are, the less the brand name is able to convey specific images or messages. For example, Gillette on razors means 'technology in shaving'; when extended to aftershaves, soaps and deodorants it might mean 'masculine products'—a less specific image.

The recent emphasis on brand extensions has meant that many eponymous brands are currently in the process of moving from eponymity to umbrellaness for the first time. For example, 'Mars' and 'Tide' used to be perfectly eponymous, but both are in the process of divesting their eponymity.

Swapping an eponymous brand for an umbrella brand is attractive to companies in the short term, as it immediately reduces the necessary investment for launching new brands. The danger that we see, and will come back to in Chapter 8, is that retailers can also umbrella brand. Strong, uncopiable, brands are the best defence for manufacturers facing retailers. As hinted in Fig. 3.3, extending manufacturer brands tends to march them into territory occupied by retailer brands. It is because of this danger that brand extension merits close examination in this book.

3.2.2.2 The Road to Hell is Paved with Good Extensions

Brand extensions fit our times with the same ineluctable logic as airport shopping and ready-cooked dinners. The logic is as follows.

Protecting mindspace

Brand proliferation means that aggressive new brands are continually finding ways to take sales from established brands. One solution is for the company owning the established brand to launch fighter brands to hold or win back sales in the new, more specialised segments and subsegments. This strategy may help to hold on to sales volume, but the new brands do nothing to protect the mindspace being eroded from established brands. Since mindspace is zero-sum, the reverse must be true: mindspace is won off the established brands. An alternative to expensively creating mindspace for new brands is to try to exploit existing mindspace by bringing out extensions under the existing brand name.

For example, if a liquid detergent takes sales from a powder detergent, the maker of the powder can offer users a me-too version of the liquid brand. The me-too can attack the new brand by capitalising on the mindspace of the original brand, and at the same time help to preserve the mindspace of the original brand. In the UK, Lever Brothers were the first to market with a liquid detergent. Following the conventional wisdom of yesterday, they launched the brand-new brand 'Wisk', which was more or less an overnight success. Procter & Gamble then launched a liquid version of Ariel, obliging Lever's to respond with a liquid Persil. Wisk is now under review for divesting.

On the other side of the Atlantic, Procter & Gamble feel that clinging to the 'new technology = new brand' philosophy all but destroyed their Ivory (soap) and Spic & Span (cleaner) brands. After years of erosion by more modern products, Procter & Gamble have decided to revive the mindspace of these two great old brands by launching new technologies under these names.[2]

There are many such cases where brand extensions seem to be the only way to rejuvenate and protect a major brand. Such a situation faced Coca-Cola Company when they launched Diet Coke in 1982.

Coca-Cola Company stayed with one version of Coca-Cola for nearly a hundred years. During the 1970s, the product field changed dramatically because of an 'anti-sugar' social movement and technological progress in artificial sweeteners. Several diet colas, lead by Royal Crown, were launched and showed the enormous potential for virtually calorie-free substitutes. Coca-Cola Company first launched Tab, sugar-free Cola, but saw that they needed to use their powerful main brand if they were really to dominate this dynamic area of the market. Coca-Cola

Company bowed to these changes by introducing Diet Coke: an astounding success. Was it a new brand (using the Family name) or a timely technological updating of the old, great, brand?

Interestingly, Coca-Cola Company have since resisted extensions to their main brand: their clear (as against brown) Cola has been launched under the Tab brand name and their 'new age' fruit drink under the name 'Fruitopia'. Coca-Cola company generally competes with separately promoted brands (Minute Made, Hi C, Sprite, Mello Yello, Fresca). Meanwhile, Pepsi have launched Pepsi Crystal and Pepsi Max, a sugar-free drink without a 'diet' designation. The time has come when to order a Pepsi in a café gets the response: 'Which Pepsi?' Coke remains, more or less, a real 'thing'.

Protecting mindspace is probably the only good marketing argument for launching extensions, most particularly when a technology becomes obsolete. Unilever would be crazy to let Lux slip down the plug hole (in the USA and the UK) with the block soap habit. Beyond this particular situation (and the people in the Coca-Cola head office in Atlanta seem to agree) you shouldn't expect to have your Coke and drink it.

Smaller segment size

There are powerful incentives to brand proliferate, and brand proliferation is what has been happening, at an accelerating rate, in all FMCG markets. As a consequence, FMCG markets are fragmenting faster than they are growing. Each new segment, sub-segment and sub-sub-segment is, on average, smaller. Launch investment has to be calculated as a function of targeted brand size. Launching new brands is expensive, and thus only viable if the brand being launched is going to reach a certain size. If a new brand has high sales targets, the cost of launching an entirely new brand will be acceptable when discounted over a reasonable period. Now the size of most new segments has shrunk to the point where manufacturers who were once reluctant to 'stretch' their brand names see no other economic way of gaining mindspace.

Short-term vision

Most major FMCG companies are under overwhelming pressure to discount the future, in favour of short-term profitability. This has a powerful impact on the question of whether to extend or build from scratch.

The exceptional returns made by FMCG companies in the 1980s raised the stock market expectations for the FMCG industry. If a company fails to fulfil such expectations its share price falls. The stock market demands profit estimates every three months. In marketing terms, three months is a very short-run strategy.

The pressure of the stock market is felt by senior managers via their personal stock options, as a take-over threat, and as a threat to their job security after explaining share price falls to the shareholders. Their concern for reaching targets affects the way they assess junior staff for promotion (which often carries with it a change in responsibilities). Thus from top to bottom the organisation is looking for actions which will show quick returns, on the cogent basis that there won't be a long term if the short term isn't on target. Brand extensions fit the bill because they give quick returns compared to launching totally new brands. The economic advantages of brand extensions are often categorical when calculated on a three to five-year time span.

The active life span of a consumer product can, on the other hand be decades. The original (and eponymous) Oil of Ulay had been turning in good profits for 40 years before all this started. Will the Oil of Ulay umbrella name still be adding value to the same degree in 40 years' time?

Below we look at the controversies over extending brands, but one thing is clear: if the decision frame is purely the short term, the extenders have it, and the shorter the term the more the argument goes in their favour.

Branding me-toos

The impact of me-toos is one reason why individual brand support is becoming uneconomic, it also means that in many cases it is superfluous.

An argument that used to be raised against using extensions, was that the established brand name restricted the positioning possibilities of the new brand, and thus potentially its sales. Me-toos have nothing to say except 'I am similar to that, of good quality and a little cheaper'. All this can be said perfectly with umbrella reassurance and presence on shelf. Some retailers refer to such brands as 'manufacturer label'. Brand extensions are frequently efforts to expand presence on shelf or to neutralise functional benefits offered by competitors and have little new to talk about.

In a market where most of the new product development is humdrum reformulations of existing products, brand extension is the fitting form of branding.

3.2.3 Rain Forest or Rice Field?

The key unknown about brand extension is its effect in the long term. In the long term, is brand capital a non-renewable resource like a rain forest, or is a brand name like a rice field, which generates a steady crop twice a year through a thousand years?

Opinion is split. Some research has been done on the value added by extensions, mostly aiming to draw the line between 'appropriate' and 'inappropriate' extensions.[3] The researchers concentrate on drawing the line, for example, between Marlboro 100s, Marlboro Lights, Marlboro Menthol, Marlboro clothes, Marlboro coffee, Marlboro mineral water and Marlboro powdered baby milk formula, and so on.

Estimating the long-term effect of extensions, once everyone has done it, is of course much more difficult. Some authorities celebrate 'capitalising' on brand names as a way of getting something out of nothing: 'A line extension is the ultimate in increased productivity' according to one analyst quoted in *Advertising Age*.[4] The opposite view (that one should suspect free lunches) is promoted, for example by Ries and Trout: 'One name cannot usually stand for two different brands . . . in the long term, line extension is usually a losers' strategy'.[5]

Actual practice is divided also. Mercedes have in recent years placed their famous star on the bonnets of increasingly middle-market cars. Ford are launching their first small model extension of their prestige Jaguar brand and GM have similar strategies for the Saab name.[6] To Mercedes, Ford and GM it is 100% clear that these almost mystical marques add value to the new, smaller models. The risk, which in these cases seems more like a certainty, is that the brands will irrevocably degrade, as MG and Alfa Romeo have already done. During the same period Toyota with 'Lexus', Honda with 'Acura' and Nissan with

'Infiniti' are following Alfred Sloan's expensive and long-term brand proliferation approach when he created Chevrolet, Oldsmobile, Pontiac, Buick and Cadillac back in the 1920s.

Viewing the brand extension spectacle as a whole, it seems that the process cannot go on indefinitely. It seems quite possible that wonderful old brand names will turn out to be a non-renewable resource like rain forests, that make their owners rich while they plunder them. The following three considerations reinforce this fear.

(1) Dilution (and Destruction) of Imagery

Stretching a brand name over different versions of products, or even different types of products generally involves a move from specificity towards blandness. As the brand recedes into umbrellaness it loses some of its original meaning. The pointedness of the brand image will decline, and its meaning will tend towards a non-specific quality reassurance.

The associations linked to a brand are dynamic. Immediately a brand name is placed on a new product, the name will be receiving a new set of input images. The experience of the new product will influence perceptions of the name just as much as those of the original brand. Nike extended their brand into casual footwear but subsequently withdrew, feeling that the move weakened the sports image of their base brand.

The example of luxury cars was given earlier, Miller beer had problems with its 'Lite' beer. Light products tend to have connotations of false, emasculated, etc., which pull decisively against images of 'the genuine article', and macho. Similarly, Oil of Ulay extended to washing products and oil-free moisturisers may retain broad values of 'conserving youth', but the idea of some 'precious Eastern oil', must start to dissolve.

In terms of communication, most particularly advertising, it is more difficult to associate clear values with an umbrella brand than with a specific product brand. The communications will seek the highest common factor linking the range (e.g. keeping your skin young-looking) and this will tend to converge on other skin-care ranges. The situation is similar for packaging, another key element of communication for FMCGs. In skin care, it is conventional to pack moisturisers in warm colours such as pink, cleaning products in watery colours such as blue. Wide ranges using both colours lose the opportunity to identify themselves with certain colours, as say the old Oil of Ulay with its 'black and pink', or the old Nivea with its 'white out of blue' certainly once did. Such aspects of branding and communication are hard to pin down, but one can only imagine that mindspace is easier to create with pointed and distinct communications than with broad and similar ones.

(2) Noun Quality

Intuitively, there seems to be a difference in going into a sweet shop and asking for 'a Coke' or 'a Mars', and asking for a cola-flavoured soft drink or caramel-filled chocolate bar from such and such a manufacturer. More concretely, made up eponymous names cannot be copied directly by competitors and, in particular, retailers. A close copy looks false and an exact copy is illegal. Conversely, competitors are very likely to have respectable umbrella brands to deploy with prosaic descriptions.

Once an eponymous brand name is extended to a second product, its noun quality is lost. There is no longer one healthy margarine called 'Flora', which caring wives know they can safely spread on their husbands' sandwiches. There are a range of light, extra light, standard and low-calorie Floras, extending even to 'White Flora'—a lard substitute for use in pastry and roasting—made from sunflower and vegetable oil. Unilever/Van den Berg Foods has certainly got good reason for expanding its range in this way. The down side may be that each Flora sub-brand is now less resistant to the onslaught of quality lines of polyunsaturated fats signed by retailers. Sainsbury can launch ranges of low-cholesterol and polyunsaturated margarine but they can't launch 'Flora'; they can launch 'Sainsbury's Micro Bubble Chocolate', but they can't launch a 'Sainsbury's Wispa'.

(3) Impact of Cannibalisation and Failure

Extending a name means primarily targeting one's own users: Pepsi Crystal is likely to attract Pepsi drinkers. An extension close to the original can give opportunities to increase margin, rejuvenate the product and counter new competition (e.g. Diet Coke). But an extension can lead consumers away from the main brand and perhaps to disappointment or even a withdrawn brand.

For example, Nivea Visage launched new products containing 'liposomes' to compete with high-tech ranges such as L'Oréal's Plenitude. If the new brand extensions are poorly distributed, or even withdrawn, what effect would such a failure have on the parent brand? A proportion of original brand users will have been attracted to the extension, for example having been convinced through familiar Nivea advertising of the necessity of liposomes. If the extensions fail (and many do) usage patterns will have been disturbed.

Similarly, Lever's leading Persil brand became embroiled in the 'clothes eating' controversy which followed the launch of 'Persil Power'. There would probably have been hardly any publicity given to the new product's teething problems, had the famous brand not been evoked to give it credibility.

On a happier note, when Heineken launched their alcohol-free beer in The Netherlands they called it Buckler, rather than Heineken Light. The brand flopped, largely due to competition from a small Dutch brewer offering a better and cheaper brand called 'Bavaria'. Had Buckler been launched as a Heineken extension it *might* (despite its quality problems) have had a greater chance of success. The downside is that it could have failed after attracting a proportion of Heineken drinkers and delivering them an inferior product labelled 'Heineken'. As it happens, no mindspace was borrowed from Heineken, and none was lost. Cannibalisation is also an issue at the trade level, where an extension can cannibalise the shelfspace normally given to the parent brand. Subsequent to failure, shelfspace may be lost.

3.3 HYPERSEGMENTATION: THE END OF THE ROAD

Great fleas have little fleas upon their backs to bite 'em, and little fleas have lesser fleas, and so ad infinitum. Such is the story of segmentation.

In theory, the scope for segmentation is almost unlimited, as every individual might want a slightly different product, and each individual likes variety. Whenever two products differ on a dimension, another product can always be imagined halfway between the two—for example, Maxwell House Light halfway between real coffee and decaffeinated, or a lemon-flavoured cola, halfway between Coke and Sprite. In most cases such compromises attract some consumers.

As all FMCG companies have progressively understood and applied the brand paradigm, every FMCG area has been transformed by an explosion of functions, formats, sizes and flavours.

The marketing approach can lead to new products that create or grow markets, but many FMCG markets are limited by population growth and human calorie needs. Current consumers already wash their clothes and hair much more frequently than their parents and grandparents did; modern consumers actually consume fewer calories (and still manage to be fatter) than their predecessors. In many FMCG markets humdrum new products mostly displace older ones. Mindspace gained for new brands is taken from older brands. Ready-made salad dressing takes sales from the traditional oil and vinegar; low-fat salad dressing takes sales from the ready made; and low-fat salad dressing in six different flavours sucks sales from the low-fat segment. Mars gains sales of ice-cream with a range of innovative new products, but these sales must be taken from other ice-cream marketers (e.g. Unilever), or confectionery or dessert sales. Consumers cannot simply eat more. The general rule is that average volume sales per SKU (stock keeping unit) keeps going down. Higher margins compensate for the lower volumes. More flexible production methods allow more segments to be served, but somewhere a new limit is reached.

Opening up new segments with branded, differentiated products worked effectively for years: it is still the creed taught to trainee brand managers. Now this approach is showing its age. Many weaker brands are becoming marginal, and new launches are more and more problematical. Articles in the business press proclaim from time to time that 'brands are dead'. This is clearly a gross exaggeration (the articles are usually about who—manufacturers or retailers—will control mindspace in the future), but it is true that manufacturers in many FMCG markets are starting to hit their heads on the ceiling of segmentation.

Our argument is that the perfectly rational policy of brand extension, carefully observing the guidelines for 'good extensions', gradually makes manufacturers more vulnerable to retailer brands. Manufacturers become more vulnerable to retailer brands as they come to rely on umbrella branding because retailers can often provide umbrella branding just as well as manufacturers. Manufacturers are in the same dilemma as the owners of rain forests: they know they should preserve them, but they simply cannot afford to. Brands are still now manufacturers' main weapon against retailers—are they rotting away from the inside? Overall, is it more exact to talk of 'spending' brands than 'exploiting' them?

FMCG was the first industry to embrace marketing orientation. As a result, most of the companies in the industry now try to expand by looking for new segments. Now, while other industries are hailing segmentation as the elixir of industrial youth, FMCG industries have drained the bottom of the glass.

FMCG producers have moved from segmentation to hyper-segmentation, from power brands to brand extensions, from differentiation to me-toos. And now they are approaching the end of the road.

Notes

(1) Table 3.2 was made up from information published in an article by Helene Suaudeau, 'Bifidus: la fortune de pot', *LSA* (Libre Service Actualités), No. 1198, Paris, 22 February 1990, p. 46.
(2) Bill Saporito, 'Behind the tumult at P&G', *Fortune Magazine*, 7 March 1994, pp. 49–54.
(3) David Aaker, *Managing Brand Equity: Capitalising on the Value of a Brand Name*, New York, Free Press, 1991, pp. 207–37.
(4) Julie Liesse Erickson and Judann Dagnoli, 'Line extensions are marketers' life lines', *Advertising Age*, 22 February 1988, pp. 3 and 76. The actual quote, 'A line extension is the ultimate in productivity', came from Manny Goldman, analyst with Montgomery Securities in San Francisco.
(5) Al Ries and Jack Trout, *Marketing Warfare*, New York, McGraw-Hill, 1986, p. 151.
(6) 'Leather, luxury and losses', *The Economist*, 17 July 1993, pp. 67–8.

4
Dealing with Hypersegmentation

Manufacturers seem to be coming to the end of the road for segmenting and sub-segmenting existing markets. Brands, to deserve that name, need a threshold of consumer mindspace and retail shelfspace. Both of these are limited resources that cannot be shared out over more and more lines indefinitely. As more extensions and sub-brands are thrown in, the consumer cannot be expected to remember all the names and propositions. Rather than make the attempt they will make the simplifying assumption that there are few differences and it is most reasonable to choose on price.

Marketing orientation, as practised for the last 50 years by FMCG manufacturers, need not lead to hypersegmentation. Traditionally, to justify a brand launch the new brand had to have some differentiating characteristic and the potential to satisfy a significant segment. It is only when companies flout these conventions and launch me-too products with small potential sales that hyper-segmentation starts. This may be a natural outcome of strategic marketing, which encourages companies to focus on the activities of their competition. Soon they feel that every move has to be matched and every advantage neutralised.

This chapter reviews the new pastures which companies are exploring to escape from the hypersegmentation in their largest markets. These are: new product development, expanding geographically or by product field, going industrial and counter segmentation, via value.

4.1 NEW PRODUCT DEVELOPMENT, OLD PRODUCT DEVELOPMENT AND BREAKTHROUGH

The supreme solution to competitors who erode power brands is still to come up with technical improvements and innovations that are based on proprietary production methods or protected with patents. Gillette has managed this in the razor market, and states the that each time a product is launched another new one is in the pipeline. There is still a regular stream of new products that do succeed to a significant level: Müller yoghurt (in the UK), Snapple iced tea and fruit drinks, Häagen-Dazs ice-cream.

Consumer companies place great emphasis on innovation, for example in their annual reports and press releases, though actual R&D spends are low compared to other industries (see Table 4.1).

There seems to be a risk that the convention to extend, to fine-tune and fiddle, and to repackage and reformulate, dominates

Table 4.1 *Comparison of R&D spending across US industry. R&D expenditure on consumer products is well below average, and in the food industry it is only 0.7% of sales*

Industry	R&D as percentage of sales	R&D as percentage of profits
Health care	8.7	47.9
Electricals/electronics	5.5	84.8
Leisure time products	5.1	125.3
Aerospace	3.7	90.5
Automotive	3.7	over 100
Manufacturing general	2.9	44.7
Housing	1.8	29.7
Consumer products	1.4	13.0
Metals and mining	1.1	17.2
Containers and packaging	0.9	24.3
Food	0.7	8.9
Non-bank financial	0.7	8.5
All industry average	3.4	46.8

Reproduced, with permission, from 'R&D statistics', *Business Week*, Special Issue, 25 October 1991.

the need to discover radically new brands and markets. In most FMCG markets, products are so highly developed that it is difficult to imagine further improvements and the improvements made are so incremental that the consumer is hard put to perceive them: how white can a shirt get? Most washing powders probably already remove stains beyond a mortal's capacity to see or smell them. But is this only because FMCG R&D departments are limiting their remit to areas already well known? The whole washing–drying–ironing cycle is still extremely onerous, and labour and energy intensive: are there truly no possible improvements?

It is perhaps better to think of new product development (NPD) as having two distinct forms. There has to be a continual effort to develop, improve and renew existing brands, aside from this there should also be more fundamental research towards radically new products.

Any brand that does not benefit from continually updated technology slowly dies. This is the conclusion, for example, of Procter & Gamble management about their Ivory soap brand. Extensions, alternative formats and reformulations are part of good brand management. Thirty years ago the typical power brand of was an eponymous, distinct product: Persil was a washing powder, Ivory a soap, Smarties were candy-coated chocolates sold in cardboard tubes. Nowadays, FMCG manufacturers are agreed that a power brand is a changing set of varieties, flankers, forms and extensions with a common link. Van den Berg's Flora ('Becel' in some countries) provides healthier, polyunsaturated fats for spreading and cooking, and as long as a product is both a fat and healthier, it can pitch its tent in the Flora camp. For better or worse, this is modern brand management: this sort of continual brand maintenance should not take over as the only form of NPD.

A survey of top UK FMCG producers gave some insights into the current thrust of NPD departments.[1] The number of launches was high: most companies were churning out at least one 'new' product a year. On the other hand, ambitions were low: two-thirds of the companies set minimum targets for new brands below £6m. In line with these low expectations, and belying the high numbers, over half of the companies surveyed were spending less than 1% of their turnover on R&D (excluding launch costs). This is exactly in line with the US figures in

Table 4.1 (averaging food and consumer products) and pretty low for an industry that believes it depends on innovation.

Perhaps the reason is that the output of R & D cannot be relied upon in any short-term period to supply a breakthrough product. Another may be that breakthroughs are not easy to protect, thus copying is a better strategy than pioneering. On the other hand, there is evidence that in markets where there are genuine innovations, own-label brands are kept at bay (see Fig. 8.2, page 183).

Innovative products are not the only possible new pastures for FMCG companies. Three alternative approaches are also sought to gain relief from the stresses of hypersegmentation, namely: increasing scope (geographically, or by expanding into related product fields), going industrial and counter-segmentation (or value). This is where we now focus our attention.

4.2 INCREASING SCOPE: EXPLOITING CORE COMPETENCIES

Compared with many other industries, the FMCG industry is both relatively fragmented and relatively national. It seems likely that this fragmentation, and national bias, will reduce in the next 20 years, as FMCG companies search for efficiency, and technological and economic forces continue to bring the world closer together.

Companies need to expand because size is still a key benefit. Economies of scale and muscle in dealing with financial, media and retail markets provide real and sustainable competitive advantage. Thus any company which does not want simply to be someone else's acquisition has to be interested in opportunities to exploit company resources and experience in new, and hopefully, less over-crowded markets. By growing larger in these new, less competitive markets, the company can hope to find economies of scale which can eventually help their competitivity back in their base markets.

4.2.1 Ways of Expanding

Expansion can come about by growth within existing markets (NPD), or by expanding across product categories or countries or both (see Fig. 4.1).

		Product field: Existing	Product field: New
Country	Existing	Managing existing brands NPD	Leverage know-how Growing markets
	New	Exploit ideas Less mature markets New resources	Diversification

Figure 4.1 *Leveraging companies' competencies into new markets*

All four routes for expansion compete for resources and the choices are fundamental to the company's future. Each company has to choose between getting a toehold in many countries and developing them all in parallel, or dominating in one or two regions and rolling out a powerful brand. Companies have to assess whether, after all, their skills, resources and brands are essentially national, and best exploited by investing in the home country to gain brand share or enter new categories.

If a company is strong in one or more markets its core competencies may well be relevant to other product fields. Expansion is not the same as diversification: the whole point is to leverage certain core competencies by applying them to new areas. For example, a company that has dealt successfully with the distribution of impulse-purchase confectionery, might be able to exploit its distribution network distributing savoury snacks or soft drinks; a company that has successfully built up health and beauty brands in one country, might have technical and marketing expertise which they could exploit in a less sophisticated, developing market. Consumer understanding and reputation in, say, the women's skin-care market might be leveraged in the men's or children's market, or equally, into health foods or slimming products. The leverage is often greatest when the level of sophistication in the new field is less than that in the old one. Sometimes a new approach and greater sophistication help to transform and expand the new market.

The point in targeting related markets is to gain synergy and economies of scale in managing brands (salesforce, distribution, promotion). Expansion, in any of the four quadrants of Fig. 4.1, can be done organically, through acquisition or through alliances.

(1) Organic

Most businesses start up in just one market. Gaining a presence in further markets involves them in risk, expense and time. The slowest route to expansion is usually organic growth from the base organisation, generating all its own ideas for new products. Mars entered the ice-cream market organically with great success and speed. However, the conjunction of distribution synergy, mindspace synergy (the confectionery brands), and technical know how was quite exceptional.

All expansion is expensive, but organic growth offers more flexibility for the rate of investment. It also offers control. The big disadvantage is that it is usually slow. Even when the capital is available (and many FMCG companies are able to invest heavily), starting from scratch is often too slow to be viable. As observed, one of the key resources for an FMCG company is mindspace among consumers and the distribution, and this takes a long time to build. In addition, products and brand concepts developed and popular in one country are not guaranteed a ready audience abroad. The British love Cadbury chocolate eggs filled with sugar fondant: the product bombed in French consumer tests. On the other hand, if the same niche *does* exist it may well already be filled by a native or international competitor. For example, Mars's Maltesers have no direct competitor in the UK, but Cadbury markets products very similar to Maltesers, under different names, in various parts of the Commonwealth. Even in less developed countries, most FMCG products exist, and people have preferences and habits. It takes a lot of time (and luck) to create and then build a brand. It can save time to buy a set of brands which have already shown some potential, and use the parent company's money and expertise to develop these existing brands.

Another limit on organic expansion is people. To adapt and develop the company's products will require excellent management. Some can be drafted in from the home company, but to understand the native market (consumer and distribution) good national executives are essential. The catch-22 is that it is difficult to attract the quality of managers necessary to deal with the new market, since the subsidiary does not have the stature or size of the parent company. A successful national company, used to exploiting a large or dominant position in its home market, does not necessarily adapt well to being a humble start-up in an alien environment.

The risk of being pre-empted or simply too small to be successful leads to the interest in acquisition of related companies already operating in the new markets, and alliances with companies with complementary experience.

(2) Acquisition

A company can buy related producers to gain or increase its presence in new markets, or strengthen its position in one of its existing markets. Philip Morris, from a start in tobacco and beer, bought General Foods and Kraft to enter the food market and entered the chocolate market by buying Jacob Suchard and Freia Maribu. Buying established brands reduces the time needed to create a presence and cuts the risk by supplying a brand concept that has already demonstrated its viability.

Acquisition targets are often attractive to several competitors and it is naive to expect to buy cheaply. The attractiveness depends more on the synergy generated by the union. These come in the form of economies—in production, in marketing and in distribution—and in the form of potential development of the brand assets gained.

It is difficult to estimate the real value of brands, for example, when a smaller company has developed an appealing product and concept but does not have the resources to exploit them effectively. It is hard to predict how well a national brand will do internationally. For companies with the vision and competence to recognise, and then actualise, global brands (say Unilever with Elizabeth Arden or Chesebrough Pond) bargains can exist.

The motivation of acquisitions is the synergy between the acquired brands and the muscle needed to exploit the full potential of an FMCG brand these days. If a company such as Nestlé takes over an excellent brand, it can provide the investment and infrastructure to exploit the brand to its limit both in its home market and internationally. When Nestlé took over Rowntree-Mackintosh they were able to make a much greater push to internationalise great brands such as Kit-Kat, Smarties and After Eights. Kit-Kat has taken massive strides towards global status, since its acquisition in 1988, and because of this, Kit-Kat, the brand, has a greater value owned by Nestlé than it does by Rowntree. Thus the selling price of the brand can be both more than its worth to the vendor and less than its worth to the buyer, and the sale increases the value of the brand.

(3) Alliance

Alliances are usually something of a compromise, and in the long term this usually shows. Organic growth and acquisition both deliver the expanding company ownership and control. Joint ventures and alliances, between companies or between a company and a government, imply not having the freedom to manage the brands as the company wishes, in the long term.

However, the joint strength of the companies can mean rapid progress with tried and trusted brands. Up-front investment is less than for acquisitions, the fact that both parties have a longer-term interest in the deal encourages commitment from both sides.

Alliances take different forms, but essentially they link companies with complementary strengths, in terms of geography, brands or know-how/people. Thus Cadbury became allied to Hershey in the USA and allied to Unilever in ice-creams. Gillette has bought into a major blade maker in India, and established joint ventures in Russia and China.[2] General Mills has teamed up with Nestlé to form Cereal Partners World-wide to supply Europeans with breakfast cereals. General Mills provides the technology and experience of their US cereal brands (Cheerios, Golden Grahams, Wheaties and Trix), Nestlé provides the umbrella brand for Europeans, and European operations and distribution strength. Individually, each of these huge food manufacturers would have had trouble matching the resources and expertise of Kellogg's, especially if they had both tried at the same time.

Pooling resources creates a new force. Controlling and optimising that new force is rarely straightforward. Deciding business policy and strategy is not simple for one company on its own. When two companies have to hammer out strategy and profit shares there is much scope for painful disagreement and costly delays in decision making. The companies involved often find they have common interests only in the medium term: a few years down the road their objectives and strategies may shift, leading to conflicts of interest. These problems can be reduced by making the management of the joint venture as autonomous and separate as possible. Unfortunately, autonomy must naturally be constrained as total autonomy would imply losing the synergy which was supposed to exist between the original partners and the new activity.

4.2.2 The International Opportunity

As hypersegmentation has reduced the average sales per SKU, trying to take brands (and their extensions) across national borders is a possible solution. Internationalisation can compensate for the shrinking size of segments by matching the same segments over several countries, with accompanying economies for production units, for R&D and in negotiations with suppliers.

The USA has long been the largest homogeneous market in the world, and for this reason segmentation has gone further there than in other developed countries. For example, a breakfast cereal brand in the USA can survive on a mere 0.5% share of the market, whereas in even the biggest national markets in Europe, a 3% share can be considered marginal. TV advertising, the cost of organising promotions and so on need to be amortised over a certain volume of sales.

It becomes more economic to service micro-segments in Europe and the rest of the world if the same micro-segments can be served simultaneously in several countries. Even packaging and advertising production, despite problems of language, can find economies by spreading across borders. Production can be centralised into factories serving several countries. Pampers are now produced for the two sexes, four ages, and in various pack sizes but one factory produces all the models for all of Europe. To be competitive in both varieties and production costs, Kimberly Clark built a £100m factory in Humberside UK to source Europe in Huggies.

The French company Clarins has favoured internationalising its European niche positioning to specialised outlets in the USA and Japan, rather than, for example, expanding into further distribution channels in France. Similarly, it has been easier for Laura Ashley to find fans of its distinctive designs/values across the world (Laura Ashley now has a world-wide turnover approaching £250m) than it would have been to become larger and larger in the UK by adding contemporary and geometric ranges. In the same way, internationalisation can be an antidote to the small segments created by hypersegmentation.

Hypersegmentation is characteristic of First World markets. First World consumers are saturated with marketing messages, spoilt for choice and adept in the use of contraceptives. Only about 15% of the world's population live in rich, marketing-saturated societies, and this percentage is dropping. It is estimated that at the turn of the century, the rich industrial nations will account for less than 50% of global output.[3] Given that FMCG products (soap, snacks, soft drinks, etc.) are some of the cheapest and most accessible consumer goods to buy, it is understandable that FMCG producers should wish to be in at the beginning in developing markets, gaining loyal buyers in the huge consumer markets of tomorrow.

It seems likely that marketing efforts have a higher payback in newer markets. This phenomenon is exploited in mature markets when companies try to influence consumers at times when they are most responsive. For example, making special efforts to gain a new mother's first purchase of disposable nappies. Similarly, the first brands to use advertising, especially television, when it becomes available in a country, often gain a unique advantage. Many companies believe that countries (such as Hungary, Vietnam, India and South Africa) just opening or re-opening to modern marketing, provide unique opportunities, both qualitative and quantitative. The first Western fast-food restaurant in Beijing or Moscow will attract many curious visitors, *who will remember that visit for the rest of their lives*. In China in the early 1990s it was possible to buy a 30-second spot on national TV for about $200. A similar spot on UK television would have cost around $100 000. The Chinese spot would reach roughly 400 million viewers, the UK spot something like 15 million. And these 15 million, slumped in front of the TV, would be jaded, mindspace-saturated, advertising sophisticates.[4]

Expanding into countries with fast growing consumer markets often means attacking national producers with the economies of scale of an international business, and offering quality honed by competition in First World markets to newly rich consumers just able to pay a premium for quality. It also means the chance to exploit marketing expertise to create durable 'mindspace' capital (even among those currently unable to buy), in a way that has been virtually exhausted in long-industrialised countries.

Sometimes international expansion may be forced on a company as a defence. Once an idea—for a new segment, positioning or even advertising campaign—is out in one marketplace it is vulnerable to being copied in another. Some market research companies offer internationally syndicated services, trading new products and promotional ideas around the world.

McDonald's, Coca-Cola and Marlboro took their time extending internationally. Today, with so many market-oriented businesses falling over each other to get to new ideas first, competitive response is much faster. Mars launched its ice-cream bar in the UK in 1988, and swept across Europe and the States in 1989. Gillette launched Sensor simultaneously in 19 'North Atlantic Region' countries. Procter & Gamble was similarly rapid with Pantène and Wash & Go once they (or equivalents) had shown their potential in the USA. As competition becomes more international, a non-international competitor is at a disadvantage. An international competitor may grow in strength abroad (through scale or experience) and then attack back home.

Widespread presence and experience in several markets can mean a foot in the door on new trends, wherever they emerge. Unilever has established multi-disciplinary 'innovation centres' for some of their most actively innovative product fields. The centres concentrate on one product area, and are located partly because of particular experience and excellence in the product field, examples being Asian hair care (Bangkok), deodorants (UK), toothpaste (Italy), skin care (Germany).[5]

A 'transnational'[6] company locates its activities strategically and shops around the world for its inputs. Some countries offer low wages or cheap energy, others financial incentives and tax breaks. Other countries offer unique skills and know-how—for example, in engineering, R&D or advertising.

Any combination of these powerful benefits can inspire a company to expand internationally. There are, of course, non-negligible hazards in this new pasture.

4.2.2.1 The Realities

All these advantages have been discussed at length, and much ballyhoo has surrounded the idea of 'global brands', as expounded in a paper by Theodore Levitt published in 1983.[7]

So far, examples of truly global FMCG brands—Coke, Colgate, Bacardi, Kleenex, Martini, Marlboro, Nescafé, Ariel, Pampers and Gillette's razors; Plénitude and Magnum on their way; at a pinch McDonald's Big Mac—remain rather few. Of the top 100 FMCG brands in Europe, USA and Japan, only seven are common to all three, and only 17 are common to the USA and Europe (see Fig. 4.2).

In the triple overlap are Coca-Cola, McDonald's, Kleenex, Nestlé, Sony, Panasonic and Kentucky Fried Chicken; the two common to the USA and Japan but not Europe are Lipton tea and Band Aid.

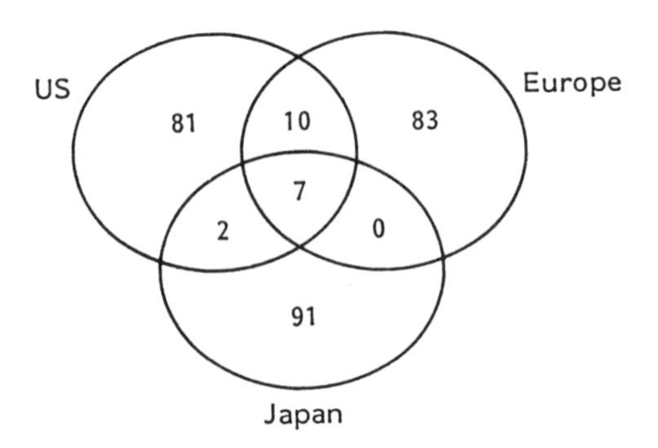

Figure 4.2 *Extent of overlap between the top 100 FMCG brands in Europe, Japan and the United States*[8]

Table 4.2 *The top ten brands in the top five European markets*

	Germany	Spain	France	Italy	UK
1	Coca-Cola	Coca-Cola	Danone Yoghurt	Barilla Pasta	Coca-Cola
2	Lagnese Ice Cream (Unilever)	Danone Yoghurt	Café Jacobs (Jacobs-Suchard)	Moulin Blanc Biscuits	Persil (Unilever)
3	Jacobs Coffee (Jacobs-Suchard)	Carbonell Oil (Carbonel y Cia SA)	Coca-Cola	Coca-Cola	Ariel (P&G)
4	Pepsodent Toothpaste (Unilever)	Ariel (P&G)	Pampers (P&G)	Algida Ice Cream (Unilever)	Nescafé (Nestlé)
5	Iglo frozen Veg. (Unilever)	Danone Deserts	Lu Biscuits (Danone)	Grandapadano Parmisan	Andrex (Scott)
6	Persil (Henkel)	La Casera soft drinks	Chambourcy Yoghurts (Nestlé)	Findus frozen fish (Nestlé)	Silver Spoon sugar
7	Milka Chocolate (Jacobs-Suchard)	Fanta (Coca-Cola)	Ariel (P&G)	Iglo frozen fish (Unilever)	Whiskas (Pedigree Petfoods)
8	Fanta (Coca-Cola)	Pesconova frozen meals	Yoplait Yoghurt	Lavazza Coffee	Flora (Van Den Bergs)
9	Ariel (P&G)	Koipe Oil	Panzani Pasta	Dash (P&G)	Dash (P&G)
10	Barenmark condensed milk (Nestlé)	Nescafé (Nestlé)	Nestlé Chocolate	Parmalat Milk	Walkers Crisps (PepsiCo)

Few brands are dominant in several different countries.
L'Expansion, No. 463, November 1993, p. 72.

Table 4.3 *Even the largest FMCG companies are far from completely Europeanised. A typical large FMCG company is only present in half of its product categories in the top European Markets*

	Home country	No of product fields in home county	Average no. of product fields in five top European markets
Allied Lyons	UK	9	2.9
BSN	France	13	5.6
Bahlsen	Germany	3	2.1
Buitoni	Italy	7	2.8
Cadbury-Schweppes	UK	2	1.6
Coca-Cola	US	2	2.0
CPC	US	5	2.7
Ferrero	Italy	3	2.4
Heinz	US	7	2.3
Kellogg's	US	1	1.0
Mars	US	4	3.2
Nestlé	Switzerland	15	9.6
Quaker Oats	US	4	1.8
Sara Lee Corporation	US	2	0.5
Unilever	Netherlands	8	5.0
Average		5.7	3.0

This chart was first presented at the ESOMAR Seminar, 'The Challenge of Branding Today and in the Future?' Brussels (Belgium), October 1992. Permission for using this material has been granted by the European Society for Opinion and Marketing Research, J. J. Viottastraat 29, 1071 JP, Amsterdam, The Netherlands.

Even true Euro-brands are rare: few major brands are major in more than, say, three leading European countries (see Tables 4.2 and 4.3)

Looking at FMCG usage across countries, it is not difficult to find explanations for the lack of internationalisation. FMCGs have long histories, compared to, say, electronics, and each country and culture has evolved its own habits and brands. Even in the relatively homogenised cultures of Europe and the USA, where cars, pop music and electronics easily cross borders, there are subtle differences in FMCGs. To take a few examples, the UK, Belgium, France and USA each have sugar syrup markets: English people use golden syrup in cooking, Belgians spread fruit syrup on bread, the French drink liquid fruit syrups diluted with water, and Americans pour maple syrup on sausages and eat them for breakfast. Mint is a peculiarly popular flavour in the UK, in the USA cinnamon is popular; aniseed, almond ('praliné') and chicory are popular in France. Germans consume six times as much beer as Italians, while Italians consume twice as much fresh fruit and vegetables (four times as much as the UK or Spain). The Spaniards use virtually no animal fats, cheese or milk in cooking, but instead consume enormous quantities of olive oil.

Brand shares and consumption often vary markedly even across regions within one country: the Scots eat significantly more chocolate biscuits than the English, while the Welsh drink significantly more tea.

Brand names bring their own set of problems: Jif is peanut butter in the USA, marketed by Procter & Gamble; in the UK Jif is a bath cleaner belonging to Unilever. Persil belongs to Unilever in Ireland, the UK and France (where its name, in fact derived from its chemical content, happens to mean 'parsley') but to Henkel everywhere else. Unilever owns Findus in Italy, elsewhere it is owned by Nestlé; Nivea is owned by Smith & Nephew in the UK, by Beiersdorf elsewhere.

Further afield the differences are more extreme. Flavours of seaweed, fish stock, green tea (for example, for ice-cream), soy bean paste, monosodium glutamate and of course soy sauce are all basic to Japanese tastes, but quite alien to Western tongues. The same types of differences exist for scents, for example in soaps, shampoos and air fresheners, and for medicines. Habits to do with personal care and cleanliness have highly cultural links—for example, Chinese children below the age of two wear split bottom pants instead of nappies; antiperspirants are not effective in very hot countries. Cultural, social and practical differences can make products completely irrelevant.

In response to the very real differences, most companies modify the pure 'global' brand idea, and pragmatically adapt their brands. Few 'brand concepts' are able to use the same product formula, brand name, positioning, etc. transnationally. Many more brand concepts are globalised with modification among product formula, production, name, positioning, target market, advertising idea, advertising execution, packaging, pricing, sales promotion, PR and distribution strategy (see Table 4.4).

However, the cup is half full, rather than half empty. As urbanisation and affluence spread, world-wide media, working women, more international travel, television advertising and ownership of household appliances are becoming the norm in developing countries. As life styles converge, ideas such as

Table 4.4 *Very few brand concepts use the same product formula, brand name, positioning etc. transnationally*

	Bacardi	Gervais Danone	Henkel Pritt	Gillette	Johnny Walker	Benetton	Swatch
Core product	yes	yes	yes	yes	yes	yes	yes
Product formula	no	no	no	yes	yes	yes	yes
Brand name	yes	yes	yes	yes	yes	yes	yes
Positioning	no	yes	no	yes	yes	yes	yes
Advertising concept (TV)	no	no	yes	yes	yes	yes	yes
TV executions	no	no	yes	yes	yes	yes	yes
Print concept			yes		yes	yes	yes
Print execution			no		yes	yes	no
Packaging design	yes	no	yes	no	no		yes
Pricing	no	no	no	no	no	yes	yes
Sales promotion	no	no	no	no	no	no	no
Sales concept (distribution)	no	no	no	no	no	yes	yes
Total yeses (out of 12)	3	3	6	6	8	10	10

Adapted with permission from Hajo Riesenbeck and Anthony Freeling, 'How global are global brands?', *The McKinsey Quarterly*, 1991 Number 4.
Yes = same; no = varies.

convenience, shaved underarms, and disposable nappies gain disciples and create markets. While the differences are very real, they are declining. Hopes of simple, efficient globalisation are re-kindled by the observation of a convergence in tastes across countries. The fact that some companies have been marketing globally for some time both illustrates that it is possible (who would have thought you could sell the Japanese hamburgers?) and may in itself have helped to homogenise tastes further.

The risk for international adventurers is not so much that their market will not materialise, but that it will materialise more slowly than expected. In some countries there are risks of political or economic upheaval, and in others the time taken to pay back years of negative cash flow will be significantly greater than anticipated. Many FMCG companies have experienced disappointing results in Spain and eastern Europe.

Despite the differences and difficulties, international opportunities for FMCG manufacturers are, logically, so great, that large manufacturers cannot afford to ignore them. In 20 years or so from now, 90% of world population (in other words, practically everybody) will live outside of North America and Europe. For companies beyond a middling size, who want to remain independent, internationalisation has to be a goal.

4.2.2.2 National Barons

Many companies are pushed towards greater internationalisation because they see the advantages and fear that they will become vulnerable if the benefits fall to their more international competitors. On the other hand, success in one country is not easily reproduced in other countries. Many partially internationalised companies, of intermediate size, now feel 'damned if they do, damned if they don't'. Once some of the competition is run internationally, the opportunity for a late arrival is diminished: if a middle-sized company is not yet international it may be well advised to stay at home.

Globalisation creates considerable organisational challenges. A company operating in only one (home) country avoids the added costs of a supra-national organisation which exists just to harmonise and co-ordinate between countries. A layer of international executives, travelling at great expense in time and money across continents, struggling to translate across languages and understand different cultures, needs to add significant benefits to be worth while. This is especially difficult when being close to the local consumer is so important to the FMCG industry.

Given the substantial advantages of internationalisation (listed earlier) companies are likely to keep on trying. The substantial drawbacks mean that there are still, and probably always will be, opportunities for focused national 'barons' exploiting their closeness to market, national pride and business connections. At the other extreme, those companies which have geographic experience as part of their strategic heritage (Nestlé, CPC, Unilever, and others) are likely to have an exploitable advantage in the rush to take advantage of new markets. Time and experience in international markets is a crucial aid to being able to grasp the advantages of internationalisation, so the companies who have followed an 'Our man in Havana' strategy over years now have a valuable asset.

Gaining experience and exposure during the formative years of markets, when mindspace bargains are won by those brands which approach markets with missionary zeal, is appreciated by stockbroker analysts, probably with good reason. These markets cannot be seen as a short-term solution for companies suffering in the First World branding crisis, but the long-term potential, if political and economic liberalisation continue as most citizens of the world hope, is exciting for all FMCG companies.

4.3 GOING INDUSTRIAL

Hypersegmentation is caused by too many competitors rushing into each of the small segments discovered in a mature market.

As the number of brands explodes and the real differences between the brands approaches zero, it becomes harder and harder to create consumer awareness, preference and loyalty.

In product fields where consumer interest is low and distribution is concentrated, manufacturers can observe that getting shelfspace has gradually become a key objective of their consumer marketing effort. In this situation, manufacturers who are finding it hard to compete profitably by creating consumer demand can see marketing directly to retailers as a viable alternative.

Going industrial may mean providing the retailer with false brands—that is, brands without any consumer promotion—or it might mean supplying own-label brands. In either case, a product sold without a consumer differential advantage is not a consumer product, but an industrial product. It is sold to a distributor, another business. The retailer will look at the product with the eyes of a professional buyer, judging the manufacturer on price and service, and the product on its ability to deliver the retailer's objectives. A company which produces FMCG goods can operate as an industrial company serving retail businesses and no more try to create a relationship with the end consumer than, say, NCR when they supply cash registers to the retailers.

Many producers will find this attractive at least for some products or some product categories. For the third or fourth manufacturer in a product category, squeezed both by the major brand producers and the retailers, going industrial may be unavoidable.

For some brand manufacturers industrial marketing is a startling new twist in their traditional relationship with retailers. Once they recognise that they cannot survive as the third or fourth player in a market, they may find that retailers actually provide their greatest opportunity to compete with their crushing competitors. Own label can offer a way of creating a differential advantage with retail customers; it can provide a profitable route to market for a high-quality product; and it can even improve relations with a retailer to the extent that their brands might be favoured in these stores.

4.3.1 Choosing the Policy Towards Own Label

Companies do not have to be exclusively consumer or exclusively industrial, and many manufacturers already use retailer brands as a convenient way of serving the unbranded, low-quality end of consumer markets or as a tactical use for spare capacity. With retail brands accounting for a third or more of sales in some European FMCG markets, industrial marketing is a new frontier even for quality manufacturers. It cannot be otherwise when the traditional branding methods cease to work for weaker brands in a portfolio, and perhaps for whole divisions of top FMCG manufacturers.

Producing for own label is a subject that often draws an emotional response. Creating consumer loyalty, developing superior, branded products is a creed, a value, a mission. However, it is important to de-emotionalise the issue, and objectively evaluate the company's capabilities in terms of cost of production, innovation and consumer franchise. It may well be that an objective and rational assessment concludes that own-label production would be a mistake, and threaten the company's long-term best interests. This will often be the case for successful branded companies.

Producing for own label involves a different type of company culture, a commitment to low-cost production and to satisfying the retailers' demands in terms of service, quality and innovation. The industrial market is itself highly competitive, and no manufacturer can expect to succeed in it if their approach is half-hearted and opportunistic. Clearly, making the commitment to devote significant resources to an activity which at some levels competes with the main activity of the company is an enormous business decision.

To succeed, manufacturers must understand how value can be created and sold profitably to retailers, and, most importantly, they must be able to harmonise the demands of 'trade' marketing with the demands of 'consumer' marketing. This topic is discussed again in Chapter 11.

4.4 COUNTER SEGMENTATION

Hypersegmentation has been the trend for 20 years or more, and swimming against a trend is often an opportunity for the courageous. It may be possible for a quality brand, or quality manufacturer, to switch to a value positioning as a way to gain advantage over the micro-segmenting competition. Value can coalesce segments.

From the consumer's point of view, a product tailored to his personal preference is the ideal. From the point of view of efficient production and distribution, serving everybody in the world with the same product would be the ideal. Consumers are willing to compromise their ideals for lower prices, and companies are willing to sacrifice some efficiency for higher prices received. Deciding where this arbitrary line falls is a question of competitive advantage for the company. Will the company leave its competitors behind by levelling consumers, providing fewer, or simpler, products and achieving uncopiable economies of scale, or will it leave its competitors behind by pandering to local differences and different needs, outbidding its competitors in its ability to satisfy the range of consumer tastes? This arbitrary line is not fixed. Consumers' willingness to compromise can increase because their interest in the product field has declined, or because one competitor decides to take an aggressive price position and promote the importance of value. The opportunity for a value proposition can grow because hypersegmentation and market orientation have pushed prices so high that the potential savings offered by a value-oriented supplier become significant. It is not a matter of fragmentation and value forming a pendulum, with the market swinging from one to the other, rather, the business strategies of value and hypersegmentation can profitably exist alongside each other in the marketplace. External influences, such as recession may act to make one opportunity greater than the other at various times.

4.4.1 The Value Philosophy

Every manufacturer is involved in a continual effort to reduce costs. Whatever business orientation dominates the firm, lowering costs is a worthy endeavour. The FMCG industry enjoyed high profits for many years, during which time it put on considerable fat. In the harder, colder times which have followed, most FMCG companies have learnt to reduce inefficiencies to sustain and even grow their profits. A continual drive for efficiency is not the same thing as a strategic refocus on value. In a market-oriented firm the challenge is to reduce costs while maintaining the same quality and service within all its high-value segments. A value-oriented firm asks: 'How far can good value coalesce segments?'

The value philosophy argues that cost advantages gained from larger volumes and simpler products may be so strong that it becomes worth while to manhandle the consumers into 'preferring' the offer. Retailers provide a classic example. Choice (large number of brands) has a positive appeal to grocery shoppers choosing a store. However, choice is expensive for stores to support. But a store can force consumers to accept less choice by offering them lower prices. To be successful the value-oriented company has to correctly estimate customers' willingness to trade off benefits against value, and to make the most of the scope for increasing volumes and simplifying products.

The company's choice of target segments and differential advantage impinge both internally on the company and externally on the market. The company's targets influence the evolution of the company, for example, the investments it makes and the direction of its R&D. Conversely, consumers are influenced by what is offered. Value segments can always be created by a product which offers lower prices and adequate delivery: some consumers will compromise and alter their preferences to save money. You can strike while the iron is hot, or you can make it hot by striking.

In a mature German pudding-with-topping market competition among major players Gervais Danone, Dr Oetker (Oetker Group), Chambourcy (Nestlé), and Elite (Unilever) led to product proliferation (sizes, flavours), and high advertising expenditure.[9] Price and profits had fallen. A regional manufacturer, Ehrmann, rolled into this crowded market with a larger sized pot—200 g rather than 125 g—priced very competitively gram for gram. This value proposition appealed strongly to many buyers across the micro-segments and Ehrmann took 20% of the market. Within six months Ehrmann was the second brand. When the competitors decided to offer a larger pot size, and compete on value, the distribution was reluctant to stock them. The market was fragmented, had become low interest, and the marketing costs assumed by the existing competition provided a strategic window for the low-cost newcomer. Ehrmann was able to establish 'value' as a differential advantage for its product. Afterwards, its hold on its channels of distribution and economies of scale made this 'value' positioning sustainable.

4.4.2 Sustainability of Value

Me-toos are less of a threat to a company whose cost structure is its source of advantage, than to one who relies on innovation or image to justify higher margins. Low price advantage is sustainable if it is based on experience and organisation. For example, the German retailer Aldi has built a low price differential advantage based on 40 years of cost control experience applied to the whole value chain (buying, logistics, store design, product range, pricing policy, consumer promotion). Similarly Mars chocolates claim that nobody in the world can produce a Mars bar of comparable quality and consistency and sell it cheaper than they do. Apocryphal tales abound of own-label suppliers who have struggled to deliver own-label mimics and end up concluding that they will have to charge the retailer 50% more than Mars to break even. Honest to their philosophy, when raw ingredients (e.g. cocoa) drop in price Mars takes the opportunity to run '10% more for the same price' promotions, rather than taking extra profits.

Value orientation is clearly a modification of the marketing concept. It is justified when competitors become willing and able to copy all product differentiation. Gaining uncopiable experience and economies of scale by adopting a mission for value is a radical opportunity which appears when competitors become obsessed with balancing another micro-brand on the head of a pin.

The drawback to 'value' as a competitive system, compared to the marketing orientation, is that it is one-dimensional. In any given market there is usually only scope for one value player. A value player can cohabit in a market with market-oriented competitors, but if more than one player tries this route for creating big segments a price war will result.

We come back to both industrial and value approaches in Chapter 11, when we talk about brand management for the future, taking into account competition from the retailer. In order to avoid repetition, we save discussion of the implications of industrial and value philosophies till then.

4.5 THE OTHER CRISIS IN MARKETING

This book is about the profound changes which are affecting marketing as practised by FMCG companies. This first part has traced FMCG companies through product orientation and selling orientation, to market orientation and segmentation. It has shown how marketing orientation reached its zenith in consumer markets, and how segmentation has given way to hyper-segmentation. Manufacturers sense that in some way they are coming to the end of the road, for example when they observe that it is more and more difficult to launch successful value-added brands in the traditional manner. In reaction, manufacturers have extended into related product fields, extended internationally, have started marketing directly to retailers and have in some cases made a forceful return to consumer value.

At the same time, manufacturers of consumer goods are having to face up to another crisis: the rise of retailing as a source of reassurance and innovation for consumer products. The arrival of market-oriented retailers who seek to provide brand-type reassurance via their own brands is having (and will have) a profound influence on manufacturers' marketing strategies.

In Part II we examine the retailers' situation and objectives in considerable detail before returning to the battle between the two in the last section of the book.

Notes

(1) William Ramsay, 'New Product Development in Food and Drink Companies', Templeton College, Oxford, October 1992.
(2) Lawrence Ingressa, *Wall Street Journal*, 14 December 1992.
(3) 'The wealth of nations', *The Economist*, 15 May 1993, p. 13.
(4) Interview with Anthony O'Reilly, CEO Heinz given to *Aim Magazine*, published by A. C. Nielsen, Vol. III, No. 1, 1991.
(5) Alan Mitchell, 'The driving force behind Unilever', *Marketing Magazine*, Haymarket Publishing, 8 April 1993, p. 20.
(6) Term coined in Sumatra Goshal and Christopher Bartlett, *Managing Across Borders: The Transnational Solution*, Boston, MA, Harvard Business School Press, 1989.
(7) Theodore Levitt, 'The globalization of markets', *Harvard Business Review*, Vol. 61, May/June 1983, pp. 18–28.
(8) This Venn diagram (Fig. 4.2) was created by comparing the lists of the top 100 brands in the US, Europe, and Japan, which appeared in an article by S. Owen 'The Landor image power survey: A global assessment of brand strength', published in *Brand Equity and Advertising*, edited by D. Aaker and A. Beil, Lawrence Erlbaum Associates, New Jersey, 1993, pp. 28–30.
(9) Reinhard Angelmar, Gervais Danone/Dr Oetker case study, INSEAD Fontainebleau, France (revised 1988).

Part II
THE RISING RETAILER

5
Retail Evolution

In manufacturers' strategic marketing, distribution is considered as a variable within the marketing mix: a crank that can be turned and the more it is turned the more distribution will be achieved. This view of distribution is reflected in the common measures of distribution strength, such as those offered by Nielsen. Nielsen's most popular 'value index' indicates what proportion of stores usually stock the brand (weighted by the value of the stores' sales), and what proportion had the brand available on shelf at the time of the survey. It is common for major brands to approach 100% on these measures. If this distribution index falls, the salesforce is usually expected to exert pressure to recover any lost distribution. Such a shortfall is not seen as a strategic marketing problem. Its resolution is expected in the short term through tactical methods—including salesforce attention and paying the retailer to re-stock. Retail evolution has made this picture of distribution completely out of date.

5.1 THE EVOLUTION OF RETAILING

For many years retailers took a back seat in the FMCG industry and manufacturers were able to dictate what retailers should stock and the terms they could expect. In recent years, the retail trade in many sectors of consumer goods has changed radically, while the conventional marketing view of the retailer has changed more slowly.

In the conventional marketing view, distribution is assumed to be passive or transparent. It assumes that retailers pass back to the manufacturers an unbiased consumer market—that is, that the consumer in a shop will behave in the same way as the consumer considering brands in a totally neutral, abstract situation. This tacitly assumes that manufacturers have control of all the marketing variables including price, promotions and presence on shelf. It assumes that if the manufacturer succeeds in targeting a consumer with the product offering, then the distribution, managed and administered by an efficient salesforce and logistics system, can be relied upon to deliver the product transparently to the consumer.

Manufacturers have become increasingly aware of the power of retailers, but this has not necessarily changed their assumptions about marketing. The crank has got stiffer, but the principles of segmenting consumers and positioning brands against brand competition have remained the same.

This assumption is frequently revealed in the market research carried out by manufacturers. In brand preference research, all the major national brands are often measured against each other. In reality, the major retailers consciously and intentionally do not offer all the major national brands and, indeed, many major store chains have a policy of stocking only a few. Similarly, it is conventional in market research to rotate the order of questions to give all brands equal treatment. Do retailers make efforts with store layout to give each brand equal prominence? A transparent retailer would rotate the brands on the store's shelves, as an interviewer rotates questions; in the real world, of course, retailers place their own brands most prominently. In reporting their purchases and preference to market researchers, consumers often underestimate the amount of own label they buy.[1] If the market is not that measured and modelled by market research among consumers, strategic marketing decisions should not be based on this market research.

Brand positioning strategies always include an idea of the price point for the brand. But modern retailers do not follow the manufacturer's recommended selling price: they price according to their own objectives. Evidently, the more sophisticated the retailer, the more likely it is to have an independent view on pricing the brands it sells. The retailer's objectives are largely independent and quite frequently in conflict with those of the manufacturer. For example, through price competition in the retail trade, many retailers make only small margins on the best-known brands. Thus retailers may not be very motivated to sell such brands even though they recognise the need to stock them.

Despite the enormous changes, 'transparency' is still an underlying assumption in current marketing theory. It underlies many marketing courses and is modelled in computer training simulations originated in the 1970s (e.g. MARKSTRAT) and early 1980s. In the 1990s it is no longer appropriate. Students should not be taught that distribution is a marketing mix variable to be bought (e.g. via salesforce pressure), just like advertising, when this is no longer the case. Pricing, promotions and merchandising are no longer controlled by the manufacturers.

Manufacturers have to consider retailers as a separate force on the market. They have to look at the decisions made by 'shoppers' in stores rather than by 'consumers' in an abstract world of brands. They have to compete with retailers for influence over the 'shopper'.

Earlier, we described how industries tended to be product oriented in their origins, progressing through a selling phase before becoming market oriented. A similar range of orientations can be observed among retailers. This chapter examines how retailers have evolved, and how they are likely to develop their business strategies in the future. We analyse the basis of retail power—that is, how modern (and future) retailers influence and distort consumer preferences.

5.1.1 The Retail Revolution (1940–1980)

The traditional 'Mom and Pop' stores and grocery shops are the retail equivalent of the cottage industry that existed before the industrial revolution of the late 18th Century, when cart wheels were made by the village blacksmith. The retail equivalent of the early, product-oriented, mass manufacturers are the 'discounters'. A discounter's 'product' is a (set of) large store(s), competitive buying and an efficient operation. Just as mass production techniques allowed manufacturers to produce goods at prices accessible to the masses, high volume, mass retailing enabled the discounters to sell at attractive prices.

Retailers were relatively late, as an industry, to become concentrated and professional. Only with the advent of the car as mass transportation could innovative and efficient discount retailers compete effectively against the traditional small, scattered retail outlet. Once the average consumer could move around enough to benefit from large, efficient stores there began a golden age for supermarkets and discounters as whole continents of consumers waited to get one of these stores near to them. Sam Walton became famously rich (indeed the richest man in the world) bringing the twentieth-century version of shopping to the newly mobile populace, and many other millionaires (Sainsbury, Cohen, Mulliez, Defforey) were created or had their fortunes multiplied as they rode the wave of concentration in retailing. Corresponding legions of independent store owners slowly went out of business, just as in the previous century factories had done away with cottage industry in the making of goods.

In the decades following World War II there was a singular opportunity for discounters:

- Car penetration made ever larger out-of-town sites preferred. Trolley and boot/trunk replaced the traditional shopping basket and, along with fridge and freezer, put paid to the daily shop.
- Breaking up of retail price maintenance agreements and other restrictive practices (e.g. not allowing supermarkets to sell over-the-counter pharmaceutical products) meant retail efficiencies could be passed on to the consumer and used to build volume.
- Information technology allowed a revolution in logistics, with huge benefits attached to size and centralisation. Greater control with flexibility also reduced the one advantage that local independents once enjoyed.
- Market share meant more power to negotiate with suppliers, especially once store-level buyers were replaced by specialist buyers, buying regionally or nationally.
- The huge increase in the range of products in every category offered by manufacturers and desired by consumers could only be stocked by much larger stores.

- Size also meant the opportunity to advertise in mass media (where available and allowed) and economies and synergy in marketing efforts.

A discount strategy is most successful and appropriate when there is share to be taken from smaller units and high-street retailers whose product offering is as obsolete as slide rules. The high-volume, low-operating cost discounters can offer lower prices, more choice and acceptable service levels while still enjoying better margins. Sam Walton's US Wal-Mart chain grew dramatically through the 1970s and 1980s by placing many of his new stores in relatively small towns, where the formula was new.

Developing large sites and maximising efficiency, building high volume with low prices and then negotiating appropriate discounts from manufacturers, investing in technology and reducing logistics costs, is the discounter strategy. This strategy has worked well in one country after another, and one sector (food, electric appliances, toys, pet care, eye care) after another. When the discounter strategy is applied specifically to one category, the shops are known as 'category killers', because they compete successfully with the generalist discounters.

5.1.1.1 Manufacturers and Discounters

This development in the retail trade was not initially a threat to manufacturers. In fact, the efficient stores were better customers, shifting greater volumes per location and often increasing overall consumption. The better deals justifiably earned from manufacturers were all part of the efficiency passed on to consumers.

Discounters' profits come from buying competitively while handling financial operations, logistics and property business more astutely than their traditional competitors.

Building share is a self-reinforcing benefit for a discounter. Increasing volume improves both efficiency and power to negotiate with manufacturers. For the manufacturers, the lower prices offered to the most successful discounters are justified by the savings involved in servicing the high-volume discounter, compared to the costs of servicing smaller, less tightly run, stores.

Logistics costs can be squeezed to save several percentage points of the final sales cost. Some large manufacturers have introduced systems where their computers are linked directly with the stock controlling computers in their clients' stores. Stock sold is reordered automatically as the goods move out of the shop. Inventories can be minimised and administration reduced. Manufacturers encouraged and favoured these 'model traders' with discounts, advantageous delivery arrangements and support for the information technology that made it all possible. The manufacturers saw these super-efficient stores as their best clients.

5.1.1.2 The End of the Golden Age for Discounters

For many years there was a pool (or even a lake) of small, inefficient retailers to put out of business. Consumer demand for large, efficient retailers was greater than supply. Operators did not need to apply resources to create demand; they concentrated on increasing supply. The game was to develop new sites servicing consumers who up to that point hadn't benefited from the retail revolution, but were out there waiting. But this game had to end. In France, consumption rose by 5% between 1985 and 1990; in the same period sales areas of supermarkets and hypermarkets rose by 50%.[2] There were 421 hypermarkets in 1980: there were 850 by 1991.[3] Once there is surplus capacity—that is, supermarket or hypermarket saturation—growth via the discounter strategy is no longer possible. New sites have to be placed not in virgin discounter territory, but in areas already served by discounters.

Discounters have powerful differential advantages compared to traditional small stores, but as protection from each other all they have is location. As long as they stay apart, and the consumer isn't too mobile, they are differentiated by the cost involved in travelling to the other store. As saturation looms, discounters (such as Toys R Us and Child World) find themselves as alike as Tweedledum and Tweedledee, and equally disposed to do battle.

Discounter strategy is a supply strategy, a product-focused strategy. Once supply has saturated demand, growth via discounting dries up. There are no 'new' supermarket shoppers.

Competitors face each other with similar offerings; similar stores selling similar products. Growth now implies taking share away from competitive stores.

The golden age of discount retailing, where developing a modern store in a well-chosen location was a formula for printing money, has come to an end. 'Mom and Pop' grocery stores, sleepy camera or hi-fi specialists, high margin toy shops and jewellers were soft targets. They were beaten on every major criterion from assortment, to price, to convenience. Facing another discounter working on the same formula is an unwelcome shock for a discounter specialised only in blowing specialists out of the water.

5.1.2 Selling Orientation

The fastest and most obvious route for keeping or gaining volume is a transition to selling, or 'hustle' strategies (see Fig. 5.1).

Hustling means holding the basic product offering (store, range, service) constant but increasing selling pressure. This means price cutting, promotions, special 'discount' days, weeks or years. The most important thing to remember about hustle strategies is that they do not create extra consumer value. Just as a second-hand car dealer increases selling pressure without increasing the value of the car, hustle strategies try to reduce consumers' reluctance to buy rather than increase the worth of the goods.

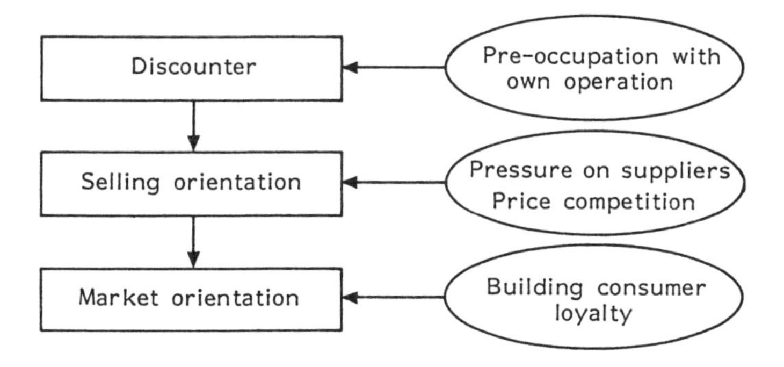

Figure 5.1 *The strategic orientations of retailers*

The hustling done by retailers is by no means crude—with the mass of data now available from scanners, promotional techniques have become very sophisticated. The retailer has to decide:

- The categories to hustle: toothpaste? yoghurt? potatoes?
- The brands to hustle: Ariel or Persil?
- How to hustle: money off, buy two get one free, buy one get a coupon for next purchase, normal price but special event—Easter chocolates, Back to School clothes, Italian foods?
- Where in the store: in aisle, end of aisle, special promotions area?
- Type of display: on shelf, special fixture, with other produce?
- For how long: one week, two weeks . . . permanent?
- What frequency: twice a year, once a month?
- Support: in terms of advertising, display feature.

The most sophisticated retailers are introducing methods for measuring the effects of different hustling techniques, the rate of wear-out, etc. The objective is to calculate how much business is done on promotion; which categories respond best; the effect on category sales and on total store sales. Most promotions have multiple effects and involve both direct and indirect costs. The sales of the promoted brand will increase, but those of competing brands will probably decrease. On top of the obvious costs, such as the cost of a price reduction or special support materials, organising and running a promotion costs management and shop floor time and may demand extra floor space. Trying to pull together the net effect of such a promotion clearly demands sophisticated data collection and analysis. It is easy to see that designing an optimal selling strategy can totally dominate the thinking of retail management.

No retailer can afford to ignore the techniques of promotion and display. However, there is a fundamental limit to the technique. As for manufacturers, 'hustle' techniques do not create greater value. Most hustle techniques are relatively easy to copy—price reduction being the supreme example. Each new technique works briefly for the first store, but once everyone is doing it all the competitors are back to square one. The total volume of the market may increase in some discretionary categories (snacks, soft-drinks), but hustle techniques escalate beyond their break-even point: the value of the market does not increase enough to repay the investments: price reductions may well have reduced its profitability for all.

Competing retailers hope to out-do each other by becoming more sophisticated. By analysing the worth of their promotions more exactly than the competition they hope to tailor their promotions more efficiently and thus end up with greater profits. This will be true for some competitors at some points, but it can't sustain the whole industry in the long term. The techniques for analysing the effects and costs will diffuse to the slower retailers, and in the end the outcome will be similar layouts and promotions in all stores.

5.1.2.1 The Beneficiaries of a Selling Phase

While discounters aim to provide better value by being more efficient and holding on to their margins, 'sellers' frequently sell popular items at cost or below. Price competition between stores drives them to make price claims using the most obvious references—widely recognised brands. In France, during the selling phase of the late 1980s/early 1990s, retailers claimed they were losing money on the top 200 retail brands. An ex-marketing vice president of Carrefour, Etienne Thil, claimed that 20% of supermarket turnover in France was being sold at zero or negative margin.

At first glance the consumer would seem to benefit from such a competitive climate. However, the oversupply is in itself inefficient: supermarkets working at below optimal capacity have relatively higher fixed costs. They also have less money to invest in efficient technology. Selling strategies also tend to breed other, more complicated, inefficiencies.

5.1.2.2 Inefficiencies

Selling strategies often lead to distortions which have a detrimental effect on overall logistics costs. One example is the habit of 'investment' or 'forward' buying. This practice is a result of regular and significant promotions, which are supposedly forced on suppliers by the price-obsessed distribution. Once an expectation of promotions is established, retailers are motivated to buy as much of their turnover as possible during promotions, often to be resold later at regular prices. If a manufacturer offers promotional prices every other month, a retailer will forward buy five weeks' supply at the end of each promotional month. It's not unknown for a retailer to buy a year's supply ahead of a major price rise. At the extreme, forward buying necessitates special warehousing capacity, and the stop–go purchasing creates inventory inefficiencies both for the manufacturer and retailer. Freelance warehousing companies can generate a separate, parasitic business. These 'brokers' buy in bulk during promotions and sell to retailers out of promotion time. Such companies also make a business out of 'diverting' (or parallel importing) when a manufacturer offers different terms geographically, rather than over time.

Retailers in a selling war sometimes ask manufacturers to create artificial differences in a product sold through competing chains (e.g. different size packs) so that direct price comparison becomes more difficult. This creates inefficiencies in manufacturing and potentially in trying to sell at least some suboptimal products (e.g. not the preferred size).

All these inefficiencies have to be paid for eventually and it may be the consumer who finally covers some of the costs. Thus while winning themselves smaller and smaller margins, the retail trade as a whole may not actually deliver better value to the consumer. An industry where retailers avoid oversupply and price wars, work with manufacturers to streamline the supply chain and generate profits to invest in technology may well also provide the consumer with better shopping facilities, on average, and equally competitive prices.

5.1.2.3 Manufacturers and Selling Strategies

Discounting big brands makes them exceptionally good value, and attracts extra users. Despite making little or no margin, retailers still feature these brands prominently in their publicity material, reinforcing the producer's mindspace and attracting attention to their prices. This both strengthens big brands and increases price sensitivity between stores—hence the losses that stores suffer on the most successful consumer brands.

Meanwhile, since these brands are so essential to selling-oriented retailers, the manufacturers can hold out for high margins in their negotiations. The profitability of large manufacturers in France during the fierce retailer price wars of the early 1990s, was better (for equivalent brands) than in the UK, where retailers were competing less on price. In effect, price wars can take place at the retail level or at the manufacturers' level (for example, computers). It is the industry that has the price war, not the product. Of course, it is possible for both manufacturers and retailers to engage in price wars at the same time, as has been the case for televisions. In the short term, large brands do not appear to suffer greatly from retailers' price wars.

The selling phase can, however, be hard on smaller brands, as the retailers try to pass back the cost of their 'hustle' strategies, demanding discounts, extended terms of payment and promotions.

In the long term it is a disadvantage for big brands to be sold at a loss for retailers because the retailer loses the incentive to merchandise the brands. The retailer features them in advertising to generate store traffic, but once the shopper is in the store the retailer has every incentive to sell that person a competitive brand—one on which a profit is made. This technique is known as 'bait and switch'. The retailer still stocks the leading brand, but the shelf position and number of facings reflect not the brand's leadership position, but its commercial value to the store—which might be negative. This negative value might be interpreted as a row of facings on the bottom shelf—the 'behind a pillar' strategy.

In the long term, manufacturers who cultivate high added-value, brand-building strategies, are undermined when the retail trade promotes the same products with aggressive price promotion. The money that retailers invest in price-oriented advertising works against the careful, slowly accumulated differentiation of brands. The exaggerated importance attached to price eventually swallows up the importance of other attributes, encouraging brand switching and substitutability.

5.1.2.4 Negotiating with Selling-oriented Retailers

Selling-oriented retailers approach negotiations with their suppliers in a belligerent frame of mind. Their objectives shift from those of the original discounter. Instead of seeking prices lower than those of smaller competitors, justified by lower logistic and transaction costs, 'selling' retailers are determined each to secure better terms than their quasi-identical competitors.

When the retail trade has fallen into price wars, negotiations take on specific characteristics.

First, there is a polarisation depending on the power of the brand. Certain brands (often called 'power brands') are 'unavoidable' for the retailer. Their brand loyalty is such that their being out of stock could lose the retailer customers (see Chapter 9). Small 'avoidable' or less targeted brands suffer, even as they provide the retailer with better margins. The margins are reversed for manufacturers. They can demand realistic prices for their power brands, while they get pushed down sometimes to cost or below on their smaller brands.

A second curious characteristic of negotiations at this stage is that retailers are so much focusing on their retail competition that they are often less astute when buying than they might be: competitive effort is directed horizontally rather than vertically. In these circumstances it is not unusual for a manufacturer to find that it is possible to raise tariffs (i.e. the list price) offered to all retailers, without being criticised. The retailers are focusing on the discount from the given list price, as the list price is known to be common to all retailers. Thus the objective for retailers in the negotiations is to win greater discounts, bonuses, promotions support, delays of payment and so on, than other retailers, but not primarily to compete for profit with the manufacturer. This in part explains how manufacturers can survive quite profitably despite retail price wars and supposedly aggressive negotiations.

A deeper explanation is that selling-oriented retailers are totally dependent on manufacturers' brands. Their price touting strategies can work only if they stock well-known brands. Their quality image is weak, so they need brands to reassure consumers on the quality of the goods which they are so noisily discounting. These negotiating inefficiencies of selling-oriented retailers also reinforce the doubt (explained above) that they do not, despite their loud declamations, provide the lowest possible prices to their customers. They are not negotiating hard on behalf of the consumer, but only trying to edge ahead of their retail competitors.

5.1.2.5 The Winners of the Selling Phase

Selling strategies can dominate for a long time, but not indefinitely. This is a transition stage. Smaller units are shut down and sold off. Eventually, weaker competitors get squeezed out or bought up. These are the real losers: those who invested in the retail industry without the clout to bring it off.

The surviving players are the real winners. Once sufficient contraction, concentration and merging has taken place, these players are free to find a new route to higher profits. They may even have the opportunity to buy up worn-out competitors at bargain prices. The winners are then free to establish a more orderly form of competition between themselves.

Clearly, there can even be an incentive for a relatively strong competitor to start or intensify a price war. If the competitor feels that long-term profits will be improved by a 'shake-out' in the industry, it can aim at a pricing policy that it knows will put a proportion of its competitors out of business or up for sale.

5.1.3 Achieving Marketing Orientation

The retailers left at the end of the selling phase, like manufacturers in the same situation, need to find a lever for differentiating their offerings. They want to create differential advantages for their stores, so that 'their shoppers' no longer see one store as substitutable for any other.

The essential purpose of a differential advantage for retailers, as for manufacturers, is to increase loyalty among shoppers. Selling-oriented retailers often say 'compare us to the competition—we offer the best deals'. The market-oriented retailer aims at inhibiting shoppers from shopping around by seeking to convince them that this particular store satisfies their needs better than competing stores, either because the prices are consistently to be trusted, or in aspects other than price. A successful differential advantage will push up the total perceived cost (actual and emotional) of going to another shop.

Following the example of manufacturers suggests that retailers should study differences between customers and develop discriminated product offerings. By offering a shopping experience tailored to differentiated customer needs, they could hope to improve margins, without losing too much volume to price competitors. In most FMCG markets the brand leaders are not the least expensive brands. This might encourage retailers to believe that consumers (who are also shoppers) are willing to pay extra for perceived 'quality'.

More 'orderly' competition in the retail market would be achieved once some large retailers had created sufficient loyalty among their users that they could profitably allow smaller competitors to dominate on price. Once some large players were setting a tone of less price competition, competitors with less influence on the market can choose to follow their lead. This situation is frequent in FMCGs where large companies such as Unilever, Procter & Gamble or Philip Morris/General Foods pursue strategies of quality, and consciously set the reference price level for a market.

This process seemed to occur among UK retailers during the 1980s, championed by Sainsbury's, Tesco and Argyll. The 'orderly' competition created allowed them to double their margins, from around 3.5% at the beginning of the 1980s to around 7% in 1991.[4]

Retailers need to be perceived by their customers as offering something different from each other if loyalty is to be built. This much is axiomatic. What has so far been much less clear is what 'different somethings' are available to retailers. What genuinely distinct yet equally appealing positions exist in the retail market? The next two chapters are devoted to assessing the possible 'levers' for diverging the offers of competing supermarkets.

Notes

(1) Wendy Gordon, 'Meeting the challenge of retailer brands', *Admap*, March 1994.

(2) Jean Claude Fauveau, 'Le Monde de la Distribution', *Les Presses du Management*, 1991.

(3) 'European Marketing Data and Statistics', *Euromonitor*, 1994, Table 1209, p. 321.

(4) Economist Intelligence Unit, *Retail Business Quarterly* trade review, No. 20, December 1991.

6
Retailers and the Marketing Concept

Substitutability destroys profits. To make profits it is essential to create loyalty among a segment of the market.

The marketing concept is based on the observation that markets are heterogeneous. Customers want different things and are often willing to pay for the particular qualities they seek. The vehicle that FMCG manufacturers use for applying this marketing concept is the 'brand'. Manufacturers, individually and collectively, create differentiated brands to satisfy all the varieties of buyers in their markets. By targeting products, giving them brand names, positioning them to complement each other, FMCG manufacturers found a way to price discriminate between different segments. Brand proliferation is a brilliant device for increasing the value of a market.

If retailers are to establish more orderly competition among themselves, they also need to create loyalty. Can they apply the marketing concept? Can retailers segment their market and differentiate their offerings? Can they follow the manufacturers and brand proliferate?

Some retail chains are clearly differentiated from others: nobody could mistake a Sainsbury's for an Aldi or a 7–11 convenience store for a Sam's Club warehouse. On the other hand, within a given format (hypermarket, discount store, warehouse club) retailers tend to gravitate to very similar layouts, promotional techniques and prices.

Some retail companies do boast a number of differentiated chains. In the vast majority of cases chain proliferation has been either the by-product of acquisition, or a defensive measure, usually against the bottom of the market. For example, Carrefour runs a hard discounter called Europa Discount (ED) alongside its quality-conscious hypermarkets; Asda has launched a discount format called Dales; Tengelmann owns a hard discounter called Ledi among a set of other chains. Belgium's GIB runs the chains Unic, Sarma and Nopri alongside their GB supermarkets and hypermarkets. In Holland, the Vendex Food Group own Torro and Konmar hypermarkets, Dagmarkt convenience stores, Edah supermarkets and Basismarkt hard discount. Such store groups exist all across Europe, but typically their existence is simply the result of often somewhat serendipitous and opportunistic mergers and acquisitions. In most cases the management is unhappy with at least parts of the group, and would like to be able to rationalise and integrate their different chains. Rare are the examples of genuine attempts to service different segments of the grocery/consumer goods market by developing planned sets of distinct chains.

To answer the crucial question of whether retailers can apply the marketing concept in a similar way to manufacturers, it is instructive to look at the differences between the situation facing retailers and that facing FMCG manufacturers as they market themselves.

Clearly there are many sets and types of differences: retailers don't produce a tangible good, retailers handle thousands of different lines, many times more than even the largest manufacturer, the retail experience depends much more on the local personnel and so on. The four differences discussed below are those which we believe have a direct bearing on a retailer's ability to apply the key marketing ideas of segmentation, differentiation and brand proliferation.

6.1 STRUCTURAL DIFFERENCES

The marketing situation of retailing and manufacturing differ in four fundamental ways: physical network, cost structure, financial structure and the role of price, as detailed below.

6.1.1 Physical Network

The first fundamental difference between manufacturers and retailers is that retailers are physically tied to a fixed set of locations. No market analysis of a retailer is complete without a map showing the locations of their stores. And how puny the pins always seem compared to the spaces between them.

Location is of the highest importance to retailers: choosing the right location, as every shop, bank or fast-food outlet knows, is critical to success. In studies on shop choice, location comes up repeatedly as the dominant reason for choice (see Table 6.1).

Location has no direct equivalent for manufacturers—the nearest equivalent would be distribution or shelfspace. Shelfspace is fundamental and concerns physical presence and accessibility, but the influence of location in retailing is more absolute than the influence of shelfspace on FMCG sales.

Most large manufacturers aim to make their brands available to the whole of their target segment. This target segment might be spread across a whole country, or in some cases, several countries. Manufacturers rely on the distribution industry to make their brands available to almost all consumers. They assume, for the most part, that direct competition will sit side by side with them on the shelves. Lack of shelfspace is fatal, but shelfspace on its own will not sell consumer products. The key for FMCG marketers is to target specific consumers, so that a proportion of shoppers will prefer their offering. Product brands, such as, say, Café Hag (a decaffeinated coffee: the whole sector worth only 14% of instant coffee sales) can afford to target very specific segments of consumers.

Table 6.1 *Reason for choosing main supermarket, among regular users*

	France		UK	
Location	36	46	56	64
Near other shops/services	10		8	
Choice	15		18	
Prices	38		19	

'Forces et faiblesses de 22 groupes European', using statistics from Secodip study: 'Scenario pour làprés 1993', *LSA*, No 1289, 30 January 1992, pp. 28–36 (these statistics on p. 30).

The physical situation of retailers is different. The set of locations determine the 'coverage' of the chain, the group of consumers who could, conveniently, use one of the stores on a regular basis. Coverage defines the store's total potential target market.

The coverage of a chain of stores depends on the number of stores, the population density around the stores, plus traffic flows and transport infrastructure. Coverage depends not only on physical aspects, but also on people's standards of convenience and willingness to travel.

Convenience is relative: it is difficult to get a shopper to drive past one supermarket to reach another. Relative convenience may change over time. A shopper may for years drive 15 minutes to one supermarket and then be seduced away overnight by a new store that offers no other benefit than being a mere five minute drive from their front door. Thus, it is necessary to consider and measure the coverage of a store in the context of number of stores available to their target households.

Willingness to travel (and thus coverage) will also depend on type of shopping trip. For a top-up trip to buy 6 items, it will never be worthwhile driving for 15 minutes, whereas for a major stocking-up trip, a 15 minute drive is often quite acceptable. This is why there will always be a market for smaller local stores as their convenience provides a sustainable differential advantage for certain types of shopping trip.

Coverage is not black and white, but should be visualised rather as a set of concentric rings, with levels of coverage going from dominant, through competitive to possible. The more attractive the store (range/prices, etc.) the larger its circles of coverage will be (Fig. 6.1, page 116, ignores the different degrees of coverage).

Coverage is clearly of huge importance to retailers—as much or more than distribution to manufacturers—but rather harder to calculate exactly. When Tesco bought the William Low chain they did so to add a large group of new shoppers to their potential market. By our rough estimates, William Low's 67 stores are within 5 minutes drive time for 2.5% of the UK homes, or 1.5 million people, but such estimates are extremely hard to make exact. For example, many shoppers shop from more than one base (i.e. not just from their homes), and willingness to travel is very variable.

Another, always rather approximate, way of looking at coverage is in terms of number of closer competitors. In the UK, the biggest chains, Sainsbury's and Tesco, can claim to be within the nearest five supermarkets to more than half of UK households. This is a notable achievement, but still means that each of these chains is only a serious competitor for about 50% of UK grocery purchases. This is less surprising when one considers that only about one out of 16 supermarkets in the UK belongs to Sainsbury's. Many supermarket chains operate successfully while competing for less than 10% of households—an interesting figure to contrast with the distribution achieved by the average grocery brand.

As the total number of large supermarkets increases, the 'coverage' given by each individual unit may actually decrease with people's willingness to travel. Thus opening new stores is a compulsion for each individual chain, but the net effect may be to deliver a better service to the consumer, without gaining in the competitive struggle to be nearest to the shopper. Only one store can ever be the most convenient to any one shopper.

The implication is that many consumers who might prefer a store, given a perfectly free choice, are inhibited by a convenience cost which is beyond the retailer's control. Conversely, many stores hold on to shoppers who would really prefer another store, just because of the physical cost of going elsewhere. In most cases shopper and store find themselves in a 'marriage of convenience'. At the extreme, shopper and store can find themselves in an 'arranged marriage'.

What is the effect of this restriction of free choice, dictated by location? First, it imposes a 'geographical segmentation' on a retailer's 'choice' of shoppers (the chain's 'target'). Second, it determines the competition.

A retailer's 'coverage' consists of a set of geographical 'patches' around its stores. This 'patchiness' causes problems for targeting in three ways:

(1) The patches will not necessarily resemble each other. For example, one store might be in an affluent area and another in a poor area, some will be in urban areas, others in rural areas.
(2) Each of the patches is itself likely to be heterogeneous. Geographic segmentation does not generally say a lot about people's preferences. No manufacturer segments its market on local geography.

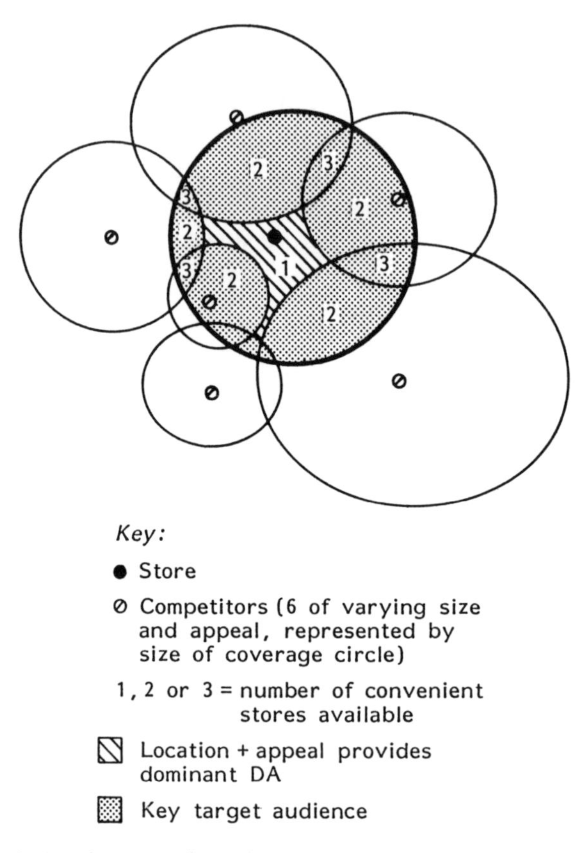

Figure 6.1 *A visualisation of retail competition. The key target audience for the store are those people living in the stippled ring. Who are they?*

(3) The key target market for a supermarket are not those people in the 'nearest coverage', but those more marginal shoppers, located in a ring at some distance from the store, who could just as easily (or more easily) visit another store. (See Fig. 6.1.)

Manufacturers create perceptual maps of brands which suggest to them how their brand should be positioned to gain users. Stores are positioned, in the first instance, on the ground, on a real map. Whatever target segment(s) a chain would *like* to choose, it *has* to serve the shoppers who happen to live (or work etc.) nearby. The key target audience are those who could conveniently shop at the store but are also able to shop

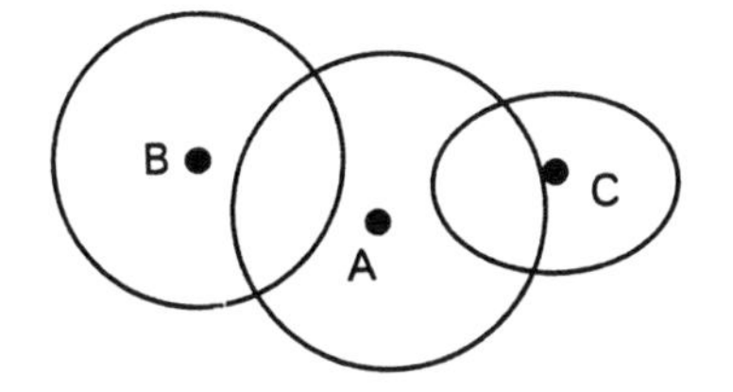

Figure 6.2 *Stores compete according to their area of coverage. Here store A competes with both stores B and C. B and C hardly compete at all with each other*

elsewhere. What is special about these shoppers and their needs? Simply that they live in this abstract doughnut. A manufacturer can hope to understand the motivations of people who like its brand but are attracted to a close competitor. How can the store understand its target people?

This target is doubly heterogeneous: across the different stores in the chain and within the catchment areas of each store. In general, a chain of stores is forced to service a widely heterogeneous target: the people for whom the store is convenient.

Aside from target market, 'coverage' determines a second key marketing input for retailers: their competition. When the 'coverage' of two stores overlap, they compete for customers. If their 'coverage' or patches are discrete they do not compete directly for shoppers. Coverage determines which chains of stores compete most directly and in which areas. (See Fig. 6.2.)

A large retail chain will have some branches that enjoy being the only large store in their area, competing perhaps against small local shops. Another branch of the same chain might be next door to a price-oriented rival. In other places, stores will have an overlapping catchment area with a huge, high-quality hypermarket. Even in a saturated market, not all stores compete against all others. Competition between stores is a 'network of sub competitions'.

Retailers do not sit side by side on shelf. They do not have an entire population from which to pick their users and, for their part, shoppers do not select stores from the complete range of retail chains on offer in the country. Approaches to marketing for retailers have to grasp this important difference.

6.1.2 Cost Structure

Modern retailing is no different from most other industries in terms of the benefits of size. Size provides economies (for example in logistics, advertising and own-label development) and competitive strength (for example in negotiating with suppliers). The difference for retailers is the level at which scale advantages accrue: company, chain or store.

When manufacturers proliferate brands, many of the costs associated with the brands can be shared, i.e. there is considerable synergy across brands. Thus Kellogg's can produce another cereal brand more cheaply than a rival setting up to produce one brand of cereal.

This is less true for retail chains, the equivalent to brands for retail companies. Many of economies are chain (i.e. brand) specific. For example, a chain with high coverage benefits from greater economies in marketing costs (advertising, promotions, merchandising), compared to two different chains with the same combined coverage, owned by the same company. Companies which have bought several retail chains complain that the economies made across the chains are less than anticipated. This can be because the managers of the different chains set up barriers to joint operations (such as logistics and buying), but it is also because different types of chains need different policies and decisions in these areas. A hard discounter, convenience store and hypermarket need different ranges, different types of goods and have different warehousing and delivery requirements. This makes it hard to achieve synergy in negotiations with suppliers or in logistics, warehousing etc.

An increasingly large element in retail costs are those associated with planning and procuring high-quality own-label products. (We shall see later that own label is a key tool for developing chain identity and loyalty.) In other words many of the costs associated with own label are chain specific. The significant cost of developing own brands means that they need to be amortised over as many stores (as large a coverage) as possible. Having several chains each with their own own-label products is inefficient.

The importance of assortment and 'one stop shopping' is a fact of retailing life that, again, has no real equivalent for manufacturers of FMCGs.

Large store size, other things being equal, improves consumer appeal. The number of brands available has jumped dramatically in the past 20 years or so, due to consumer interest in choice and novelty. This exciting variety and choice can only be provided by large units.

Assortment also benefits the retailer in terms of profit margin. Retail competition is fiercest on the most basic grocery items—some 400 lines. If a store stocks only 1000 lines, relatively few can be sold at a higher margin. A store with several thousand lines has more scope for making good margins on some of its lines (in particular fresh foods and non-food). Thus a larger unit, other things being equal, will make better average margins.

As retailing becomes more sophisticated, the fixed costs in property and technology at each location increase. Significant economies of scale are attached to logistics, technology and even to labour within a store. For example, an in-store butcher or bakery cannot be scaled down indefinitely.

The result is that retailers increasingly have to generate volume sales in each unit to justify the high investment in property and technology.

To summarise, significant scale economies accrue at the chain level so a chain must have critical mass (i.e. needs to attain a minimum, large size, just to be competitive) within a country. In particular, retailers need critical mass for their own label(s) which are generally chain specific and also to support marketing investments. A small chain is at a disadvantage compared to a large chain, economies across chains are small, so in general it is significantly more efficient for a company to run one numerous chain rather than several less numerous ones.

Simultaneously, every store must produce volume to justify the high fixed costs in the fabric (technology, property) of the store. Generating volume is vital for retailers right down to the level of the individual store.

6.1.3 Financial Structure

Retailers are able to run highly geared operations because of 'free' credit from their suppliers. This credit comes in the form of 'Delays of Payment' (DOP). For example, in France and Belgium 90 days—one-quarter of a year—is common. Combined with a fast asset turnover these retailers may hold a significant proportion of their annual turnover in 'free' loans, at any one time. These delays of payment terms are a convenient instrument for equity-poor retailers to fuel their growth. Not surprisingly, it is independent, franchised retailers such as Intermarché, Leclerc and Super U in France (together accounting for around 30% of the market) who insist most strongly on these extended terms.

In fact delays of payment are not free at all. Their level depends on the overall power of the retailers compared to manufacturers, and on their respective costs of capital. If the cost of capital is higher for retailers than for manufacturers, it is efficient for the manufacturer to grant longer delays of payment to the retailer. In that case the benefits to the retailer are greater than the cost to the manufacturer, i.e. it forms a basis for joint gains.

As an illustration, it is interesting to compare retailers in France with their counterparts in the UK. In France, several chains have expanded very quickly with financing from manufacturers, but with control still maintained by the family founders. These retailers have not developed the sophisticated financial structures needed to keep control of their organisations while sharing the equity with non-family shareholders. The desire to keep control makes them reluctant to increase their capital via the stock market. French banks, on the other hand, demand equity investment equal to the loans granted (debt/equity ratio not greater than one), and see retailing as a volatile, rather risky industry. Instead of being owed to banks, the debt owed by French retailers is currently spread widely among their manufacturer suppliers. Each owns a small part of the credit, and this spreads the risk. Given the precarious nature of a business prone to price wars (see below), most banks (or even a collection of banks) would be reluctant to take on this debt. They are more willing to do so for manufacturers, who are seen as more financially secure. Thus bank funding for retailers is limited and the cost of capital for French retailers is relatively high.

UK retailers are quite a contrast financially. British retailers have developed financial structures which allow them to issue equity without giving up control (though they do then become forced to generate and declare high and consistent profits to satisfy the financial markets). Through the 1980s, rapid gains in sales and profits made the large chains the darlings of the stock market.

Besides relatively high equity (i.e. money raised from shareholders) these retailers find that UK banks are about as willing to lend to them as they are to finance manufacturers. The cost of capital to UK retailers is thus lower than for French retailers.

Given that the cost of capital is higher for retailers than for manufacturers in France and vice versa in the UK, DOPs should be longer in France than in the UK.

Once long delays of payments are established it is hard to reduce them. To reduce the delay of payment the retailer generally demands a higher compensation than manufacturers are willing to give, partly because the sudden change in cash flow will be hard to bear. Since the costs of capital (real or perceived) are not constant across retailers, some retailers will resist a reduction in delay of payments more fiercely than others, and it is difficult in practice to reach agreements that are perceived to be acceptable by all parties. This poses problems for retailers, apart from the risk that they are being financially inefficient.

New entrants (or new franchisees) can more easily enter in a market where long delays are normal. The new entrant retailers do not need to persuade investors or banks of their creditworthiness. Thus the price of entry is small, which is a well-known break on profitability.

Possible financial inefficiency and openness to new entrants is only part of the problem with extended DOPs. The most important consequence is that high leverage tends to make retailer profits extremely sensitive to volume.

The long-term effect of extended DOPs becomes clear when one examines the fundamental financial equation for a selection of retailers and manufacturers: competitive pressure between retailers, gorged with free capital, brings down their operating profit margin to a level which would be unacceptable in manufacturing companies.

$$\text{Return on equity} = \frac{\text{Net profit}}{\text{Shareholder equity}} = \frac{\text{Net profit}}{\text{Sales}} \times \frac{\text{Sales}}{\text{Assets}} \times \frac{\text{Assets}}{\text{Shareholder equity}}$$

$$= \text{Net profit margin} \times \text{Asset turnover} \times \text{Leverage}$$

Table 6.2 *Return on equity for manufacturers*

Manufacturer	Net profit margin	Asset turnover	Leverage	Return on equity
Quaker Oats	4.3	1.7	2.8	20.9
Ralston Purina	5.6	1.6	4.8	42.9
United Biscuit	5.4	1.7	2.4	21.4
Pernod-Ricard	5.8	0.9	2.6	13.0
Reckitt & Colman	8.8	1.2	2.2	23.9
Sara Lee	4.3	1.6	2.8	19.2
Heineken	4.4	1.1	2.4	11.4
Cadbury-Schweppes	6.7	1.3	3.2	28.4
Coca-Cola	13.1	1.1	2.2	33.9
CPC	6.6	1.4	2.9	26.0
Guinness	15.4	0.5	1.9	15.4
Nestlé	5.2	1.3	2.6	17.5
L'Oréal	6.6	1.2	2.1	17.0
Colgate-Palmolive	4.1	1.4	2.8	16.0

Table 6.3 *Return on equity for retailers*

Retailer	Net profit margin	Asset turnover	Leverage	Return on equity
Carrefour (Fr.)	1.8	2.3	4.0	16.8
Casino (Fr.)	1.3	2.3	4.7	14.1
Promodes (Fr.)	1.0	3.0	6.2	19.0
GIB (B)	1.5	2.7	4.7	19.6
Aholt (N)	1.2	3.9	3.4	16.5
Asda (UK)	4.1	1.5	2.2	13.7
Sainsbury's (UK)	4.7	2.0	2.1	19.7
Argyll (UK)	4.5	2.1	2.3	21.8
Tesco (UK)	5.2	1.9	1.8	18.0
Kwik Save (UK)	3.9	3.6	1.8	25.8
Kroger (US)	1.4	4.0	4.1	23.2
Winn-Dixie (US)	1.3	6.2	1.9	15.2
Southland (US)	−0.8	1.5	3.4	−4.1
Lucky Stores (US)	2.2	5.4	3.9	46.5
Albertsons (US)	2.1	4.2	2.1	18.8

These are average figures over a four-year period (1988–91) based on data published by Dafsa, London (different accounting rules, diversified companies, data only for publicly owned companies).

The equation shows how return on equity (ROE) can be described as the product of three key ratios: net profit margin; asset turnover; and leverage. Tables 6.2 and 6.3 show these ratios calculated for a convenient sample of major manufacturers and retailers.

Tables 6.2 and 6.3 show that continental European and US retailers work on small profit margins and rely on high asset turnover and leverage to generate ROEs comparable to those of manufacturers. (They also show that the UK is an exception to this rule.)

In contrast to most retailers, the ROE of manufacturers is generated more evenly across net profit margins, asset turnover and leverage. The two tables show average manufacturer net profit margins to be three to four times those of continental retailers.

This skewed financial structure may not affect shareholder profitability. In terms of return on equity (the overall profitability of a company, as considered by shareholders), retailers may still be as profitable as manufacturers. However, it does affect the way these retailers operate.

Since the actual profit margin is tiny, in some cases under 1%, profits are very vulnerable to small changes in operating costs (for example, increased wages) or changes in volume, or forced changes in prices. With profit margins as thin as these, profits turn to losses if the retailer loses control of costs by even one or two percentage points.

Take for example, a typical (non-UK) retailer with an ROE of 18%, and compare this with a manufacturer also with a ROE of 18% (see Table 6.4).

A reduction of the net profit margin (NPM)—through, say, lowering prices to face hard discounters—of one percentage point will reduce the retailer's ROE by 67% (two-thirds). A similar one percentage point reduction in the NPM of the manufacturer will reduce its ROE by only 15% (one-sixth).

Retailers are very sensitive to small changes in volume because it unfavourably affects both the NPM (high break-even volume) and asset turnover. It is imperative for a retailer to be optimally efficient and to be very sensitive to any drop in sales volume.

Table 6.4 *Comparison of ROE between a typical retailer and manufacturer*

	Net profit	Asset T/O	Leverage	ROE
Retailer	1.5%	2.5	4.8	18%
Manufacturer	6%	1.6	2.1	18%

Naturally, this sensitivity to volume translates into vulnerability towards price wars.

British retailers, as apparent from Table 6.3 operate more similarly to manufacturers. Their overall shareholder profitability is comparable to that of their continental counterparts, but they are much less sensitive to small changes in their net profit margins. We will see below how retailers such as Sainsbury's accomplish this through manufacturer type strategies.

Long DOPs will tend to spawn a more volatile operation, very sensitive to small changes in price, costs and volume. If retailers want to move to a more stable financial structure, with a higher NPM, to make them less prone to price wars, they should reduce their dependence on long DOPs. The first step is to introduce the financial mechanisms to ensure control as equity is sold off. Once equity is increased, debt can also be negotiated from banks.

6.1.4 Pricing and Price Perceptions

It is striking to any observer how price plays a much larger role in the positioning of stores than in the positioning of product brands. Even supposedly high-quality chains, such as Sainsbury's, continually remind shoppers of their commitment to price. Sainsbury's slogans—'Good food costs less at Sainsbury's', and 'Essential for the essentials'—carry price messages. At any one time Sainsbury's have price promotions on about 1000 of their 15 000 lines.[1] More generally, 90% of all retail advertising in Europe is price related and 70% is exclusively on price.[2]

Price rarely provides a differential advantage for product brands: often the more expensive brands are category leaders. In contrast, the price perception of a large retailing chain is a cornerstone of its image. This is not just the case for hard discounters with an unambiguous price positioning, but also for those who aim at a mainstream compromise between price, quality and assortment.

There are four clear differences in the pricing of a product and the pricing policy of a store, described below.

(1) Split Baskets

Many shoppers regularly visit two or more different stores and they can 'split their baskets', or 'cherry pick' promotions.

Suppose a supermarket decides to invest in giving 'wide choice', and reflects the costs incurred in generally higher prices. Nearby, a competitor develops a low-choice, low-cost strategy. The more expensive store finds many of its shoppers develop the habit of visiting the cheaper store to stock up on basic products (milk, eggs, soft drinks) while continuing to buy more exotic and quality-sensitive items from them. They cannot destock basic products (as this would inconvenience loyal shoppers), and find they have profitability problems as the basic items still account for 40% of their operating costs.

Marks & Spencer are a singular exception. They sell high added value foods—cakes, prepared meals, exotic vegetables—but do not sell sugar or washing powder. A typical hypermarket cannot afford to destock the basic items for fear of alienating the 'one-stop' shopping segment. When retailers stock directly comparable national brands this 'cherry picking' is particularly feasible.

(2) Breaking the Price–Quality Relationship

In product marketing the price of a brand usually has an influence on its perceived quality. When stores sell the same brands, this price–quality relationship can be broken. A store can position itself credibly as selling good-quality products, but through its own efficiency and good faith, delivering those products or brands at low prices. In the words of Kwik Save's founder, Albert Gubay, 'Our objective is not to sell cheap groceries, but to sell groceries cheaply'.

(3) Complexity

The third clear difference which increases the importance of price for retailers above that experienced by manufacturers, is the complexity of judging and comparing the overall price positions of competing stores. Comparing prices between chains implies remembering prices over time, and choosing equivalent items to compare. Even a research company trying to make an objective comparison has to pick an arbitrary basket of goods, and a particular instant. Thus the consumer is more inclined to rely on global impressions gained from advertising, the store's promotional activity, the presentation of the store or comments in the media, as well as an idiosyncratic selection of actual price comparisons. Retail price perception is correspondingly more open to influence (e.g. from advertising) than is the case for a brand. The flip side of this observation is that managing price perception is a vital and fruitful part of retail marketing.

(4) The Value of the Shopping Experience (Is Low)
Consumers bring different attitudes to different purchases. For example some products are sold on functional benefits (washing powders, insecticides) while others (beer, soft drinks) are sold on more emotional and subjective qualities. The type of decision is important because it dictates what motivates the purchase decision and, in particular, the role of price. For example, prestige is important in products which project an image of you (e.g. jeans, whisky); thus, being known to be expensive adds value to jeans or whisky. Similarly, when consumers feel unable to judge the quality of a product (e.g. a washing machine) price is used as an indicator of quality and can actually make a brand more valued. Consumers seeking pleasure—when they buy treats such as confectionery—are also known to be less price sensitive than when buying, say, household bleach.[3] Turning to retailing, it is striking to note that in a six-month period, 90% of German households visit an Aldi store.[4] In other words the brand with the cheapest positioning in the market has an almost universal penetration among the richest population in Europe.

There are very few upscale food stores. Marks & Spencer is the only exception, and their store traffic was originally built via clothes. Fortnum & Mason in London, Fauchan in Paris, and Rob in Belgium can perhaps more realistically be considered curios and tourist attractions. When you look at major supermarket chains, there are no 'Rolls Royce' chains; there are not even 'Mercedes' chains. Traditional 'high service' grocery stores have been shown to compete most unsuccessfully with cheaper 'self-service' supermarkets.

It seems that for most shoppers store choice is rational rather than emotional, and shopping is a functional activity rather than a pleasurable one. If this is the case, a greater degree of price sensitivity can be predicted. Retailing is generally a low added-value activity. Shoppers seek neither prestige nor pleasure from the experience. Shopping is a rational decision where price (or rather the shopper's perception of price) is destined to play a major role.

Sir Jack Cohen, founder of Tesco, summed up both the volume imperative and the price imperative of modern retailing in his maxim 'Pile it high, sell it cheap'.

6.2 IMPLICATIONS FOR RETAIL MARKETING

The last, lengthy section, contrasted retailers with manufacturers, but avoided drawing implications as to how retailers might apply the marketing concept. Now it is time to pull together the four key implications. We propose to show that:

(1) Retailers cannot segment consumers to anything like the degree that manufacturers do, and must therefore favour bland rather than pointed images.
(2) Brand proliferation is strictly limited when applied to retail chains.
(3) The quality of the shopping experience (store values—service, cleanliness, convenience, image) provides a much weaker source of differential advantages than the qualities and associations that provide differential advantages for many product brands.
(4) Price is an imperative and an opportunity for retailers; they must keep their real prices competitive and must sustain appeal by permanently managing their price perceptions.

6.2.1 Retailers and Segmentation

The art of segmentation as practised by FMCG companies, is to group together homogeneous subgroups of consumers in order to serve their needs more precisely.

The most fundamental implication to draw from the differences listed above is that a retailer cannot group customers by need to anything like the same degree as can manufacturers. Retail 'coverage' dictates the target audience for each store. This 'geographic segmentation' means that the target audiences are likely to be heterogeneous. *But* a large mainstream store has to generate volume, right down to the level of each unit. A retailer benefits strongly from this increasing volume.

The implication is that a store cannot afford to alienate any substantial segment of the shoppers who live within its 'covered area'. While a product brand can target a specific subgroup of consumers, and still take a viable volume of sales, a supermarket must aim to take a maximum proportion of the sales of all shoppers with easy access.

If a leading product brand holds 20% of its market, more targeted, niche brands can come along and attack parts of the leader's target audience. To attack Sainsbury's 20% of the UK supermarket sales, it is not possible to launch a niche supermarket that 2% of shoppers will prefer—because it is physically impossible to offer this competitor to all Sainsbury's shoppers. While L'Oréal/LaScad can target 'Mixa baby' shampoo at Mums with children under five, no supermarket can open a chain, equipped with crèche and changing room etc., targeted at shoppers with young children. Retailers do not sit side by side on shelf.

Conversely, Sainsbury's will not win 20% of UK grocery sales by appealing to one out of five shoppers. Sainsbury's must aim to take the maximum sales possible from all the people with easy access to one of their stores. A small store in a densely populated area (e.g. a boutique in a town centre) can afford to target a homogeneous segment in the way that a product brand does. A supermarket must appeal to as many of the heterogeneous people in its catchment area as possible. It cannot afford to deselect any major segments. The only exception to this is the hard discounter. A price proposition tends to coalesce preference segments and, by not competing on range, fixed costs and break-even point are lower.

Looking now at the supermarket chain, it is clear that it must attract a large proportion of potential shoppers around *each* of its stores.

A retailer will not wish to position separate stores of a chain too differently from each other for fear of losing any coherent image (and thus economies of scale in marketing) for the chain.

The chain has to generate volume in each of a set of heterogeneous 'patches'. Again this leads to the conclusion that the offering of the chain cannot afford to alienate any major segment of shoppers, who might be very important to one or two stores in the chain.

The presence of competition naturally impinges on positioning decisions such as pricing. (This is equally true for product brands as for retail chains.) For retailers, however, different competition will impinge in different places (network competition).

The retail chain could choose to develop a separate (more pointed) positioning for each store, to suit its local competition. This would mean no global positioning, no national advertising, no national pricing policy. If by contrast the retail chain wants to create a homogeneous set of stores, the overall positioning has to be some sort of average. A consistent pricing policy and advertising campaign throughout the country and centrally run strategic thinking, means compromising the ideal position for each individual store. The aggregated 'ideal positions' for each of the main chains are likely to converge on each other, as averages tend to do.

Most retailers naturally resist de-selecting any group of consumers (i.e. segmenting). Intuitively, retailers (as usual with the exception of hard discounters) feel obliged to compete on all major dimensions: always trying to offer low prices, while at the same time striving to improve service, the quality of products and the convenience of the stores. This contrasts with manufacturers, who increasingly target their brands at specific segments. In marketing terms, manufacturers aim at more pointed positionings ('rifle brands'), while retailers either create a pointed positioning on price or cultivate more bland, umbrella positionings: build a broad church.

Mainstream retailers are driven towards a bland image partly because their positioning must attract all significant groups in their 'coverage', and partly because the same brand has appeal across a range of different competitive situations. Bland national image that is capable of some reinterpretation at the local level is the only solution for a large, non-price, chain.

6.2.2 The Role of Brand Proliferation

Manufacturers try to position their brands in a complementary way to other brands in the minds of their consumers. Their aim is to differentiate their brands. A retailer's competitive position, by contrast, is primarily defined by location.

Suppose a hypermarket opens just outside a certain town and is highly successful. Suppose a competitor decides to open a hypermarket serving a similar town, 100 miles away. Assuming that the first retailer got its product offering and consumer positioning exactly right, the second retailer's optimal offering will be the same as that of the first (i.e. to be a perfect me-too). This is because at 100 miles apart there will be minimal direct competition, and if the towns' populations are similar, the optimal offering for one town will also be optimal for the other.

In contrast to manufacturer brands, competitive stores may do best with exactly the same 'product formula', 'image', pricing etc., as long as the stores are geographically separated. Identical product brands will fight for each others' sales, but for retail chains that overlap little in terms of coverage, being identical in format, quality and so on, does not imply direct competition.

There may be several hard discount chains in a country without many of the stores actually overlapping with each other. On a perceptual map, borrowed from product-oriented marketing, these 'chain brands' look like me-toos who will compete directly against each other. Viewed from a retailing perspective, the stores can be considered as acting as one brand, owned in different places by different people. And they will *not* compete directly with each other.

Within grocery retailing, several shop formats have been found to correspond to significant shopping needs. The following typology broadly captures this differentiation:

- *Superettes and convenience stores* offering a limited range, mostly food. Prices are higher but compensated for by convenience: proximity shopping and extended opening hours.
- *Supermarkets* concentrating on food and offering quality produce at good prices.
- *Hypermarkets* selling about 35 000 lines on floor space of over 2500 m^2.
- *Hard discounters* offering less than 1000 lines, a Spartan atmosphere and the promise of rock-bottom prices.

Many retailers see that these different formats appeal to different shopping needs and are attracted to the idea of offering a differentiated store format to different segments of shoppers. For example, Promodes in France has five separate chains: Continent (Hypermarket), Champion (supermarkets), Shopi and 8 à Huit (convenience stores), Dia (Hard Discounter). As mentioned before, several large supermarket chains have launched discount formats.

The technique of brand proliferation is, however, limited when applied by retailers, because of the physical locations of stores, and by the retailers' cost structure.

Much as a company such as Promodes might like to offer its full range of 'chain brands' to each of its consumers, it cannot find locations. It may wish to place its differentiated stores side by side in true brand proliferation style, but for the most part it will have difficulty doing so, because of the limited availability of sites and the saturation of local trading areas.

The number of sites (with planning permission etc.) in an area is limited, but even if sites were available, the number of competitive stores in one area is limited by the retailer's need to generate volume sales at each unit. Store costs are high (and increase with technological progress) and so retailers have to respect the density of stores which an area can justify: they cannot proliferate stores if the expected volume of sales is too small.

Thus, an area might provide enough business for, say, a hard discounter, a hypermarket, and a supermarket, but these positions may well be occupied by different retailers. The owner of the hypermarket might own a string of discount stores, but in this area the hypermarket might have to compete against the hard discounter owned by another retailer. A hypermarket does not compete against other hypermarkets in the way that a premium whisky competes largely with other premium whiskies.

Chain-specific costs are high and centralising buying or logistics to the company level is beset with problems. Promodes support a range of different chains, but they complain that the synergy between the chains is less than could be hoped.

The more costs are centralised, and the less they are chain specific, the more possible it is to brand proliferate. If chain-specific costs are relatively small, a retail company can proliferate brands in a way almost analogous to a manufacturer. Burton's clothing, for example, do maintain a portfolio of shop chains targeted at different segments (see Table 6.5).

Table 6.5 *Burton's chain portfolio*

Chain name	Products	Target
Burton	Town clothes, accessories	Men, 20–40
Alias	Fashionable clothes	Men, 25–40
Top Man	Inexpensive fashion	Boys, men, 11–30
Top Shop	Inexpensive fashion	Girls, 11–30
Principles for Women	Classic fashion, higher prices	Women, 25–40
Principles for Men	Classic fashion, higher prices	Men, 25–40
Champion Sport	Sports clothes	Men, women, and children
Dorothy Perkins	Clothes, night-clothes and lingerie	Women, 18–40
Secrets	Lingerie	Women, 15–45
Evans	Outsize clothes	Large women

Brand proliferation is more feasible given a more centralised cost structure.

Brand proliferation for Burton's approaches the level of that for FMCG brands, each one being targeted at a group of consumers with homogeneous wants.

This difference in the potential for retailers to brand proliferate is seen most acutely when one store chain takes over another. When a manufacturer takes over another manufacturer it often buys it for its brands, and through these brands it gains valuable mindspace. It then retains and supports the bought brands. Many of the famous brands owned by Unilever and Nestlé were bought and developed in this way.

When a retailer buys a competitor, it has to choose between keeping the 'goodwill' that might exist for the bought brand and the chance to extend the 'coverage' of its main chain. Generally it is no contest. Carrefour bought Euromarché in France and is steadily upgrading the sites and re-christening them 'Carrefour'. Whether William Low was acquired by Tesco or Sainsbury, the name, one of the most respected brands in Scottish retailing, was bound to be relinquished. When BSN (now Danone) vied with Nestlé for Perrier, it was equally obvious that the Perrier name would be developed. Supermarkets follow banks or building societies in this respect, not brand manufacturers.

The mechanism is different simply because the physical market is so different. Two brands of toothpaste can happily sell alongside each other on a shelf. Consolidating them into one brand would make few savings and no sense. Brands of toothpaste often achieve almost complete distribution in a country. A store buying another store has an incentive to consolidate the two as this will create one chain with much improved coverage. A retail chain needs critical mass.

Thus, it is clear that retail chains are not equivalent to grocery brands and retailers cannot segment shoppers by proliferating chains. Brand (i.e. chain) proliferation is not the key tool for segmenting shoppers that it is for manufacturers.

While concluding that chains cannot segment shoppers via brand proliferation, it would be a mistake to think that there is no variation in consumers' requirements from stores. The inability of chains to provide pointed positionings does not imply uniformity in shoppers' preferences. Some shoppers will demand a wide choice of brands, some convenience, some will be primarily price sensitive, some sensitive to the quality of fresh food. All it means is that retailers cannot serve these different segments by developing appropriate supermarkets. Later we look at the approaches that retailers must use to deal with this heterogeneity in their target market.

6.2.3 Store Values as a Differential Advantage

Store values are frequently the subject of pontification on how to differentiate stores and create added value. In practice, retailers have been reluctant to follow theorists who recommend investment in particular aspects of retail service in order to differentiate their offers. Intuitively retailers recognise the fundamental problems in creating a differential advantage based on store values.

First, store values cannot be limited to the segment attracted by those store values. A retailer cannot provide carpets for one shopper and tiles for the next. Nor can it increase the staff available to shoppers selecting high margin brands but teach them to ignore shoppers looking for discounts and promotions. It would be feasible, but controversial, to put up prices after 6 p.m., when richer working people might dominate the clientèle.

Some services, for example trained staff who advise customers, suffer from the problem of being separable from purchase.

If customers are advised and allowed to browse without buying, nothing stops them from subsequently comparing prices in a number of stores (including hypermarkets who only stock a very limited range) and taking the cheapest offer.

Some services are not separable from purchase. This is the case for late opening hours, after-sales service and guarantees. A store that offers its purchasers a 'no questions asked' money back policy is building a stronger bond with its purchasers than a store which offers friendly advice to all-comers. Retailers should bear this in mind when evaluating the usefulness of services as a differential advantage.

As we saw above, a supermarket cannot target too tightly. Life stage will indicate certain preferences (families with children: supermarkets with play areas; old-age pensioners: small amounts of shopping and home deliveries) or life style (e.g. trendy versus conservative, healthy versus convenience), but whereas these are all used successfully to target product brands, they are all too pointed to work in a retail context. A supermarket cannot afford to become too specific in terms of style. For example, playing loud rock music, dressing the check-out girls in funky outfits and tiling the floors black and pink will alienate certain important segments, even if it is strongly appealing to others. The store values chosen have to appeal to all the heterogeneous target.

Specific styles are out, but what about a generally better shopping experience? How could any shopper object to investment in personnel, systems and technology, number of check-outs, range of products stocked and quality property (car parks, wide aisles)?

Widely appealing (as against polarising) benefits may well attract more shoppers. The problem then becomes one of sustainability. Successful modifications will tend to be copied by any competitor who loses volume to the improved store. Since the improvements are broad in appeal, the improvements the competition make in response are likely to keep the stores similar, rather than to differentiate them. Competitors are forced to match, plastic bag for plastic bag. The net effect will be 'back to square one' at a higher cost level than before.

The nature of grocery shopping (see earlier) is such that many shoppers are unwilling to pay for a better experience. Indeed, some shoppers will actually be put off by high store values (spacious aisles, cleanliness, smart decor) because it will affect their perception of the store's prices. Once several competing chains have bid up the overall quality of shopping in a country or region, there opens up at the bottom of the market an opportunity for a lean, low-cost, low-service operator. No market has shown itself uninterested in the price proposition of chains such as Kwik Save or Aldi, indicating that the price-sensitive segment of grocery shoppers is always significant.

The absolute level of quality is thus always limited by the threat of a low-price store entering the market. The high store-value stores know they are playing with fire once they get into a position where the mainstream shopper can be won over by a low store-value competitor with a clear edge on price. This explains the furore caused by the appearance of Aldi, Netto, Lidl and Costco in the UK.

6.2.4 The Price Imperative

There is always a significant price-sensitive segment of shoppers. This price segment gets larger as the perceived price difference between retailers increases. It can also grow larger during times of recession, or due to marketing efforts which draw attention to prices.

As we have seen, because of the strong benefits of volume, no large store can deselect any important segment in its catchment area. Thus a large supermarket cannot allow its price perception to rise far from the bottom of the market: it will lose a significant segment of business (or run the risk of attracting new competitors to the area). Given the financial structure of most retailers, losing any share will jeopardise profits. This explains why it is so easy for retailers to slip into price wars and why all retailers are scared of starting a vicious circle of price rises and lost customers.

One implication of this is that price is an imperative for all mass retailers. The price imperative consists of two musts for retailers:

(1) Retailers must be genuinely price competitive on products where the shopper is able to make direct comparisons.

(2) Retailers must permanently make efforts to manage their price image and must consider the impact of all marketing actions on that image.

Another important implication is that price cannot provide a differential advantage for a mainstream, large-range store. This is surprising, but follows from the fact that low price is an imperative for everyone. Any competitor who tries to make a differential advantage of price, forces the other competitors to match because no competitor can afford to be beaten on price, given the importance of price, and their sensitivity to volume. The most likely outcome is that all the competitors get inveigled into a price war. Large stores must find other ways to make consumers loyal.

For mainstream, wide range store chains, price and store values are necessary but not sufficient: they are 'success factors'. They can never be ignored, but neither provides the solution to consumer loyalty and increased profits.

6.2.5 Retailer Marketing

With the exception of hard discount operations, large retailers have to cultivate a mainstream brand (chain) proposition. Every supermarket which does not go for the extreme price position, has to be attractive to all the main market segments in terms of quality, convenience and price perception. They have to cultivate a broad image which attracts old and young, rich and poor, male and female, black and white. A mainstream store cannot afford to alienate the health-conscious, time-conscious, price-conscious, or fashion-conscious consumer.

Retail brands, in the sense of a chain with a distinct image, will always be a blunt instrument for segmentation and differentiation compared to the finesse achieved by product brands. Retailers cannot follow the key marketing ploy of manufacturers: segmentation via brand proliferation.

A large store always has to restrict its investment in store values to a level affordable by the price-sensitive segment of shoppers. In terms of 'image', in contrast to manufacturers, stores must aim to alienate nobody rather than to strongly appeal to a targeted segment. They cannot become too specific (e.g. young and trendy) because of their need to win volume within their coverage area, which is bound to be heterogeneous.

6.2.6 Differential Advantages for Stores

So far we have discovered some interesting implications for retail marketing: the overall store image has to be bland, the fundamental importance of price for all stores and the need to segment and price discriminate within the store. We have dismissed both price and service as potential differential advantages for mainstream (as against hard discount) stores. Price cannot be a true differential advantage as every store must try to excel on this dimension. Investing too markedly in service will affect prices and price perception, while successful service improvements will simply be copied. Location, though essential, does not give an absolute differential advantage in a saturated market.

We have still to answer the key question: 'How can retailers differentiate their offerings and create loyalty?' Following the implications of this chapter means that supermarkets, at least within formats, are destined to remain fairly similar to each other. We have not shown how two similar supermarkets (say Sainsbury's and Tesco) are able to create loyal usage, non-substitutability and higher profits. We do this in the next chapter.

Notes

(1) Mark Skipworth and Alan Ruddock, 'The truth about Sainsbury's "50% off" sales gimmick', *Sunday Times*, 3 January 1993, p. 1.
(2) From a study by Ayer Reflexion, 1991, quoted by Mathilde de Bouard, *Marketing Mix Magazine*, Paris, No. 56, October 1991, p. 24.
(3) For a more detailed discussion, see Richard Vaughan, 'How advertising works: a planning model', *Journal of Advertising Research*, Vol. 20, No. 5, 1980, pp. 27–33.
(4) Secodip, 'Scenario pour l'aprés 1993', reported in *LSA*, No. 1289, 30 January 1992.

7
Creating a Sustainable Retail Differential Advantage

7.1 RETAIL DIFFERENTIAL ADVANTAGE

Retailers, like manufacturers, need to find some way of differentiating their offerings. Location often used to be a decisive differential advantage for a store, but as saturation and consumer mobility increases, location gives less protection. In saturated markets location continues to be a differential advantage only for small 'convenience' stores. Other retailers, like manufacturers, must aim to differentiate their offerings to create loyalty among their shoppers. Once stores are differentiated one from another, retailers can improve their profits. This was the conclusion reached at the end of Chapter 5. In Chapter 6 we dismissed segmentation via chain proliferation, we dismissed service levels and store quality, and we even dismissed low prices for creating differential advantage for a mainstream store. In this chapter we propose two alternatives to replace location as a retailer differential advantage: own label and fresh produce, and hard discount.

7.1.1 What Counts as a Differential Advantage?

In every market there are certain 'key success factors' without which a competitor cannot expect to survive. In retailing, good prices and good locations are essential. Achieving these minima is often in itself a very considerable challenge. Looked at from the outside, these necessary success factors are often those elements described as 'barriers to entry' for new competitors. A differential advantage is what a company can offer on top of the necessary. A differential advantage is obtained when a product is successfully differentiated in the minds of consumers, so that it is no longer totally substitutable with competitive products. If an advantage is to be a true differential advantage it must have three vital attributes. It must be:

(1) *Perceived as unique.* The idea of a differential advantage is to set the retailer apart from the competition in the eyes of the consumer. The offer must be distinct in some way. Uniqueness in itself will not necessarily motivate purchase, but it is a prerequisite. A product-offering has to be perceived as distinct before any added value can be attached to it. A product-offering can be perceived as being unique without being particularly attractive: the East German Trabant is as distinct in its way as the Volkswagen Golf. The second condition for a successful differential advantage is that the unique offering must be important to the target market.
(2) *Important to the target market.* The differential advantage has to be important to consumers when they make their buying decisions. Since the target market of a large store is broad, the differential advantage must motivate a whole range of segments. Retailers have a habit of assuming that price is important to all buyers. More often price is important for a certain group of shoppers, but relatively less important to others. Since retailers must go for many segments, they must find benefits which motivate each type of shopper to become loyal to the store.
(3) *Sustainable.* If a retailer finds some differential advantage that attracts and holds shoppers, competitors will immediately wish to match and neutralise the benefit. To be worth anything, a differential advantage has to be sustainable against the competition. To be sustainable, a differential advantage must be based on some resource that is unique to the company, and difficult to copy. In general, services (such as smiling check-out staff) are copiable, and worth copying if they are profitable. Low prices on manufacturer brands are copiable unless the store has a structural and

sustainable lead in efficiency. The most sustainable differentiator found to date has been the procurement of unique and exclusive products sold under the store's name.

7.2 DIFFERENTIAL ADVANTAGE VIA OWN BRANDS AND FRESH PRODUCTS

Through most of history, merchants, wholesalers and shopkeepers dominated the relationship with end consumers. They negotiated with suppliers and carried out the functions of dividing into small lot sizes and packaging (rather rudimentary). They also provided whatever guarantees and reassurance on quality the consumer had.

Manufacturers created brands initially to wrest power from the middlemen. By naming and making their product offering distinct (literally by burning a 'brand mark' on their packing cases) and by advertising its qualities, manufacturers built a bridge over the heads of the merchants to the consumer. They created consumer loyalty for their particular brand. Consumer demand put pressure on retailers to stock the item and the manufacturer was able to hold out for a higher price.

With the invention of brands manufacturers took over the role of lot size, packaging and, most important, of reassurance. As manufactured consumer goods became more sophisticated, with better and more attractive packaging, the relative power of distributors fell. Using more sophisticated advertising (culminating in TV advertising) and promotional techniques, the strength of manufacturers grew with their hold on the consumers' minds. The power and influence of the retail trade declined steadily for over 50 years. At this point various sociological changes (notably the car) encouraged the rise of large efficient retailers. Retail power concentrated and the discounters grew in size until they found themselves back in a position to challenge the hegemony of the manufacturers.

7.2.1 Own Label

Discounters grow by taking sales from small, inefficient shops. Discounters are happy to handle respected manufacturers' brands. These brands are those distributed by the traditional retailers, and the developing, more efficient stores can compete very successfully on breadth of merchandise and, above all, competitive prices compared to the traditional shops. Discounters actually needed national brands to convince shoppers that the products they offered were as good as those in traditional stores. This was particularly true in white and brown goods, where discount warehouses were trusted little initially.

Once competition hotted up, with large discounters competing with other large discounters rather than 'Mom and Pop' stores, selling strategies took hold and it became difficult for stores to make good margins on leading brands. This was the original impetus for own brands. Own labels were originally introduced in a selling climate as a means of countering the power of national brands.

The increased size of retailers meant that, for the first time, many had become large enough to commission 'own brands', sold exclusively through their outlets.

At first, own labels reflected the philosophy of their inventors: the discounter could buy them cheaper, and even after taking a healthy margin could offer them to their shoppers at a relatively low price. These were 'type-1' own labels.

7.2.2 Type-1 Own Labels

Own labels imply cutting out the consumer marketing machinery of manufacturing companies, and going directly from production to presence on the shelf. By buying competitively, and minimising packaging and marketing costs, supermarkets can make better margins on such products while also offering their shoppers significantly lower prices. A supermarket might sell a branded version of a commodity such as milk at a margin of 2–3%. Typically they can make margins at least five times as good on own-label milk.

Type-1 own labels help the retailer control the manufacturer. They are not designed to differentiate the store against retail competition.

Own label became an important negotiating tool against dominant national brands. By taking up some shelf space with own brands, the retailer increased the competition between national brands. The retailer could afford to sell the major brands at a tiny margin, by making much larger margins on their own labels. The major brands, though, were the reason people came into the shop.

If, in addition, the own label provided some alternative to the leading brand, the threat of non-supply wielded by the manufacturers became a double-edged sword. Thus there was an incentive for the retailers to aim for a reasonable quality for their own labels. At the extreme, own brands might even be packaged to resemble the national brands they were intended to weaken.

Mimic brands, close copies of particular manufacturer brands, are the most aggressive form of this tactic. Carrefour (France) used to offer a Carrefour bath additive reminiscent of the well-known brand 'Fa'. It dropped that own brand in favour of a new design, reminiscent of the Obao brand and called this one 'Iloa'. Superdrug (UK) markets 'Frequent Wash Shampoo' in a bottle strikingly similar to that of Timotei. The Belgian retailer GIB chose the colours of the 'J & B' whisky for their own whisky, naturally called 'GB' whisky'. A typically US twist is to print on the packaging, 'This is *not* Johnson & Johnson© Baby Oil'. Arguably, these stores are doing something unfair, and even illegal. In the UK, top FMCG manufacturers are lobbying for a tightening of trademark legislation. But the damage done by mimic brands is a gnat's bite compared to the savaging that is to come from the market-oriented retailer.

Generics are another type-1 own label. The marketing proposition for these brands is that the lowest possible price is achieved by saving money on packaging, advertising and marketing. They adopt a 'commodity-style' presentation, for example minimalist white packs, with black print stating contents. Generics have, in fact, tended to be something of a fad gaining momentum during periods of intense price competition and falling by the wayside later. Since they don't actually cost less to produce than 'false' brands, with a brand name and an appetising photo on the pack, they tend to be superseded by the latter once their novelty value has faded.

Most manufacturers resented the invention of own labels. However, manufacturers of quality brands were confident that the techniques (advertising and innovation) which protect their brands from cheaper manufacturer brands would work against this new form of low-quality competition. Cheaper and weaker brand manufacturers took on own-label business to keep up their volumes. The premium brands remained the most profitable, and the manufacturers still dominated the premium market sector.

Since the bottom of the market is limited in size (most people seek average or premium quality) type-1 own label, however it is presented, can take only a limited market share (dependent on product field). In markets where consumers are sensitive to quality differences (e.g. washing powder, instant coffee, sanitary protection) the share for type-1 own labels usually plateaus well below 20% of volume. In segments where differences are more marginal (such as paper products or basic cooking ingredients), type-1 own label sometimes took as much as half of the market. In most markets, own label kicked off to a good start, but ended stable or declining after the first decade, in most countries and in most product fields. Low-quality own labels, generics and false/price brands threatened cheap, unadvertised manufacturer brands most.

Branded manufacturers felt they had 'seen them off'. In fact, like a virus that mutates and adapts to the defences of its victim, own brands came back in a far more deadly form.

Thoughtful retailers began to realise that the low quality of their own labels limited their potential market penetration and that more profits could be made on higher-quality products. Slowly, the true potential of own label began to dawn on them and they began to accumulate the know-how to launch 'type-2' own labels.

7.2.3 The Transition to Type-2 Own Labels

Retailers saw the potential for offering high-quality products procured by themselves and without a manufacturer's reassurance, but they had image problems. With a few exceptions, the history of own label was associated with the bottom end of the price–quality spectrum. Retailers themselves, due to their broad appeal and the price imperative do not have prestige images to lend to high-quality own label. For certain items (for example, a jumper or a tie), carrying a supermarket name would actually reduce its value.

A number of supermarkets hit on the idea of launching 'sub-brands' with a name distinct from the store name. Thus Carrefour used 'Tex' for its textile brands and 'Net' for cleaning products. Monoprix launched 'Gourmet' food lines, Prisunic sold quality housewares under 'Kilt', Woolworth's bought the 'Ladybird' label to put on their children's clothes, while keeping 'Winfield' on other lines. In the UK, own label had a better reputation for quality, and sub-brands were less necessary.

Sub-brand or no, most consumers would begin to associate the brand with the store. Sub-brand or no, if the quality was good and the price attractive, the brand would develop its own (positive) imagery based on the value perceived by its users.

In some cases, the quality of the products and the trust in the created retailer brand came to be perceived as a differential advantage for the store itself. *The brand was making shoppers loyal to the store*. This is the fundamental difference.

It is possible to identify many different approaches to own label but only this difference is important (see also Fig. 7.1): type-1 own labels are supported by the store—fed by the store's traffic, guaranteed (to a modest extent) by the store's credibility. Type-2 own labels feed the store—build its traffic and improve the store's appeal. If own label products are particularly liked and are not found elsewhere then they can have a very strong influence on store choice and loyalty.

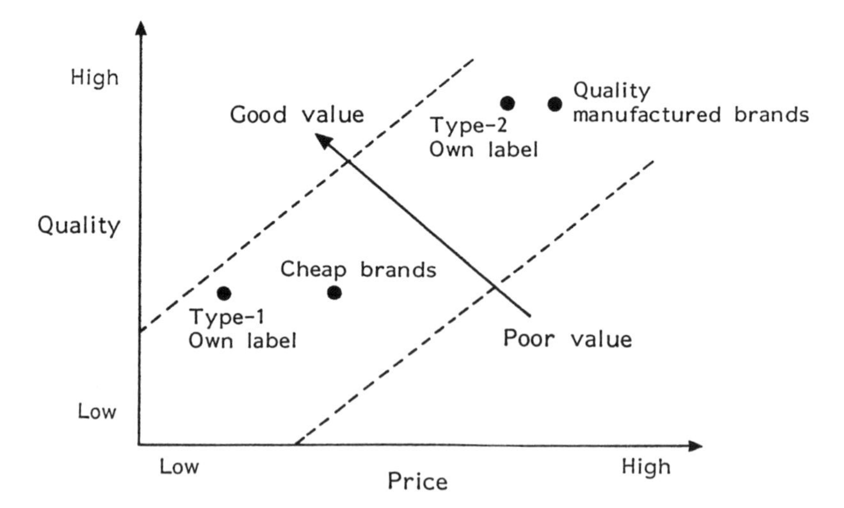

Figure 7.1 *All viable products fall in the 'value corridor' between the two diagonal lines. Type-1 and type-2 own labels fall at opposite ends: the former offering good value at low quality, the latter good value at high quality*

Faced with a 'cheap and nasty' own label (say a 400 g tin containing four watery peeled tomatoes) a type-1-oriented retailer will say: 'It'll still sell to a certain proportion of our customers'. A retailer building a strategy on type-2 own labels will accept only products capable of creating loyalty among their buyers. Although creating loyalty among shoppers was not the original objective of own brands, own brands have so far proved to be the most effective means for creating shopper loyalty.

7.2.4 Type-2 or 'Flag' Own Brands

Benetton, Body Shop, Sock Shop, Tie Rack, Next, Baskin Robbins, IKEA, The Gap, good sandwich bars and restaurants are among many examples of retailers with a strong differential advantage obtained by offering a unique and superior product. The products are unique and since they offer particularly good value or particular satisfaction, they attract buyers to the store, develop loyalty and create goodwill for the retailer.

In the cases cited above the product sold in the store so dominates, that they are not automatically perceived as own brands. These are the extreme of type-2 own brands. We suggest that this integration of brand and store is the most successful differential advantage for a retailer and the only sure way to build loyalty.

Sub-brands are not necessary to type-2 own label strategies, and the benefits and disadvantages are finely balanced (we return to this topic later). Several stores which developed sub-brands, including Marks & Spencer with their famous 'St Michael' brand, are now pushing their store name back on to their labels. Thus jumpers from Marks & Spencer once boasted 'manufacturer like' labels using the name 'St Michael', but now bear the label 'St Michael [written small] from Marks & Spencer [written large]'. On the other hand, several important chains (notably Sainsbury's and Asda) are moving towards category sub-brands.

While Sainsbury's and Marks & Spencer, the most consistently profitable food retailers in the UK, are moving in opposite directions on sub-brands, they share two important characteristics: (a) the high proportion of sales accounted for by own label, and (b) the high perceived quality of that own label.

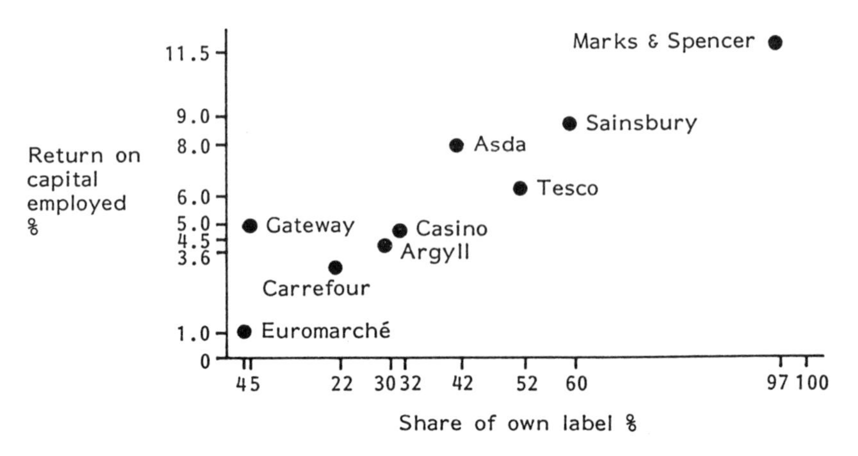

Figure 7.2 *Correlation between proportion of own label sales and profitability. Antoine Boudet, 'Marques Propres: jusqu'ou monteront-elles?', LSA, No. 1253, 18 April 1991, pp. 36–7, analysis of annual (company) reports, carried out under the supervision of Philippe Kass of OC & C (consultants)*

Some analysts have noted a correlation, within UK chains, between profitability and proportion of sales accounted for by own label. (See Fig. 7.2.)

Sainsbury's and Tesco, the leading supermarkets in the UK, sell more own brands than they do manufacturer brands. In these chains, in most product categories, the store brand is the brand leader. Many of their shoppers are loyal to brands which they can only obtain from one supermarket chain. How awkward for such a shopper to stock up elsewhere: in effect an alternative supermarket would be out of stock on more than 50% of the brands the shopper was looking for. Once manufacturers held sway over retailers because of the effect of non-stocking on the shopper. Now retailers create loyalty because competitor stores do not stock their own label. For these stores, own label has become the main vehicle for building loyalty.

The interesting thing about this loyalty is that it can provide differential advantage for more than one player in the market. Just as loyalty to, say, brands of coffee, increases the value of the coffee market and creates profitable coffee brands, loyalty to shop brands increases the value of the retail market, and makes retailers more profitable. Sainsbury's and Tesco's instant coffee may be of equal quality, but as long as shoppers develop a preference for one or the other, both are protected from substitutability, the bane of suppliers.

This is not the same thing as saying that own-label is the embodiment of the store image; no more than saying that Maxwell House is the embodiment of the image of Kraft General Foods. Store images are by definition bland, Sainsbury's Vindaloo curry is not. Shoppers need to go to Sainsbury's, or to Tesco, because they want to find Sainsbury's curry, or Tesco's muffins, not because the retail experience is so pleasurable or memorable.

Type-2 own label is invaluable to retailers because, as with product brands, several chains can each use this differential advantage. The whole retail market improves once store-brand loyalty begins to take over from manufacturer-brand loyalty in people's buying habits. Of course, the manufacturer's interests are diametrically opposed.

Actual innovation is a necessary step in the evolution. Sainsbury's now introduces about 1200 product modifications each year, up from 300 in 1987. Far from wanting to mimic manufacturer brands, Sainsbury's supports an extensive research and development department to develop innovative, quality products. Its close contact with the consumer has allowed it to sense trends to healthier eating and continental foods. Meanwhile, Sainsbury's advertising has continually featured their own products, often devoting a whole double page spread or TV spot to a single line. Many retailers are now sponsoring original brands. In the 1980s UK retailers pioneered ready-to-eat meals, and now dominate that market where consumers are highly sensitive to quality, and willing to pay considerable premiums.

One drawback for retailers developing strong type-2 own brands is that they reduce their sales of branded goods, and thus lessen their negotiating strength with major manufacturers. On the other hand, in these stores the major brands play a different role to that played in 'selling oriented' stores. In a price driven store the popular national brands are discounted to create a good price image and generate traffic; in a quality store they are there to satisfy those shoppers who are truly brand loyal, and less swayed by price. The more value conscious shoppers will usually opt for the private label alternative. Thus, not having the keenest prices is less of a problem, and the retailer is able to generate good profits even on the most popular national brands.

Type-2 own label raises the interesting question of whether a retail brand needs to be distributed only through one chain.

Boots' own label cosmetics are distributed abroad—No. 7 is apparently brand leader in Finland—but Boots has always been a significant manufacturer as well as retailer. Dixons (electrical goods) use their sub-brands (though not the Dixon name) in their acquired chain of Curry stores. If the retailer brand provides a reason to go into a shop, but is not the embodiment of the shop's image, it is reasonable to consider distributing it through other chains owned by the retailer, or even through non-competing outlets. For example, Marks & Spencer sandwiches could be distributed through independent sandwich bars or, say, British Rail. As own labels develop, the idea of retailers owning brands which extend beyond their own chain becomes more and more feasible.

7.2.5 Fresh Foods as Type-2 Own Labels

Perishables have also proved to be an area that retailers can use to differentiate themselves. Producers have occasionally succeeded in creating 'fresh food' brands (Jaffa oranges, Chiquita, Fyffes and Dole bananas, Bernard Matthew turkey products) but generally, manufacturers have been weaker in this area, because of a lack of control over logistics and distribution. This is an area where retailers have a definite edge over manufacturers as they control the handling and presentation. The French chain 'Casino' boasts that fish reaches its stores less than 24 hours after purchase on the quay-side. The average high-street fishmonger buying through a wholesaler gets the same fish two days later. Shoppers used to go to greengrocers and market stalls to buy high-quality vegetables. Now these smaller outlets cannot get hold of the best produce because it goes straight to the supermarket chains. The chains specify what they want, how they want it packed, and they send it back if it flunks their quality checks. Some supermarkets have developed this area as a strong differential advantage. In-store bakeries, delicatessen, fishmongers, and butchers can be of sufficiently high quality to tip the choice of supermarket.

These 'fresh own labels' are definitely type-2, aimed at creating a sustainable differential advantage for the store. They lend their appeal to the store. The best bakery in town always has a queue outside. If that bakery is in a store, that queue represents shoppers visiting that supermarket because of that bread.

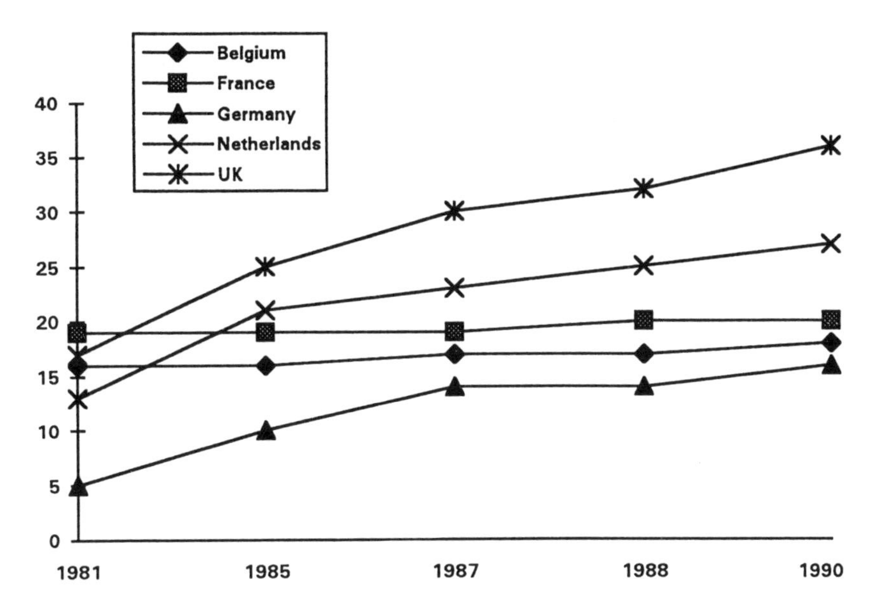

Figure 7.3 *Share of food sales going to retailer-controlled brands is steadily increasing throughout Europe*[1]

There are two bonuses in developing fresh foods as a differential advantage. First, fresh own labels build the frequency of visits to the store, because purchases of fresh food are more frequent than for dried groceries. Second, fresh produce competes with specialist greengrocers, markets and bakers who continue to sell a significant share of these foods. This is thus an opportunity to grow supermarket sales into a premium price area. For newer 'pre-packed' products, such as ready-to-serve salad, supermarkets have an advantage in terms of refrigerated transportation and display.

It is not surprising, given all these incentives, that own label share is growing throughout Europe, see Fig. 7.3.

7.2.6 Multi-segmentation In-Store

Retailers cannot segment the shopper market with retail brands, so they have to find another method for catering to the variety of shoppers. Retailers have to develop marketing methods which discriminate between different segments of customers within the store.

Multi-segmentation is used by most marketers who are tied to certain locations, and cannot fundamentally change their product. For example, McDonald's 'core' segment was defined by its president, Ray Croc, as families with children, and tailoring a restaurant to their specific needs is generally held to have been key to McDonald's success. Subsequently they have directed marketing efforts systematically to many different segments: older people, teenagers and working people. Similarly the product has been 'augmented' with salads, candlelit dinners, breakfasts etc., to cater for multi-segments. Another example of multi-segmentation is Euro Disney. Their number-one target is families with children, but they also package their attractions to attract couples without children, groups of young people and even business people. These latter groups are offered sailing and golfing facilities and sleeping accommodation tailored to their needs—varying from log cabins to luxury hotels.

In addition to benefit segments (convenience, price, choice, quality) retailers have to think in terms the segments created by shopping behaviour and local geography. Shopping trips vary so that a useful variable will be 'regular stock-up shop' versus 'emergency top-up shop'. Similarly 'lunch-time shoppers coming from work' might have different wants to 'evening shoppers coming from home', 'daytime shoppers' might have different priorities to 'evening and weekend shoppers'. Shoppers can be segmented by their geographical location compared to the store. Variables might be 'five-minute access versus ten-minute access' or 'nearer to competitor versus nearer to us'. Shoppers from one housing estate might be comparing the store to one competitor, while those from another estate might make a comparison with a different store. How does the brand share compare in the two estates?

Retailers have to appeal to all the segments present in their catchment area(s), and cater for the wide range of shopper segments attracted inside the stores. That is, retailers have to satisfy each of their multi-segments so well that each becomes loyal. Each segment attracted to the store needs to be understood and offered a shopping experience that satisfies its particular needs. Multi-segmentation also means price discriminating between shoppers so that the most price sensitive can be satisfied, while also achieving a higher margin from quality or service-sensitive shoppers.

For example, fruit and vegetable sections of supermarkets can be pre-packed. Pre-packing offers convenience and speed, but is off-putting for many shoppers concerned with quality, who prefer the choice and flexibility offered by specialist greengrocers. Supermarkets can offer 'choose your own' vegetable sections, where shoppers choose, pack and even weigh their own vegetables. This pleases the majority of shoppers, and takes business from specialist stores, but some shoppers resent the lost convenience, and are willing to pay (or are indifferent to paying) for that convenience. The 'multi-segment' solution is to provide both options, and thus to serve the different segments (convenience and quality). Similarly, many supermarkets now have in-house, staffed butchers which operate in parallel with a nearby pre-packed meat counter. The in-house butchers provide a better-quality product, and are there to seduce the consumers who previously went to a specialist butcher for their meat. This duplication within the store is (at last) what brand manufacturers offer with their substitutable brands, side by side on shelf.

Some supermarkets have organised themselves so that top-up shoppers can enter part of the store for bread and newspapers without having to go round the main store. Similarly, fast check-outs for people with less than ten items is a rather rudimentary attempt to satisfy the top-up shopper segment.

Price discrimination is a particular form of multi-segmentation. The overall image of a store must always include a promise of competitive prices, so as to attract the widest possible group. Inside the store the retailer has to price discriminate, in other words, multi-segment on the price variable. Managing price perceptions, and price discrimination is such an important marketing task for retailers, that we dedicate a large part of the next chapter to that subject.

A multi-segmenting retailer has to vary the store experience for each segment coming into the store. Beyond the elementary suggestions made above, the key to multi-segmentation is developing the appropriate mixture of product brands within the store: own brands, cheap unnamed brands and national brands.

7.3 PRICE AS MARKETING

There is always a position in the retail market for the hard price promoter. A hard discounter is the one type of grocer which can and does segment the shopping market: they have a pointed image which alienates some shoppers. For one player in any (local) market, price can be a differential advantage. Aldi is the classic example, being to hard discounting what Marks & Spencer is to high-quality retailing. Aldi promises an exceptional ratio between low price and acceptable quality, made possible by low store-values, a small assortment and cutting costs hard—so hard that for many years its stores did not even have telephones. The impressive thing about Aldi is that they have stayed lean enough to occupy this differential advantage for over 35 years.

In most markets (consumer and industrial) the price–quality spectrum provides a series of viable positionings. Retailing, for the reasons discussed in the last chapter, is anomalous. No mainstream, high-volume store can ever allow the price gap between themselves and the bottom of the market to become significant, but none can hope to make price their differential advantage. Price remains a *sine qua non*. The rest of this chapter is devoted to managing retail price image.

7.3.1 Determining Price Image

Shoppers often have only a vague feel for the objective price differences between stores, despite strongly held subjective beliefs. Table 7.1 shows how perceptions of price compared to an objective measure of prices in one French survey.

Table 7.1 shows that consumers are incapable of making accurate objective assessments of the prices offered by different stores. According to the survey, Carrefour is, objectively, highly price competitive. The consumers failed to perceive this and Carrefour fails to communicate its achievement. By contrast, Leclerc manages to charge much the same prices (94 against Carrefour's 95, on the objective measure), but has a price image par excellence. Monsieur Leclerc frequently appears in the media arguing the pro-consumer side of issues such as price

Table 7.1 *Comparison of objective and perceived prices of French supermarkets*

Store chain	Price image index	Actual price index
Leclerc	183	94
Intermarché	161	94
Continent	138	92
Rallye	116	97
Euromarché	112	99
Auchan	112	93
Franprix	109	105
Mammouth	104	98
Carrefour	97	95
Lion	81	104
Cora	78	101
Super U	76	100
Champion	74	97
Geant Casino	33	103
Suma	26	108

Denis Stoclet, 'Quelle Politique de Prix pour les Grandes Surfaces Alimentaires', *Points de Vente*, No. 380, 15 February 1990, p. 34.

maintenance and right to sell legislation: his store's price image is a tribute to his charisma and entrepreneurship.

It is interesting (and consistent with other similar surveys) to note how little real variation there is in prices among the large supermarket chains. The differences in terms of perception are huge in comparison: consumers are inclined to exaggerate price differences. A survey in the USA found that 21% of shoppers could not quote a price for an item they had just purchased, and that on average those who gave a price were 15% out: a huge margin compared to the variation between stores.[2] Of course, the problem is subtle: while the average consumer may be pretty vague, the price-conscious segment certainly do check prices more carefully.

Consumers form their impression of a retailer's relative price position in five main ways:

(1) *Direct price comparisons* on a subset of brands/products. The reasons for being in this privileged subset of brands can be high unit cost, frequency of purchase, frequent retail promotion, or an idiosyncrasy of the shopper. The problem for the retailer is that the set of brands varies over shoppers and may be magnified by word of mouth.

(2) *Promotional activity.* Getting one item at a noticeably lower price may register more forcefully than getting ten items at competitive prices. A shopper experiencing two stores with the same net prices, may feel that the one signalling more reductions and special offers is giving more bargains.
(3) *Store presentation.* An atmosphere of 'no frills' improves price perceptions. Discount stores have developed certain conventions: 'walls' of stacked product and cheaply made price banners are now associated with low prices. Conversely, efforts made to improve the store experience (tidiness, spaciousness) may have a negative effect on price perceptions. This happened to the department store Byenkorf in Amsterdam. When the store was upgraded in the early 1980s its price perception was dramatically increased, much to the cost of the store.
(4) *Direct communication.* Advertising with price claims reassures shoppers that the store does everything possible to be among the most price competitive. Public relations campaigns where retailers take the part of the consumer (such as those run by M. Leclerc on behalf of his French hypermarkets, or by the late Sam Walton for Wal-Mart), and price guarantees (see below) can similarly improve perceptions.
(5) *Positioning of own brands.* If a store uses its own brands to offer a cheap alternative to brands it is more likely to foster a price image than a store which uses type-2 own label to create loyalty.

Maintaining the right balance of image between quality, range, convenience and price, to attract the largest possible proportion of all the shopper segments is a hugely delicate operation for the mainstream store. There are many examples of stores that have chased around after different images, and ended up with a poor overall image as a result. GIB in Belgium blame their eight years of declining share largely on repeated changes of course. It is tempting to react head-on to every challenge, but when one day the attack is on price (Aldi or Colruyt) and another day on quality (Delhaize) the resulting lack of consistency can destroy the development of any coherent image. It is extremely long and costly to re-establish a price image, for any store which once loses their price credibility.

The ideal balance will vary across individual stores, vary over time and be affected by competitive actions. Every communication on each attribute will have an impact on other attributes, and past actions and image will hang around and affect current perceptions. Positioning a store is much more of a balancing act than positioning a brand.

7.3.2 Every Day Low Prices and High–Low Pricing

Every Day Low Prices (EDLP), has moved from being marketing jargon to gaining currency in normal language. In the process it has lost much of its precise meaning.

The idea is that instead of complex pricing schemes, coupons and exceptional promotions, the store maintains a uniform policy on mark-ups giving permanently competitive prices. This has an honest, consumerist ring about it, guaranteed to cull favourable media coverage. This has meant that many organisations (manufacturers and retailers) have loudly espoused the notion, sometimes adding the weasel phrase 'on a limited range of products'. In reality, EDLP is relevant to, and can only be practised by, a small proportion of claimants.

EDLP contradicts all ideas of price discrimination, but if the philosophy of the vendor (store or producers) is value then EDLP fits with the company's philosophy. The most compelling argument for EDLP is that it is the most cost-efficient pricing strategy (for both retailers and manufacturers). EDLP cuts the costs of mounting special promotions (materials, staff time) and the costs associated with continually changing prices. Fewer promotions smoothes out demand, reducing stock-outs and inventory costs. Relatively less advertising is necessary as true good value builds consumer loyalty, wins trust, appeals to one-stop shoppers. EDLP reduces the need for promotion wars run with expensive advertising and door-to-door brochures.

The second strategic reason for loudly adopting EDLP is that it can signal to retail competition that you are single-mindedly following a price orientation, and that they are free to take your stable and predictable prices as a baseline. For reasons explained in the section below, they are ill advised to attack any store with a serious EDLP positioning.

Because EDLP is efficient, and because it warns off competition, EDLP is the best pricing policy for hard discounters whose raison d'être is price. They have the cost structures to back it up and, indeed, EDLP is part of that cost structure.

A less convincing argument, but one that often lies behind attempts to drop prices across the board, is that each shopper is sensitive to a different set of prices, and an unfortunate comparison on any one price could lose some shopper's whole basket of goods. Word of mouth also influences shop choice, so one or two unfortunate comparisons could be expensive. This risk of being caught out on one or two items drives the retailer seeking a good price image to be competitive on a wide raft of products. Wanting to make the fashionable EDLP claim, and then afraid to be found cheating, is in itself an argument for adopting EDLP.

The question for retailers without a hard discount positioning is how to cultivate the best possible price image without detracting from their quality rating, and without destroying profitability.

A mainstream retailer facing competition from hard discounters cannot usually afford to lose its price-sensitive customers. Dropping prices on a wide range of lines (i.e. approaching EDLP) is often perceived to be the only way to redress the problem. The larger store runs price advertising and tries to match or beat the hard discounter's prices. In this situation management often feel this strategy is forced on them by their need for volume. Bearing in mind the evidence that price perceptions are subjective and unscientific (Table 7.1), it may not even work. A large store following this solution usually only increases its problems, for three distinct reasons:

(1) *Plausibility.* It is very difficult for a large assortment retailer to earn the same price image as hard discounter, even with comparable prices on comparable goods. It may be impossible to bring subjective perceptions in line with the objective reality, simply because the large store looks more expensive.
(2) *Profitability.* The large store may gain some sales on the discounted lines, but it will lose money on sales to less price-sensitive customers who would still have bought at the previous price. The volume gained on the discounted lines

is unlikely to compensate their lower prices. Profitability will be preserved only if the discounted prices serve to protect volume on non-discounted lines. To maintain EDLP in the long term the large mainstream store must develop the cost structure necessary to offer hard discount prices. This may be impossible for historical reasons.

(3) *Competitive reaction.* If large, mainstream stores advertise their intention to join the discounting game it can reinforce price sensitivity. A large store is admitting that quality and low price can exist together, and endorsing the belief that it is right to be more price sensitive. Thus the group of price-sensitive consumers is likely to increase, and the group seeking the qualities of the large store will diminish. Most sinister of all, if a mainstream store attacks a hard discounter on price, the discounter has only one weapon of defence. The discounter must preserve differential advantage by cutting prices further. Faced with retaliation the large store cannot quickly and painlessly withdraw (having advertised its intention to compete). The total cost of the price cuts will increase well beyond initial estimates if the action triggers a price war.

Low prices across all products is an appealing consumer proposition if you are a hard discount retailer, with cost structures to match. Any mainstream retailer facing such a competitor with higher costs (and hopefully qualities) will shoot itself in the foot trying to support claims that it offers low prices across the board.

A non-price retailer has to develop its price image through a strategy of continual, but unpredictable, promotions. The point of high–low pricing is to discriminate, both across consumers and across product lines. High–low gives the opportunity of improving margins by selling to non-price sensitive consumers at higher margins, and also providing higher margins on some less key lines. Low prices are appropriate on lines which are known to be price sensitive, and/or which are easy to use for comparisons. This is not 'limited EDLP'—it is the low half of high–low pricing. Promotions and the occasional real bargain are used to impress the shopper, supported by competitive prices on easy to compare items.

High–low pricing appeals to price-sensitive consumers as it gives them the chance of finding some genuine bargains. Thus it gives a price-based appeal to a store competing against a price-oriented EDLP operator. EDLP may even seem boring for some price-sensitive consumers because they enjoy special offers.

One could argue that a high–low pricing policy is more high minded even than EDLP: every consumer gets what they really want (or need) and the rich help the poor, Robin Hood style.

High–low pricing needs relatively more data (local competitors' prices) plus a (local) management system to operate an efficient discrimination strategy as prices have to be fine-tuned locally. Tesco is known to have a particularly sophisticated system for 'area pricing'. However, the overall price image has to be managed centrally.

High–low pricing is necessary if a store is developing a high-quality own label range, as management will wish to retain a high degree of flexibility in pricing differentials. For example, to price premium products above own label, to encourage trial, or to use brand-style, short-run promotions to develop own-label use. A high–low strategy is more flexible across a country, facing a range of competition. High–low will generally be more compatible with a higher-quality perception.

Managing prices will always be one of the highest arts of retailing. The EDLP fad is certainly not going to put an end to the fun.

7.3.3 Price Guarantees

Price-matching tactics can help to curb the price-cutting zeal of the competition. In one example, a large supermarket in the US, called Big Star, was suffering from the price attacks by another supermarket, Food Lion (a practitioner of EDLP). Big Star announced that it would 'match to the cent and for all time', Food Lion's prices on a named set of competitive lines, listed in their *Price Finder* magazine. The results of the price matching are shown in Tables 7.2 and 7.3.

The study found that the prices of the products being *matched* tended to *rise* under price matching. Food Lion seemed to recognise that any price cut would indeed be matched and,

Table 7.2 *The effect of Big Star's promise to match prices on items subjected to price matching and included in the* Price Finder *magazine*

Product lines subject to matching	First week		Last week	
	Food Lion	Big Star	Food Lion	Big Star
Hellman's mayonnaise	1.49	1.49	1.69	1.69
Chef Boyardee pizza	1.39	1.39	1.44	1.44
Hunt's whole tomatoes	0.60	0.60	0.50	0.50
Pillsbury flour	0.79	0.79	0.79	0.79
Mazola oil	1.99	1.99	1.73	1.73
Maxwell House coffee	2.19	2.33	2.89	2.89
Comet cleanser	0.69	0.69	0.74	0.74
Nabisco Oreo cookies	1.89	1.85	2.46	2.46
Mrs Smith's apple pie	2.94	2.94	3.35	3.35

Reproduced, with permission, from J. D. Hess and E. Gerstner, 'Price matching policies: An empirical case', *Managerial and Decision Economics*, August 1991, p. 307.

Table 7.3 *The effect of the price matching on products* **not listed** *in the* Price Finder *magazine*

Products not subject to rigorous matching	First week		Last week	
	Food Lion	Big Star	Food Lion	Big Star
Cut green beans	0.35	0.35	0.33	0.33
Thin sliced bread	0.59	0.55	0.55	0.69
Head lettuce	0.89	0.69	0.89	0.99
Pork loin chops	3.69	2.49	3.49	2.99
Ground beef	1.69	1.69	1.49	1.69
Swift hostess ham	8.99	8.99	9.99	9.99
Coke	0.99	1.29	1.09	0.89
Pepsi	1.47	1.19	1.29	1.39
Large grade A eggs	1.33	1.37	0.78	0.49
Miller beer	2.71	2.71	2.84	2.84

Reproduced, with permission, from J. D. Hess and E. Gerstner, 'Price matching policies: An empirical case', *Managerial and Decision Economics*, August 1991, p. 307.

conversely, that price rises would also be matched. Thus making price cuts on these lines was futile. Under price matching, the average price of non-matched lines fell relative to the matched lines.

Price guarantees ('Never knowingly undersold', as John Lewis in the UK puts it; 'Le Contrat Confiance', says Darty in France) are a way of simultaneously creating a good price image and discriminating between price-sensitive and non-price-sensitive customers. The stores reassure all their customers that if they find the same goods on sale at lower prices elsewhere, they will be refunded the difference. In practice, only the price-sensitive customers claim on the guarantees, while the less diligent price followers pay the higher price in the belief that the store is doing its utmost to be at the lowest current price.

Price guarantees are highly compatible with type-2 own label strategies.

7.3.4 Price Discrimination

Manufacturers price discriminate by developing and positioning their brands on a price/quality axis. This is very clear in cars or video recorders where the luxury model can cost double the price of the basic model, and each intermediate price point is filled by a model with more functions. The different models ask the consumer: 'How much do you want to spend?'

Retailers have to create a pricing structure within product categories that allows each price segment in the market to be satisfied. This might mean a predictable set of price levels within each category. For example having a pricing policy which sets the relative price levels for generic (unbranded) brands, cheap brands, quality own label and premium brands. Stores can also arrange themselves into separate sections or boutiques, which operate different pricing rules. Stores can mark certain brands as offering the rock-bottom price position. By flagging 400 basic lines in this way a large store can guide a shopper to a subset of lines which together add up to a 'hard discount' experience.

The retailer can impose a non-monetary cost on the price-sensitive consumer: e.g. waiting for promotions, buying in larger quantities and stocking at home, clipping coupons or bagging up their own apples.

Coupons giving price reductions on specific brands, distributed by retailers, but paid for by manufacturers, can be a technique for discrimination.[3] In the USA, statistics collected by Nielsen show that the face value of coupons has steadily increased since the mid 1980s, and also that more and more coupons are being distributed (see Fig. 7.4).

Only a tiny proportion (less than 3%) of coupons are redeemed, presumably by the most price-sensitive shoppers. The total value of savings has gone up, and these significant discounts are being targeted via coupons to a self-selecting subgroup, i.e. the coupon

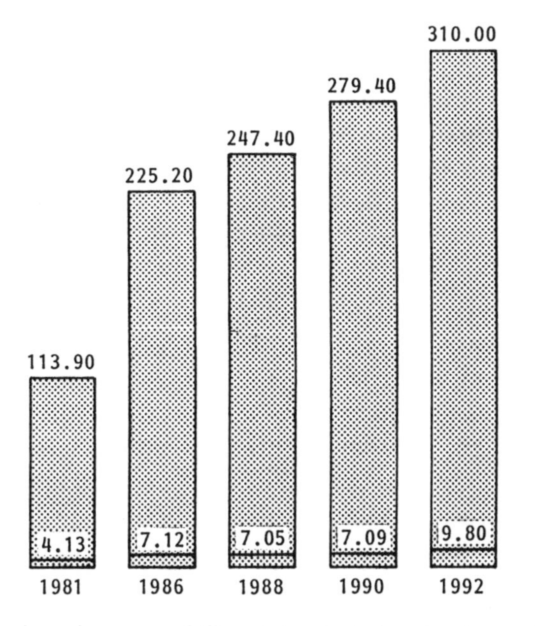

Figure 7.4 *Number of coupons (billions) distributed and redeemed in the USA. Europe is far behind in the use of coupons. Yves Puget, 'L'explosion du couponing',* LSA, *No. 1388, 10 March 1994, p. 38.*

issuers are managing to deliver strong incentives to purchase to the most motivated bargain hunters, while charging higher prices to those less price sensitive. Discrimination has increased.

The key aim is to find socially and legally acceptable ways of allowing price-sensitive shoppers to pay less, while leaving the less price-sensitive customers to pay more. This is exactly what manufacturers achieve with their portfolios of brands. Retailers can use their own quality brands, cheap and false brands and manufacturer brands to price discriminate. Coupons, price guarantees and convenience can also be used creatively by retailers. The objective is both to avoid giving product away for less than its value and to avoid losing a profitable sale through setting the price too high.

7.4 CONCLUSIONS

A retailer has a range of assets, starting at the most physical with location and property, through systems and people to the more intangible: information on the consumer and control of the in-store marketing variables. As retailers have become more sophisticated, they have made use of each of these assets in turn to create competitive advantage for themselves.

At one time large supermarkets and discounters (K-Mart, Comet, Darty) relied on their location, size and efficiency, to give themselves a winning edge over high-street competition. In time, these assets became necessary conditions. Similar stores with similar property and technology easily enter into price and promotion wars. This can lead to a selling orientation where retailers use sophisticated promotional calculations in an effort to out-price each other.

The last stage, 'market orientation', comes when retailers use their information and control of in-store marketing variables to build brands: the traditional weapons of their suppliers. Own brands have turned out to be the most powerful tool for developing consumer loyalty, and price discriminating between customers.

The art of branding, creating and owning mindspace, has been developed and tested by manufacturers. Retailers are coming (or will come) to the conclusion, that no better way of marketing themselves exists, and no more subtle tool exists for price discriminating among their shoppers.

In summary, for major retailers:

(1) *Store values* do not create sustainable differential advantages. Any appealing store value will be copied, bringing all the stores back to parity at a higher cost level. Continual price competition, and split baskets, limits the investment possible in a superior store and service.
(2) *Segmentation* of shoppers has to take place within each store, rather than between competing stores. Deselecting major segments of shoppers who live nearby is not an option for large stores because large units have to attract as many shoppers as possible from their covered area. Retail chains cannot become 'brands' which 'segment' the shopper market. What retailers can do is to multi-segment within their stores. The retailer has to plan each of their categories, pricing and promotions to satisfy the wants of a varied clientèle.
(3) *Low price* can only provide a true differential advantage for

one player (in any area). There is a uniquely differentiated position available at the bottom, profitable to an operator with a single-minded determination to create the lowest cost structure. The presence, or potential presence, of a hard discounter, combined with the volume imperative, means that positionings far above are not viable.

(4) There are only two *price points* in retailing: EDLP and high–low pricing. Only the committed hard discounter can go for EDLP. Every retailer has to be competitive on easily compared, regularly purchased lines and every retailer must continuously manage its competitive price image. This is an imperative of retail marketing which is different from FMCG marketing: product brands which are perceived to be premium priced can do very well, supermarkets cannot.

(5) *Type-2 own labels.* Those brands (including fresh produce) which build loyalty for themselves and attract shoppers to the store, are the only alternative to a hard price positioning for creating a sustainable differential advantage. The main source of differential advantage for mainstream retailers, with high–low pricing, is to build their own brands. A retailer with a 'flag' own brands can build loyalty, differentiate itself from its retail competition and hold a sustainable position against price rivals.

Location was once the major differential advantage for stores, but increasing mobility and the vast expansion in supermarketing in recent years, have reduced this traditional protection. In mature retail markets, most consumers choose from at least two major stores when making their shopping choice. Location is still a major factor in choice, but it no longer holds sway, except for small local shops trading on their convenience.

Our conclusion is that retailers in a mature retail market have two alternatives to location to create sustainable differential advantage. One is quality own brands and fresh produce, and the other is price, based on ruthless control of costs. These three possible strategies lead to three retail formulas that can be successful and can coexist: convenience stores, hard discounters (both limited range and warehouse) and large 'value-quality' retailers. A retailer trying to straddle any two of these formulas is likely to lose out to more focused players.

Market orientation leads major retail chains to develop their own quality brands and their own philosophy of consumer reassurance. Hard discounters often handle only a very limited range of premium manufacturer brands. Convenience and local stores still rely on their location and manufacturer's brands to attract shoppers, but their volumes are small. Following from this, a marketing orientation among retailers will inevitably lead to a head-on confrontation with manufacturers over mindspace. This battle, the battle over the ownership of FMCG brands, is the subject of the last part of this book.

Notes

(1) This graph (Fig. 7.3) was created using figures published in 'European Marketing Data and Statistics', *Euromonitor*, 1994, Table 1220, p. 332.
(2) Peter Dickson and Alan Sawyer, 'The price knowledge and search of supermarket shoppers', *Journal of Marketing*, July 1990, pp. 42–53.
(3) Chakravarthi Narasimhan, 'A price discrimination theory of coupons', *Marketing Science*, Vol. 3, No. 2, Spring 1984.

Part III
MATRIX MARKETING

8
The Battle for Mindspace

8.1 THE BRAND IS DEAD— LONG LIVE THE BRAND!

Manufacturers invented new or better products, gave them names and made those names household words. Some brands become so familiar that their names become generic: Hoover, Mars, Kleenex, Coke, Nescafé, Sellotape, Pernod.

Keeping a brand name dominant in its field is not a rare achievement, but it is not automatic. Top brands stay on top because of the continual investment and commitment of their owners. Brand names do not constitute a permanently acquired capital, perennially earning a predictable rent. Rather, they represent a position in a market that can be defended. Top brands are able to defend their positions because they can afford more R&D, more advertising, more salesforce etc., and not least because large brands are able to attract the best brand management.

Manufacturers have become so used to the idea of owning space in the consumer's mind, that sometimes they seem to believe this is a law of nature. It is not a law of nature: famous brands are owned by manufacturers because they grasped the opportunity when the technology of branding and creating mindspace became available in the recent past. Now competition for the consumer comes as a shock.

Cigarettes long had the reputation of being one of the most loyal brand markets, and confident manufacturers used this knowledge to increase their prices and margins. Thus when 40% of the US cigarette market went over to retailer controlled brands and generics, manufacturers and their shareholders were shocked and shaken. Journalists, stock analysts and other marketing soothsayers were quick to explain this phenomenon in terms of fundamental changes in consumer behaviour. The *Financial Times* observed: 'If penny pinching consumers were willing to substitute "discount" smokes for a well marketed brand such as Marlboro . . . would they not do likewise with less renowned names?'[1] *The Economist*, with its particular brand of self-righteous consumerism chipped in: 'Many cynical American and European shoppers have concluded (correctly) that there is scant difference between (supermarket products). Price sensitivity is waxing and brand loyalty is waning. This is taking a toll on even the savviest marketing machines, such as Philip Morris and Procter & Gamble'.[2]

Another instance of the 'revolution' in branding concerns Coca-Cola, another brand darling of the FMCG world. Coca-Cola regularly comes out top in surveys designed to measure brand equity (see Table 8.1), and is frequently the object of adulation in the business press.[3] Despite this, in countries where retailers have obtained high-quality cola drinks, the combined marketing nous of Coca-Cola and Pepsi has not been able to hold back the sales of the retailer-controlled brands. Broad statistics indicating the inroads made by own label in this market are given in Table 8.2.

Table 8.1 *In assessments of brand equity, Coke regularly takes first place*

World-wide	Europe	USA	Japan
Coca-Cola	Coca-Cola	Coca-Cola	Sony
Sony	Sony	Campbell's	National
Mercedes-Benz	Mercedes-Benz	Disney	Mercedes-Benz
Kodak	BMW	Pepsi-Cola	Toyota
Disney	Philips	Kodak	Takashimaya
Nestlé	Volkswagen	NBC	Rolls Royce
Toyota	Adidas	Black & Decker	Seiko
McDonald's	Kodak	Kellogg's	Matsushita
IBM	Nivea	McDonald's	Hitachi
Pepsi-Cola	Porsche	Hershey	Suntory

Landor Associates 1990, based on a survey of 10 000 consumers, measure based on a combination of familiarity and esteem. Reprinted from *European Management Journal*, Vol. 10, P. Barwise and T. Robertson, 'Brand portfolios', p. 278, Copyright 1992 with kind permission from Elsevier Science Ltd, The Boulevard, Langford Lane, Kidlington OX5 1GB, UK.

Table 8.2 *Volume sales of flavoured soft drinks (including colas) in a selection of major countries, year to May 1993*

Market shares (% horizontal)	Retailer brands	Total Coca-Cola	Total Pepsi Cola
United States	8.8	32.6	31.0
Canada	21.7	31.0	32.1
United Kingdom	30.0	26.6	9.4
Switzerland	26.9	44.1	8.5
France	16.8	40.6	5.3
Germany	2.8	55.8	4.1
Belgium	0.0	47.7	11.3
Spain	0.0	51.7	7.3
Italy	1.1	55.0	4.6

A. C. Nielsen, reproduced, with permission, from appendix A to David Nichols' speech at Oppenheimer Store Brands Conference, Wall Street, USA, June 1993.

While the soothsayers wail that brands are dead, retailers, supposedly their executioners, avow that brands are their very salvation. Retailers have shown that if a consumer is offered the same quality at a lower price, with a name that identifies and assures consistent quality, they will switch brands. Is this a revelation? Is it fair to accuse the consumer of transmogrifying into a penny-pinching cynic (or were they always such)? There are many examples of a brand offering a better overall package and overturning an established brand. Kao nappies reduced Procter & Gamble's brand share in Japan from 80% to 8%,[4] Bic's disposable razor had Gillette on the run. Once the original brands took care to restore the value they offered, they won their users back. In societies where 50% of marriages end in divorce, one can hardly expect the average housewife to remain loyal to a brand which offers less than its neighbour on shelf. As David Ogilvy might have put it: 'Never forget the consumer is your *ex*-wife.'

Consumers have a limited (though not necessarily decreasing) need for brand reassurance. If one supplier can provide 'branding' (identification, quality, image as needed) at a lower price, consumers are willing to reconsider their brand loyalties. Retailers have merely shown that they can procure high-quality goods and deliver them to the consumer with cost-efficient branding.

The trouble is that whenever brand reassurance is provided by a retailer, some manufacturer's role is correspondingly diminished. Retailers are challenging manufacturers for control of their traditional source of profit: mindspace. This is different from saying that brand loyalty is dead. It may well be worse: the idea that ex-Marlboro smokers might have become loyal to some own label brand, would be exceedingly bad news for Philip Morris. To win a smoker back would not simply mean reducing the price premium to below that which triggered the original switching. At the extreme, if the smoker was satisfied with the new brand, it might mean that the smoker would need to see a financial advantage in switching loyalties once more. That is to say, Marlboro would have to offer a price *lower* than the smoker's new brand!

So has brand loyalty disappeared? Or have smokers become loyal to their new packs, whatever colour they are? Did brand loyalty ever really exist, or is brand choice permanently under review, stable only as long as the consumer is satisfied with the overall value delivered?

8.1.1 Brand Management with Retail Characteristics

Once retailers start competing with manufacturers for consumer trust, manufacturers really have to justify their existence. This poses the question to manufacturers as to what they really are. Van Schaik, once chairman of Heineken, described his firm as 'a marketing organisation with production facilities'. This idea is also illustrated by the following quote from an American brewer:

> If I had to choose between losing my factories, and losing my company reputation . . . I would surely say: burn the factories. Tomorrow I would raise the capital to rebuild them, for our advertising has created a collateral of consumer demand that would bring us new capital. . . . A factory can be rebuilt in 90 days, but our awareness has taken years, and no capital can substitute for the effect created over that time.[5]

A brewer producing for own label cannot make the extravagant claim that all could be restarted from scratch if the factories were destroyed. The reverse is true: the brewer's working life is spent worrying that a retail client may swap supplier, if it finds one giving better terms.

So the question exercising the minds of alert manufacturers is: What is to stop retailers becoming 'marketing organisations with retail outlets'?

Retailers can see that, in recent years, manufacturers have been more profitable than they. The reason is that manufacturers build consumer trust, via brands. (How much have China and Taiwan 'lost out' to Western firms for the same reason?) The retailers see no reason why they cannot do the same thing. They want to own mindspace. Much is made of retail concentration, but this merely makes the challenge possible. The important change is that retailers are becoming active marketers themselves. They want to own the consumer. Retailers want to weaken consumer attachments to manufacturer brands and replace them with attachments to the brands managed by their friendly local superstore.

Some retail chains now generate sales volumes enough to justify huge advertising budgets, while manufacturers find it harder and harder to justify a national advertising budget for any but their largest brands (see Table 8.3).

In some respects retailers already have more consumer trust than manufacturers. Retailers and manufacturers are equally motivated by their own profitability, but in battles for the consumer's sympathy retailers regularly out-manoeuvre manufacturers. Retailers often promote their strategies as being 'in the public interest'.

Table 8.3 *Brand advertising expenditure in the UK in 1993*

Rank	Brand	Media spend £m
1	Tesco	27.4
2	McDonald's	27.3
3	Sainsbury's	24.7
4	Texas Homecare	24.5
5	Comet	24.0
6	Boots Retail	23.0
7	B & Q	22.3
8	MFI	20.2
9	Curry's	19.9
10	Woolworth	19.8
11	Safeway	18.7
12	Do it all	17.9
13	Asda	17.5
⋮	⋮	⋮
37	Nescafé coffee (highest ranking FMCG brand)	9.4

Source: Tracey Taylor (editor), 'Top 300 Brands' Special Report, p. 2, *Campaign*, Haymarket Publications, 29 April 1994.

8.2 RETAILERS' ADVANTAGES FOR CREATING MINDSPACE

Market-oriented retailers are a threat to manufacturers because of the relationships they develop with their shoppers. Retailers have three advantages over manufacturers when it comes to influencing consumers. The first is their direct, physical, contact. The second is their control of 'point of purchase' marketing variables. The third, as yet almost untapped as a source of power, is their access to data on consumer buying behaviour.

8.2.1 Communication with the Consumer

Marks & Spencer is one of the best-known 'brand names' in the UK. They dominate several UK clothing markets with an overall 15% share, have 5% of UK food sales and claim 14 million regular shoppers. All this was achieved with negligible advertising.[6] Their reputation has developed over a hundred years, during which their sober green facia has become familiar on practically every high street in the UK. In the USA, retail entrepreneur Leslie Wexner has dismissed the value of advertising in building his chains 'The Limited' and 'Victoria's Secrets'. He views the stores themselves as advertising and the 'look and feel' of the stores as a vital part of his retail concepts. The physical presence of shops following a uniform design, name, logo and style is equivalent to a permanent poster campaign on premium sites, perfectly targeted.

When shoppers enter a shop they form a strong impression of size, function and personality, as strong perhaps as the exposure to a TV ad. Each visit from a shopper provides the retailer with an opportunity to communicate something about the company and products. Most shoppers in the UK will speak to a Boots' employee several times a year. Manufacturers, by contrast, have to pay for every opportunity to communicate with their consumers. They have to spend money just to stop their brands being forgotten.

Many retailers are becoming increasingly involved in in-store and local advertising. In-store media are burgeoning: 'radio', videos for demonstrating and selling, brochures distributed locally and in-store, posters on shopping caddies. Advertising seen during the shopping trip and at the point of sale has certain advantages over advertising seen during other leisure activities.

Some cosmetics manufacturers have experimented with interactive computers to advise customers in-store. The computer administers a questionnaire and then recommends appropriate make-up and skin care products. Other new in-store media include electronic shelf-edge signs and coupon dispensers. Retailers can choose whether they want to allow a manufacturer to use these facilities, or to use them themselves. Supermarket media are still in their infancy and, as yet, rather unsophisticated, but this will change.

One retailer which has taken media-type initiatives is Canada's Loblaw. They promote their brand 'President's Choice' through link-ups with restaurants, cookery books, store samplings and even a video of barbecue recipes (which sold at $5.00 each in-store).[7] These are exactly the sort of promotional tactics that food brands have used for years, but they are particularly natural for retailers, because of their direct contact with the target audience.

Retailers are learning to carry out media-type strategies (creating awareness via stores, backed up with communication in-store) at just a time when manufacturers are finding it harder to reach their segments via mass media. Traditional media (particularly television) is becoming fragmented, and cluttered with messages from new sources—financial services, tele-selling, government, retailing. This is putting up the price of communication in real terms, and reducing its effectiveness. The retailers' best and cheapest medium is their store. It represents a major 'mindspace' economy over the manufacturers.

8.2.2 Control of Marketing-Mix Variables

Retailers control a number of key marketing-mix variables: presentation, price, promotions. The more retailers become interested in running their own brands in competition to manufacturer brands, the more they can benefit from taking the control of these variables.

The brand perceptions of a consumer in the store will be different from that measured in the abstract, say in market research in a shopping centre or homes. A retailer can influence the positions on the perceptual map of its and competitors' brands, not just by the drastic act of delisting, but also by its position in layout, pricing, promotions and 'flagging' with information ('This week's best buy', 'Special purchase', etc.). The opportunities are as follows:

Presence and prominence in store. In markets where impulse buying is important or variety-seeking the norm, eye-level location or an end-of-gondola feature will often be a critical factor in purchase, sometimes more critical than absolute brand preference. Brand preference research often ignores the physical facts of presence in store: the weight of lifting heavy bottles down from a high shelf or the extra second needed to notice a brand on a low shelf. One retailer told us that, as a rule of thumb, sales of a brand will be reduced by two-thirds if it is moved from an eye level to a foot level position. As a rule of thumb, retailer type-2 brands occupy the eye level shelf space in stores. Presence in store is particularly critical for new products. Retailers can always guarantee distribution for their new products, which gives them a special advantage in this vital activity.

Promotions and prices. Manufacturers used to plan promotions as part of 'their' marketing mix, while selling-oriented retailers tended to follow an everyday low-price strategy for their type-1 own label. Nowadays, retailers often use promotions as part of their own-label marketing. Since the setting of prices and control of promotions lies with the retailer, pricing and promotion strategy is likely in future to be dictated largely by the objectives of the retailer and its controlled brands.

Sampling, merchandising and special displays. Sampling is frequently used by manufacturers to increase trial of their high-quality brands. Retailers enjoy a similar advantage in costs for sampling and merchandising as they do in presence. For example, consumers give as a reason for not trying new coffee brands (including own label), that a 4 oz/100 g jar is a high-price item, and the risk of buying and then not liking is off-putting. Brooke

Bond/Unilever have sold mini jars at launch to minimise this risk. A retailer could quite easily serve own-brand coffee to customers, perhaps in an in-store cafeteria. At virtually no extra cost, customers could try the store's own-label biscuits. Sampling is a powerful tool in FMCG and the means to do it are clearly more cheaply available to the retailer than to the manufacturer. Sampling is more efficient for own labels because: (a) the retailer already has staff in the store, and (b) the retailer can amortise the extra cost over so many brands. Exactly the same reasoning applies to special displays and other in-store activities beneficial to brands: the brand-building retailer has the choice of selling the opportunity to national brands or using it to support own brands.

8.2.3 Information

Scanner-equipped check-outs tell the retailer exactly what is being sold. Scanners have many efficiency-oriented applications—improving speeds at check-outs, saving the labour of sticking on price tickets, reducing inventory, simplifying reordering. Many stores now link their check-out data to their warehouses, so that the mix of lines delivered each day depends on the sales communicated the day before. Wal-Mart is famous for maximising its turnover of stocks and minimising inventory. It is these immediate and tangible benefits which justify the initial investment in the systems.

The next range of applications tend to be selling oriented: planning store layout and promotions. Scanners provide the data needed to evaluate promotions or assess the effects of arranging layouts in imaginative ways.

A brand manufacturer would automatically use scanner data to achieve brand-building objectives. For example, each shopper buying a competitive product would be handed a free sample on leaving the check-out. Why don't retailers do this for the brands they want to promote, particularly their own? The answer is simply that as yet they haven't the expertise to put it into practice. It is coming, helped by new till technology.

For many years department stores have provided their shoppers with charge cards. This idea has now spread to multiple chains and supermarkets. Cards always had a role in creating loyalty, but up to now this role has been rather passive. With information technology revolutionising data analysis and personalised mail, these card bases can be used much more actively.

Enrolling card holders gives a retailer the chance to find out more about their customer base (where they live, family composition, family income). By integrating this information with known purchasing behaviour, retailers should be able to target direct marketing activities with a precision and success rate well above that of manufacturers.

Once the scanner data is linked up, via payment cards or credit cards, to names and addresses the marketing-oriented possibilities are endless. Average weekly purchases could be monitored. Customers who spent less or disappeared for a few weeks could be paid extra attention. Direct mail could be tailored: to those who regularly spend in the garden section, who spend most on clothes, who buy children's products, to those who expect to buy a new television in the next three years. The effect of marketing actions could be traced over time: was consumption increased or were purchases simply brought forward? How effective are each of the in-store media? Which (retailer) brands respond best to merchandising, advertising, sampling, price reductions?

As the price of 'smart' cards (cards with chips that can store data) falls, some retailers are introducing cards that have even greater flexibility. Smart cards can be used in a similar fashion to 'Green Shield stamps' or 'Air miles' to encourage heavy and loyal use, they can also be used to run promotions: for example, certain products or combinations of products can gain the card holder points which are stored in the card.

As retailers gain information, manufacturers lose it. There was a time when small stores welcomed Nielsen's visits because they provided the stores with inventory information. The stores now have their own (more accurate) information on tap (of a keyboard). Retailers with central warehousing, and especially those who forward buy and stock promoted goods, put extra distance between the manufacturer and the data once obtained quite easily. How much sales are own labels taking? Is it the type-2 or the type-1 own label that is growing fastest? Uncomfortable and unfair as it might seem, retailers also have excellent and in depth knowledge of their brand competitors, their suppliers, and the manufacturers.

These three advantages (contact with the consumer, control of marketing mix variables, information) mean that once retailers decide to challenge the manufacturers' hold on mindspace, they are awesome opponents. Bullish retail executives argue that within 20 years manufacturers of branded goods will be a thing of the past. Manufacturers are already finding it increasingly difficult to get retailers to support their new products. Competing for shelf space with retailer own brands, and cheap 'false' brands created by 'industrial' suppliers is already hurting many smaller manufacturers.

As retailers become more committed to developing their importance to the consumer, they will take tighter control of the marketing variables which fall into their hands. Any mindspace they succeed in creating with the consumer is both taken from some manufacturer and translates into negotiating power against those same suppliers. Greater marketing orientation among retailers will increase their influence on the market. Retailing will never again fit the 'transparent model' assumed in traditional marketing theory.

Despite the media hype, manufacturer brands are hanging on in there and many are still turning in impressive profits. This is because while retailers are efficient in providing branding for some brands in some markets, manufacturers also have sources of efficiency and know-how which remain crucial even in the changing climate.

8.3 WEIGHTLESS BRAND OWNERSHIP

Brand management is a complex function. Obtaining the right quality product, naming it, designing packaging and display material and creating the right associations are all tasks which demand knowledge and time from experienced and creative people. New product development agencies, packaging agencies, advertising agencies and people who own creative properties (such as film companies or sports-star managers) all jump at the opportunity to help brand management, but the initiation, co-ordination and control have to be provided by somebody.

That somebody might work for a company with production facilities, might work for a company with retail facilities or they might work for themselves.

The idea of free-floating brand owners has already been put into practice in several different ways. Franchise operations such as Mr Minute shoe repairs, Midas exhausts, Body Shop International or 7–11 convenience stores are now a familiar concept. What do these organisations own really, but the information technology to run a network, experience and mindspace? In the FMCG industry, Cadbury-Schweppes is a 'weightless brand owner' in several countries. It licenses out brands such as Canada Dry and Schweppes to bottling companies, who carry out production and distribution without owning their brand.

Speilberg's Jurrasic Park, Sega's (computer game) Sonic Hedgehog, and Mattel's Barbie all brand soft drinks and ice-creams, in deals involving various combinations of producers and distributors. The branding property is not sold to the producer or distributor. Such branding is strong in product fields where image and novelty is important. They certainly compete with more orthodox brands, and though they may not be long lived individually, they are instantly replaceable with the next craze that comes along. Grocery brands are becoming part of the multi-media scene: you've seen the film, played the computer game, worn the socks, now eat the spaghetti . . . and wash your hair in Ninja Turtle Mutant Gel (such an obvious one, this last, it's amazing that Mirage Studios missed it). Such licensing is likely to become a permanent part of brand competition.

Another 'third party' opportunity for brand management is to provide brand management as a consultancy service. Retailers have to be huge before they can devote enough management time to understanding consumer wants in each of their different categories. In the UK, larger stores have their own brand management skills. For smaller UK chains, and many (even major) chains in continental Europe and North America it makes sense to buy in brand management expertise.

Some advertising agencies have broadened their remit to include parts of the brand management task. Cott Corporation of Canada goes a step further and actually finds or buys producers capable of producing high-quality goods (mostly food and soft drinks) and sells their products within a total 'own brand' package to retailers. Cott owns subsidiaries specialised in various brand management tasks (naming, packaging, design, etc.) and can offer retailers a complete, exclusive own brand at the level achieved by Marks & Spencer or Sainsbury's in the UK. Cott will provide a name or use the established own-label name, such as Sam's Choice for Wal-Mart, declined through a complete package including merchandising, promotions, category analysis and communications to store employees. The retailer can negotiate some limited exclusivity (flavours, local geography) on the product lines supplied by Cott.[8]

Advertising agencies and Cott do *not* end up owning the brand, but hope, at least in the short run, to share the opportunity made possible by the retailers' resources (shelfspace etc.) and their hard work and imagination. Brand management consultants have to be well versed in copyright law and the drafting of contracts, but they have experience and expertise that is probably as sustainable as that in production or running a retail chain.

Overcapacity has become a chronic problem in much of the FMCG industry. When a brand takes share from its competitors it can often justify investment in new capacity. New capacity can be justified by new production technology or radically new products. Coke often creates bullish, expansionist bottlers as its inexorable marketing expertise sweeps country after country. Whenever a bullish company builds capacity in a static market some competitor is left with spare capacity.

The overcapacity beast is hard to kill. A retailer (or weightless brand owner) comes along to the producer with spare capacity and negotiates a contract to buy a product at a price which covers its marginal cost. Relieved of all marketing costs (consumer and trade) the producer, producing on written-off, spare, marginal capacity produces a good quality product which is sold at extremely competitive prices. Promoted through a retailer's shelves, the brand takes share back from the bullish manufacturer, bottler or brewer. Hey presto, spare capacity appears in another production unit. Overcapacity is displaced but not removed. It may be displaced back into higher-quality production facilities. For brand management no-capacity may be better than overcapacity. Operating on other people's excess capacity may be an opportunity for weightless brand managers of the future.

From the viewpoint of manufacturers who own capacity, whether retailers manage their brands themselves or whether they 'out source' their brand management may be somewhat semantic. The bottom line is that if a manufacturer loses control of mindspace it can get left with nothing but a proud history and the fixed costs.

8.4 MANUFACTURERS' MINDSPACE ADVANTAGES

Exploring the advantages and efficiencies of retailers in the battle for mindspace makes depressing reading for manufacturers. Brand ownership, long the key source of power for manufacturers, is in some ways under threat. On the other hand, manufacturers also have considerable sources of efficiency and know-how when it comes to providing the consumer with brands. However competent and enlightened retailers become there are certain things that are difficult for them to do. In particular retailers (or their own-label agents) cannot:

- always get the quality they want
- advertise specific functions of a brand
- create image as against functional reassurance
- give a sense of wide choice
- provide products with high ubiquity
- invest in in-depth understanding of consumer behaviour in all product fields in which they operate.

The more these six things are important in a product field, the less retailers are able to win mindspace away from manufacturer brands.

Image is a special problem for retailers, related to the broad positioning of retailers. Aside from this, the main obstacles for retailers are related to critical mass. There is a key difference in the way manufacturers and retailers become large (see Fig. 8.1).

Own brands become viable when retailers become large enough to enjoy some of the economies of scale enjoyed by manufacturers. Even so, most individual retail brands remain puny compared to most national brands sold across retailers and

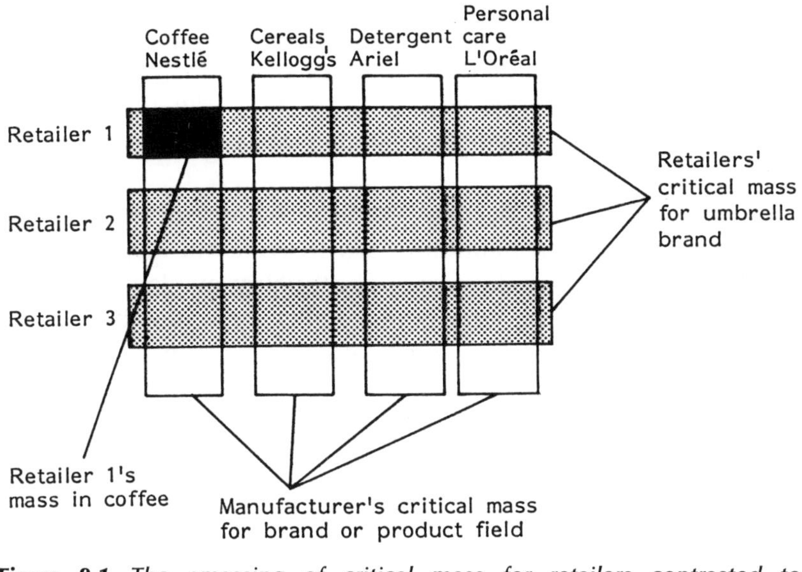

Figure 8.1 *The amassing of critical mass for retailers contrasted to manufacturers*

often across countries. Even when own label is the 'overall brand leader' in a category, with perhaps over 30% share, each retail brand takes only a fraction of the total category.

Manufacturers find economies and synergy within one, or sometimes a number of related, product fields. This specialisation gives them particular strengths: in technology, in communication and in consumer understanding.

8.4.1 Technology

Everyone, including Gillette, was surprised when their strategy to de-commoditise shaving worked, turning millions of men away from disposables back to high-quality system razors. The fact that it did work may be a timely reminder of the power of big companies to add value to their markets. Sensor offered a significantly better shave at significantly higher prices—it costs about $10 a year to remain clean shaven using a disposable, about $20 to do so using Sensor. The market had been drifting towards commodity status for a decade, and Gillette was tempted to accept this. One strategic option was to become the world's lowest-cost producer of disposable blades and take on own-label business. Another idea was to launch a low-price, disposable Sensor. A strategy combating the trend and refusing to produce own label proved to be more profitable: Gillette are now committed to promoting added value in shaving and refuse own-label deals.[9]

Every brand needs access to the necessary technology: no brand builds up or maintains worthwhile mindspace if its physical delivery is below par. The quality available to retail brands is limited to what the retailer can negotiate from manufacturers. In markets where products are technologically sophisticated, this can strongly limit own-label progress. For example, Proctor & Gamble, Unilever, Henkel and Colgate hold on to all but the cheapest segment of the washing powder market; Nestlé, Kraft General Foods (PM) and Unilever hold on to the instant coffee market. In both cases their technological lead, backed by communication focused on the functional/taste superiority (see below), has kept own-label share below 10% in most countries.

As a general rule, innovation in a product field limits own label penetration (see Fig. 8.2).

Sometimes it is tempting to believe that heavyweight advertising itself protects brands—this is often said of Kellogg's, whose media budgets regularly exceed 10% of sales. The evidence suggests that advertising backs up technology, and not the reverse. Coca-Cola and Pepsi were for years unmatchable in taste, and untouchable by own brands. Incredible as it seems, say compared with the spread of nuclear weapons technology (about 20 countries in 50 years), only three companies in the world can produce a cola syrup with real taste, a whole century after its invention. The third manufacturer, Royal Crown, is now supplying own label via an intermediary (Cott Corporation). Results to date (see Table 8.2, on page 169) indicate that once retailers can match taste quality, despite the high levels of brand investment (advertising, sponsorship, etc.) undertaken by Coke and Pepsi, they make significant progress.

In product fields such as chocolate confectionery, detergents, breakfast cereals, sanitary protection and coffee the number of top-quality suppliers is strictly limited, perhaps down to two, three or four suppliers in most national markets. Retailers who

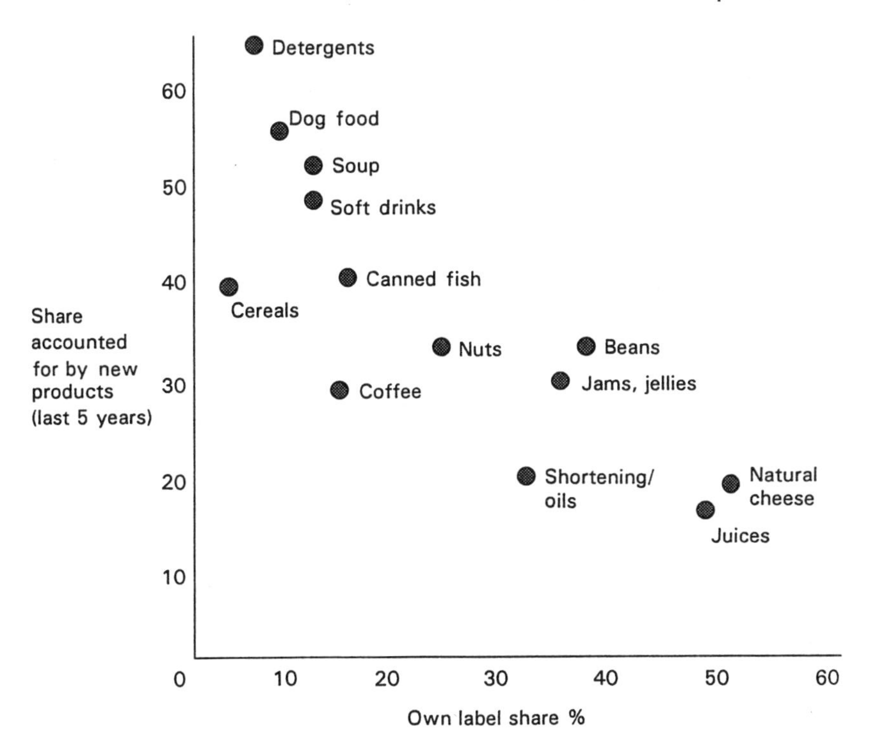

Figure 8.2 *Product category showing penetration of own label compared to technical activity. Reproduced by permission of The Boston Consulting Group.*

want to compete with the top brands, have only the choice of these top suppliers. Any manufacturer who has invested in the technology wants to be paid for the investment made. In addition, these suppliers are usually involved in the branded consumer market and not ready to see the overall price level jeopardised. Thus technically sophisticated product fields are usually weak areas for retailers because the only people with the technical know-how to match the big brand owners are other big brand owners. The competition in the market is still controlled by the producers even if the retailers nominally own brands.

There are many supermarket products which are not high-tech and which can be produced to indistinguishable standards by a large number of producers. This divide, technical sophistication, is one of the factors which decides who is going to own the brands, or at least who is going to make profits out of them.

8.4.2 Pointed Communication

In Chapter 3 we looked at the difference between 'umbrella' brands and 'eponymous' brands. This difference is an important issue in the battle for mindspace between retailer and manufacturer. We talk about retailers 'creating brands'; we tend to gloss over the difference between umbrella brands and eponymous brands.

Retailers follow a policy of umbrella branding. The retail name can be seen as one brand with brand extensions into many fields. There may be some linking theme across products—often a 'good value' positioning—but basically the retailer's name acts as an umbrella brand giving a general (even if strong) reassurance on quality. Where awareness and reassurance are all that is required, umbrella branding will be as effective as individual branding. This is the case for most low-tech, low-image product categories such as basic cooking ingredients: rice, tinned fruit, frozen vegetables, fruit juice, etc.

Even when manufacturers create additional brands in exactly the same way, their umbrella brand names tend to give rather more specific imagery. More importantly, manufacturers also pursue a much more specific type of branding where they discover new consumer wants, satisfy them with a functionally or emotionally superior product and attach the benefits via advertising to a specific brand name.

In product fields where specific functional benefits or specific images are key, retail brands are held back by their wide scope. A retailer has trouble generating the same credibility as a brand such as Crest toothpaste, which reinvests year by year in its 'healthy teeth for children' positioning, or Radion detergent, which shouts out its specific functional claims 'Cleans and destroys odours!' Even manufacturer umbrella branding is still more specific than that of retailers. Findus (Stouffer in the USA) 'Lean Cuisine' has more specific associations in frozen food than, say, Safeway.

Retailers recognise this limitation, and sometimes try to create sub-brands to overcome the barrier. Thus Sainsbury's have the 'Novon' range of detergents, and Asda have launched a similar range called 'Integra'. Dixon's use the Dixon name on blank tapes and low value accessories, but the 'hint of Eastern promise' names 'Matsui' and 'Saisho' on more expensive electrical goods. Following the logic, retailers have to advertise these sub-brands, for presence on shelf is unlikely to give them much more specific meaning in the consumer's eyes than the retailer's own name.

Advertising is expensive and thus needs to be amortised over a large market share to be viable. Many manufacturers are moving towards international advertising partly in order to spread the high cost of advertising development and production. Negotiations with media suppliers are also helped by huge size.

Manufacturers can justify significant advertising budgets to support individual brands, budgets which the retailer cannot afford for any one brand. Even in the UK, where retailers are the biggest advertising spenders, they do not compete in ad budgets on a product category basis with their largest suppliers. In 1990, Unilever UK spent £84 million spread over 24 brands—Tesco supported some 7000 lines with its budget of £26 million.

Instead of amortising advertising investments internationally, retailers must amortise the cost of advertising over a wider range of goods. Retailers are constrained to create an overall image to support all their own labels: they are right at the extreme of umbrella branding. The most they can hope for is some quality reassurance. The name 'Carrefour' is used on food products, financial services, holidays, insurance, car centre, garden centre, petrol, home deliveries of heating oil, hardware, sports wear and more besides. Critical mass at the brand and category level are essential in product fields where specific values or claims are critical in the purchase decision. This is a second factor which makes manufacturers more efficient in branding in certain product areas.

8.4.3 Image

If specific brand messages are important for some functional products, they are even more crucial for products chosen for their image or emotional values.

For products with functional benefits retailers have only to communicate certain information, which can be done in store or on pack. For prestige benefits, retailers also have to dissociate their own functional, low price, images. Retailers tend to have images which jar on prestige or sensual products. One can't imagine Brooke Shields in Wal-Mart ('We Sell for Less . . . Always') jeans or passionate couples using Tesco ('Every Little Helps') ice-cream as an aphrodisiac. Perfumes are not technically sophisticated products. The essential oils are available from industrial scent companies to anybody who wants to mix up a perfume and market it—witness all the design houses who cook up their own scents. Aldi, Albert Hein or Asda could do this just as easily ('Asda Perfume: Pocket the Difference'). Even a Marks & Spencer suit lacks a certain something, while supermarket imagery seems almost the antithesis of 'cool'. Nike advertising encapsulates 'cool' : 'Just do it!' Do what? Go shopping?

The same problems arise for beauty products where appeal is a mixture of mystique and optimism. Elizabeth Arden inspires more hope than Woolworth's/Winfield or even Marks & Spencer/St Michael. Not all consumers demand prestige, or sensuality, or hope. *Economist* journalists probably wash their hair with generic label shampoo to avoid being the dupes of Elida Gibbs or Colgate-Palmolive, but large segments of the market are willing to pay for arguably more qualitative benefits in health and beauty aids.

It is ironic that some of the product categories most dependent on advertising for their added value, tobacco and alcohol, are also those where health lobbies are particularly attacking the right to advertise. The health lobbies are not trying to help the retailers gain share, but this will be an incidental effect each time they succeed in further restricting advertising or sponsorship.

The role of retailer sub-brands in image-sensitive areas, such as clothes, can be to avoid the embarrassment of a 'retail' label on, say, baby clothes given as a present. The more ambitious aim is actually to add prestige. Hoping to create a little prestige, some retailers advertise their clothes sub-brands. C & A have gone through a wardrobe full with Sixth Sense, Rodeo, ClockHouse and Incognito; Sainsbury's are putting a toe in the water with 'Lifestyle', as is Asda with the 'George' range. France's largest supermarket chain Leclerc, advertise their clothes brand, Tissaia, in prestige magazines (TV being unavailable to retailers in France). They sign off with the cavalier line: 'Proud to be sold in Hypermarkets'. In fact it is debatable whether retailer brands can gain prestige through advertising. The advertising itself has to link the brand with the retailer, creating an image oxymoron. The idea of the 'independent' brand was to separate, indeed liberate, a certain product line from the store; the advertising is constrained to re-associate it with the store. Why has C & A moved through several prestige labels? Because they get tainted. A retail brand by any other name would smell as suspect.

In middling cases such as alcoholic beverages it may be possible to persuade people that a middling image is all that they need for certain purchases—for example for family as against guest usage. This is less challenging than persuading consumers that the store name really carries prestige. The fact remains that most people are far from accepting C & A (by any other name) on the pockets of their jeans, or offering the boss a Sainsbury's Whisky at a dinner party. Retailers have not yet (*yet*) crossed the Rubicon to creating product brands totally independent of their store names.

In some product areas manufacturers are facing the dilemma of legitimising retailer brands by seeking distribution for their own prestige labels in mass merchandising chains. This is a manoeuvre that needs careful planning, such as demonstrated by L'Oréal. In 1982, L'Oréal took the plunge with the launch of Plénitude, signed with the L'Oréal name, into supermarkets. Previously, high-tech, high-price face care had been sold only through chemists and specialist/department stores. Plénitude made these products available to a new, broader market, and also moved some sales from specialist outlets to self-service supermarkets. L'Oréal enjoyed enormous success with Plénitude, creating and dominating a new supermarket category. Ten years later, Carrefour introduced a range of face-care products called Les Cosmetiques, priced at the same level as L'Oréal's Plénitude, and packaged to an equal level of luxury. It is arguable that Carrefour could not have created its brand, demanding the same very high prices, without the lead taken with Plénitude.

L'Oréal have at the same time invested substantially, through other divisions, in brands distributed through specialists, pharmacies and department stores. Thus the whole quality skin-care market has expanded enormously in value, while L'Oréal still hold the high ground with Lancôme, Biotherm, Helena

Rubinstein, Guy Laroche, Ralph Lauren, Vichy, Phas and Laboratoires D'Anglas, sold exclusively through the high-added-value outlets. These high-value outlets will co-operate to the maximum only with a supplier who understands their retail brand needs as well as the brand needs of their customers. L'Oréal are now selling into supermarkets a second high-tech face-care range, Synergie (from Garnier), and, for the first time, a high-quality cosmetics range ('Perfection'), signed by L'Oréal. Again, they are reserving their stable of prestige cosmetics brands for the duty frees and in-store concessions.

Other big names, such as Levi's jeans and Scandale underwear at first shunned then flirted with and now seek distribution in hypermarkets. The incentive is volume, the risks are dire, both at the consumer and retail levels. For the consumer, once the prestige names are debased by sharing the caddie with the carrots and floor polish, it is, perhaps, a smaller step to trade down to the own brand (as with Plénitude). Thus the big names in a supermarket open the way for the stores to market their own competitor alongside. The other danger comes from alienating the specialist retailer, struggling to compete with the large discounters and supermarkets. There is no attraction for specialists in a recognised brand sold in the self-service emporiums. Once the specialist retailers turn away from, say, Levis, and try to find more exclusive brands with which to justify their higher prices, Levi's will lose the influence of these opinion leaders and advisers.

8.4.4 Consumer Understanding: Variety, Choice and Novelty

Successful brand management depends on a continually updated understanding of the consumers' needs and wants in a product category. This understanding is more difficult to achieve for a retailer, than for a manufacturer, due to lack of specialisation by product category.

It is true that retailers now have access to the most detailed shopping behaviour data ever held by man, but data on its own is next to worthless. Translating this data into ideas for new brand development and brand management demands marketing specialists. A generalist retailer cannot employ sufficient numbers

Table 8.4 *Even the largest FMCG companies specialise in only a few product categories.*

Manufacturer	No. of product fields
Allied Lyons (UK)	9
Danone (France)	13
Bahlsen (Germany)	3
Buitoni (Italy)	7
Cadbury-Schweppes (UK)	2
Coca-Cola (US)	2
CPC (US)	5
Ferrero (Italy)	3
Heinz (US)	7
Kellogg's (US)	1
Mars (US)	4
Nestlé (Switzerland)	15
Quaker Oats (US)	4
Sara Lee Corporation (US)	2
Unilever (Netherlands)	8

This chart was first presented at the ESOMAR Seminar 'The Challenge of Branding Today and in the Future?' Brussels (Belgium) October 1992. Permission for using this material has been granted by the European Society for Opinion and Marketing Research, J. J. Viottastraat 29, 1071 JP, Amsterdam, The Netherlands.

of specialists to cover all the major product fields in which they wish to market own labels. Manufacturers can afford (indeed, can't afford not) to carry out category specific research (see Table 8.4).

Understanding consumer attitudes and behaviour in a category should be an asset of the manufacturer and a source of power in the battle for mindspace.

In many FMCG markets the consumer demands a sense of choice and variety. The critical mass and specialisation of manufacturers allows them to service this need for variety more effectively than retailers. For example, swapping around between brands and product forms within the hair care sector is an outlet for the frustration many women feel about their hair. A retail brand, even a sub-brand, fails to generate the same sense of choice. In the hair-care sector of the supermarket, L'Oréal offers the consumer between two and four (depending on the national market) company pedigrees (such as L'Oréal and Garnier). Each 'pedigree' offers a series of ranges such as Studio Line, Energance, Rayonnance, Elseve, Free Style, Vivelle, Graphic Line, each targeted at slightly different psychographic groups (fun/conservative, older/younger, brash/sophisticated, good value/high tech). Often these ranges offer virtually identical products (mousse, gel, spray, etc.). This cornucopia allows consumers to match their various image needs or to seek variety. More important, it allows L'Oréal to hold a much larger share of the market than one company with one family brand and one non-self-duplicating range could ever do. To run the cornucopia efficiently demands up-to-date information on the consumer (attitudes and beliefs, changing preoccupations, current hair styles) and creativity on the part of brand management in responding to this information. These inputs are affordable to a specialist, but not to a generalist.

In many other product fields (e.g. computers, washing machines) consumers prefer to feel that at least half a dozen companies are competing for their money. A producer with one brand will have less chance of satisfying the consumer than a producer with three or four specific brand names. Managing several competing ranges, often targeted on psychographic and qualitative variables, is subtle and time-consuming: it cannot be financed by the critical mass of one store.

In yet other markets (toys, confectionery, breakfast cereals, soft drinks) there is a significant 'novelty sector' which sells alongside the staples. This novelty sector is similar to image brands in that it is largely animated by paid-for communication. Novelty demands paid-for communication, or, in the case of something like Mutant Turtle Ninja Hero accessories, a whole co-ordinated multi-media package. Novelty implies risk and therefore demands high margins. This does not fit with the retailer's value proposition any more than the activity fits with their areas of competence.

In some product areas (canned peas, frozen chips) the consumer does not seek variety, choice or novelty. In these areas, stores offer small ranges and their own brands can win high shares. Where the shoppers' appetite for variety, choice and novelty are greater, the specialisation of manufacturers into product categories gives them the critical mass and know-how to dominate in the battle for mindspace.

8.4.5 High Ubiquity, Small and Alternative Outlets

In Western societies, there seems to be a continual shift to mobility, informality and spontaneity. Meals and shopping trips are unplanned, eating out has increased in every industrialised nation. As consumers drift around finding food to replace missed meals and shopping in odd moments left in their busy work schedules, there must develop an increasing need for brand assurance across outlets, counterbalancing the general trend towards hypermarkets. It is not possible for every garage or cinema foyer to create their own-brand cola. Cafés, convenience outlets and vending machines all depend on widely recognised brands. This market is, naturally, more important to impulse products such as confectionery, but alternative sources of distribution have to be considered as brand opportunities.

Alternative channels can also be opportunities for current distribution giants: who will take control? When home shopping on a TV screen becomes a reality, will the consumer visit the Nestlé virtual shopping environment or that of some European (or global) buying group of retail partners? Or will it be some new entity which offers pre-selected (and branded) shopping packages, resembling set menus in Chinese restaurants: 'The *Presto* shopping caddie (food and basic household) for single parent (male) family of three for one week, (cold breakfast, 20 individual meals, 40 snacks)'?

8.4.6 Pressure on Second-tier Brands

In many national (and global) consumer markets manufacturer brands still have a major role, but the hard truth is that there is space for fewer of them.

The critical mass advantages that manufacturers enjoy compared to retail brands are much less forceful, or even non-existent, for smaller brands. To be a nationally advertised brand with a fifth of the voice of the brand leader is not the same thing. Technology, advertising muscle and consumer understanding are the raisons d'être for manufacturer brands. Each is highly sensitive to economies of scale. Once the funding for innovation and advertising is in retreat, a consumer brand can only weaken further. This vicious circle is almost impossible to redress unless there is some special protection through niching, say by locality or consumer segment. In general, second-tier brands are most threatened by the retailer's appetite to create brands themselves, and traditional consumer marketing offers little to hold back the tide. The more market oriented retailers become, the more able they are to satisfy branding needs on more sophisticated and 'image-sensitive' goods. This situation, squeezed between, say, Philip Morris and Sainsbury's is an uncomfortable and possibly fatal nutcracker.

We come back to the issue of the implications for small national brands in the last chapter. The simple truth is that in the battle for mindspace, having neither a retailer's contact with the market nor the muscle of a brand leader leads to a negative spiral for most consumer brands. We look at some alternative ways of managing these second-tier brands in Chapter 11.

The pressure from retailers also has interesting implications for the value of brands in the future. The areas which demand only quality assurance of a rather general and functional nature are likely to be dominated by retailers. Areas which demand specific or prestigious communications can be serviced best by pan-retail brand owners. When Unilever purchased Fabergé, Elizabeth Arden, Max Factor and Calvin Klein it got hold of a clutch of brands which look considerably more retailer resistant than Lux, Birds Eye, Brooke Bond or Stork. Again, this is unfortunate for manufacturers who happen to find themselves exposed in areas where the retailer has the advantages.

Individual executives who work for companies suffering under the current shifts in power, still have a bright side to look on. If they have learnt the principles of consumer marketing in manufacturing companies they will find plenty of opportunities to apply them in the industries, including retailing, that are now adopting marketing approaches. Any professional who has learnt the art of listening to consumer needs, and has the skills to translate this understanding back into action to produce what is required, will always find a job.

8.5 SUMMARY: ALL BRAND MANAGERS ARE EQUAL BUT SOME BRAND MANAGERS ARE MORE EQUAL THAN OTHERS

Whenever products offer differences in quality or taste or function, then consumers need brands. Although some commentators and retailers are scathing about image and associations, these are things which all but the most cynical consumers use and enjoy. The need for brands is actually, now, more widely understood and accepted than ever before. People living at subsistence level do not need brands. The more choice and quality exists, the greater the role for brands.

There is nothing to stop retailers or 'weightless brand-owning organisations' from wanting to provide brand reassurance. The question is, in what circumstances are they able to do so more efficiently than manufacturers?

There are some FMCG categories where retailers are destined to control mindspace. These are the low-technology, low-image, low-novelty areas. In product fields which are perceived as being 'commodity', retailers are likely to be the most efficient suppliers of umbrella reassurance. They provide umbrella branding efficiently because they amortise advertising costs over their broad range and sustain awareness by simple presence on shelf. There are other categories where manufacturers have efficiencies which will tend to leave them in control. There are further categories where fun and novelty are so dominant in importance that owners of trans-media properties (e.g. Stephen Speilberg) can offer branding.

In areas where image and/or innovation are important and brand-specific advertising is crucial, manufacturers are likely to be more efficient due to their size and specialisation. High ubiquity products—impulse products such as drinks and snacks bought for immediate consumption, which need to be very widely distributed, are also somewhat protected.

From the manufacturer's point of view, the situation also varies according to whether a brand is leader or follower in its market. A brand leader is more likely to be able to hold consumers through investing in brand building actions and be able to motivate distribution via consumer demand. Less popular brands will be squeezed both by the branded competition and by the retailers' brands.

At the moment, retailer-controlled brands are having something of a free ride. In many countries we have the bizarre spectacle of retailers losing money on national brands (because they sell them virtually at cost), but recuperating their profits on own label which they are able to buy off manufacturers at ridiculously low prices.

The costing of much own-label production is done on a marginal basis, on 'spare capacity' already paid for by now ailing brands. The technology currently used to produce own brands has often been paid for over many years by manufacturers' brands. Similarly, the consumer's understanding and desires are still being paid for by manufacturer advertising. The own label proposition is still, for the most part, that the retail brand provides the *same* functions and quality as the advertised brands, but at lower prices.

Retailers are getting this free lunch because a shift in shopping habits and consumer attitudes has made retailers the most efficient suppliers of branding, for some FMCG products. Once retailers have eaten up the shares (and production capacity) currently accounted for by smaller and commodity brand companies, further development of own label, in competition with the biggest manufacturers will become harder. Retailers will eventually compete as brand developers with other retailers as well as manufacturers, and, perhaps, with fixed-cost free marketing organisations who own no retail outlets, no production facilities, but just brand names, knowledge and information. At this point the free lunch will be over, and the equilibrium between these three will depend who can provide branding most efficiently. This depends on all the factors mentioned in this chapter and also on the efficiency and competence of the parties themselves.

Notes

(1) Martin Dickson and Nikki Tait, 'Old loyalties tested by price war', *Financial Times*, 23 July 1993, p. 21.
(2) 'Shoot out at the check out', *The Economist*, 5 June 1993, p. 65.
(3) 'The world's best brand', cover story, *Fortune Magazine*, 31 May 1993.
(4) M. Yoshino and P. Stoneham, Procter & Gamble, Japan. Case history, Harvard Business School, 1990.
(5) Re-translated from Eric Maillard, 'Vive la Marque', Institut du Commerce et de la Consommation, Paris, June 1991, p. 19.
(6) John Thornhill, 'A European spark for Marks', *Financial Times*, 13 July 1992, p. 10.
(7) David A. Nichol, President Loblaw International Merchants, Toronto, 'The Boston Tea Party—Part II', speech made to the

Annual Convention of Private Label Manufacturers, Miami, 26 March 1993.

(8) Don Daniels, Robert Kaplan and Ray Goldberg, 'Cott Corporation: Private Label in the 1990s', Case History, Harvard Business School, 1993.

(9) Keith Hammonds, 'How a $4 razor ends up costing $300', *Business Week*, 29 January 1990, p. 62; Patricia Sellers, 'Brands: It's thrive or die', *Fortune Magazine*, 23 August 1993, pp. 40–1.

9
The Battle for Shelfspace

Retailers realise that their shelfspace, nourished by their store traffic, is a resource. In the past they gave it away; then they thought of selling it to manufacturers. Manufacturers either paid directly, via slotting allowances etc., or paid in materials and manpower to make the shelves more attractive and better organised.

More sophisticated retailers will exploit the resource for their own use. If shelfspace is such a valuable marketing input, a retailer who is actively marketing own brands in competition with the manufacturer will want to use it to promote the own brands. Frequently now, manufacturers are denied the freedom to operate in-store. As one retailer put it, 'They are no longer free to dance in our cathedrals', 'they' being the manufacturers, the 'cathedrals' being the stores.[1] Still, it is paranoiac to see the threat of not stocking simply as a 'weapon' in the hands of the retailer. Retailers are more like Hamlet, inheritor of power, agonising over a painful dilemma:

> To stock or not to stock: that is the question.
> Whether 'tis nobler not to make the shopper suffer
> the pain and dilemma of out-of-stock products,
> or to take up arms against the manufacturers,
> and by winning mindspace, end them?
> To delist: to self-promote; no brands;
> and by rejecting brands to say we end
> the low profits and the selling oriented market

that stores are heir to.
'Tis a situation devoutly to be wish'd.
To destock, to self-promote; to control,
perchance to sell more own brands!
Ay, there's the rub—for in that low choice store,
what shoppers will come,
once we have shuffled out the major brands?

Retailers are afraid of destocking manufacturers' brands. Stocking products is the retailers' business: *not* stocking a product sought by shoppers is a failure in the service to their clients. The downside of wielding stocking power against a manufacturer, is losing assortment appeal against the retail competition.

Deciding how many lines to stock is an important strategic choice for retailers: Aldi offers about 600, Warehouse clubs typically about 3500, Carrefour about 5000 grocery lines, Casino about 9000.[2] Depending on the size of the branch, Sainsbury's and Tesco stores stock between 10 000 and 20 000 lines.[3] But whatever the size, a grocer cannot stock all brands, in all sizes and varieties. The number of brands available has drastically increased. About 3000 new lines are launched each year—a similar number to the total number of brands stocked in a typical supermarket in the early 1970s.[4] From tampons to crispbread, from rice to bleach, hypersegmentation has taken hold, and every FMCG product now comes in at least six varieties. In addition, many retailers want to allocate an increasing proportion of shelfspace to their own brands. Typically, retailers give eye-level shelfspace to their type-2 own label and in addition grant less valuable space to low price 'tertiary' or 'false' brands, which have taken the place of the type-1 own labels of yesterday. Many retailers have segmented the own label market themselves (Wal-Mart, for example, have the type-2 'Sam's Choice', and the type-1 'Great Value') and so have further intensified the demand for shelfspace.

Clearly, retailers have to be highly selective about what products to stock and about the new products they will allow in. To a greater extent than ever before the retailer has to use skill and judgement to allocate scarce shelfspace.

FMCG purchases rank among some of the least important decisions we make in our lives. According to one American survey 69% of people do not use shopping lists, and 66% of purchases are not planned,[5] indeed many shopping trips are not planned.[6] It seems reasonable to assume that when shoppers do not plan, the selection of brands on offer will tend to set the agenda for the purchase decision and non-stocked brands will not even be considered. Winning presence in store is gaining relative importance compared to the manufacturer's traditional priority, winning consumer preference.

Clearly, for both the retailer and the manufacturer, the decision of what to stock is of critical importance. Stocking is usually a key issue in negotiations between manufacturer and retailer. These negotiations are underpinned by the perceived costs of non-stocking to the two parties. This question turns primarily on what the customer will do if a brand is not stocked.

9.1 THE POSSIBLE OUTCOMES OF AN 'OUT OF STOCK'

Imagine a consumer shopping in a store, with its incomplete selection of SKUs (stock keeping units—brands in all their different sizes, flavours etc.). Suppose the SKU that would have been chosen by the shopper, had the shopper been offered the complete set, is missing. There are basically four possible outcomes. The shopper can:

(1) substitute an alternative SKU (brand, flavour or size)
(2) resolve to seek the missing SKU at another store
(3) defer purchase until the current store restocks
(4) drop the purchase altogether.

We posit that the outcome will most often be of type (1), (2) or (3), and will correspond to the balance between two factors: cost of switching brands (CSB), or cost of switching stores (CSS).

9.1.1 Cost of Switching Brands

Loyalty is never absolute. Brand loyalty is usually a matter of degree, with some brands preferred and others less preferred but acceptable none the less. The CSB is the marginal satisfaction given up when the shopper substitutes the next best SKU for the unavailable favourite brand/SKU.

The marginal satisfaction depends, first, on relative brand preference—the more one brand is preferred over the available alternative, the more satisfaction is given up switching. Marginal satisfaction also depends on the choice behaviour in the product category. In fact, marginal satisfaction may be negligible for reasons related to this choice behaviour. At the point of purchase, marginal satisfaction can be brought down to zero, despite brand preferences, by promotions.

9.1.1.1 Brand Choice Behaviour

Brand choice behaviour is often classified into levels:

- *brand loyal,* where the shopper tries always to buy the same brand
- *repertoire,* where the shopper switches between a repertoire of accepted brands, and
- *promiscuous,* where the shopper is open to consider any brand on any purchase occasion.

Table 9.1 shows how brand choice behaviour can vary across product fields. It shows the results of a French study which compared loyalty to brands with the importance of brands in forming the purchase choice. As one would anticipate, there is a correlation between the importance of brands and loyalty. However, the importance of brands does not systematically dictate that choice behaviour will be loyal. In some areas, brands are very important to consumers, but many consumers are repertoire buyers or even promiscuous. For example, 'brand' is of great importance when choosing champagne, but only about one in four shoppers are *loyal* to a sole brand. Brand appeal is very important for a champagne, but presence in store is clearly critical to capitalising on that appeal. The implication is that even for a popular champagne, the marginal satisfaction of one brand over the others (i.e. its CSB) will be low for 76% of consumers. In contrast, 54% of French consumers try always to buy the same

***Table 9.1** Importance of brands compared to brand choice behaviour (French consumers)*

Brand choice behaviour	Importance of brand	% of buyers Loyal	Repertoire	Promiscuous
Champagne	high	24	68	8
Mineral Water	high	44	37	19
Coffee	high	52	41	7
Washing-up liquid	medium	54	39	7
Chocolate (tablet)	medium	30	56	14
Washing powder	medium	45	40	15
Jam	low	32	51	17
Yoghurt	low	23	49	28
Tights	low	23	29	48
Dress	low	4	33	63

Adapted from Jean-Noel Kapferer and Gilles Laurent, *La Marque,* Ediscience international, Paris, 1989, ch. 3, pp. 96–8.

washing-up liquid, implying that marginal satisfaction will only be negligible in 46% of washing-up liquid purchases. Hence a lowly washing-up liquid brand may weigh in more heavily with the retailer than a prestigious champagne when demanding shelfspace.

If several brands are bought with varying frequency (e.g. biscuits), the absence of any one, for a short period, should not cause much dissatisfaction. In markets where consumers actively seek variety, CSB for each individual brand will be small or non-existent. As long as consumers feel they have a rich choice, the absence of even one or two well-liked brands, will not cause a loss of satisfaction.

9.1.1.2 Point of Sale and Promotional Effects

In those cases where the shopper does have an absolute brand preference, the marginal satisfaction may still be brought down to zero by point of sale activities, initiated by the store or by competitor brands.

Price or other promotions mounted by competitive brands are expected to cause some brand switching. This is another way of saying that marginal satisfaction is reduced to zero or below by the promotion. This brand switching can happen hypothetically when the losing brand is not in stock. The shopper will say: 'Normally I would stick out loyally for brand X, but since this alternative is on promotion I'll take it.'

Promotions and merchandising (such as sampling) are often undertaken with the objective of increasing volume sales or brand switching. They also have an important role (for the retailer) in reducing the CSB of a delisted brand.

There are, of course, categories where consumers are much more likely to have a single preferred brand. Brands such as Benson & Hedges, Campbells, Coca-Cola or Maxwell House would certainly expect a significant proportion of their customers to be uncompromisingly brand loyal. When a consumer is confronted with a stock-out of a brand for which they have a high marginal satisfaction they will register dissatisfaction with the store, whatever action (options (1) to (4) above) they decide to take.

9.1.2 Cost of Switching Stores

'Store loyalty' is a rather ill-defined notion, for most consumers have patterns of shopping which involve more than one store. A consumer can feel loyal to a shop, visit it loyally once a week and still visit one or more competitive outlets each week. Different stores may serve different roles, either by shopping occasion (Friday night, lunch hour fill up) or by 'speciality' (e.g. vegetables, meat, frozen, discount). Some shoppers take shopping very seriously and are willing to invest time visiting different stores, 'cherry picking' for good value and tracking down the precise items preferred. Some shoppers visit different stores on a regular repertoire basis, both to review prices in competing stores and because they enjoy a sense of variety, choice and change. Many shoppers regularly visit two or more stores simply because they arrange shopping trips from different geographic bases (e.g. home and work). One snapshot of shopping habits, gathered in a US survey, is displayed in Table 9.2.

The same survey found that 27% of supermarket shoppers visited only one supermarket each week, 46% visited two, 22% visited three and 5% visited four or more. In the UK, AGB's Superpanel indicates that the average shopper visits over five

Table 9.2 *A snapshot of shopping habits*[7]

	% of shoppers visiting at least once a week	Weekly trips	Weekly expenditure
Supermarket	100	2.0	$68.04
Mass merchandisers	67	1.0	$25.64
Convenience store	43	2.9	$12.79
Warehouse clubs	27	2.1	$75.99

Source: 60th Annual Report of the grocery industry, *Progressive Grocer*, April 1993.

different outlets for grocery purchases within an eight-week period.[8]

A more objective measure for the propensity to switch stores is the (perceived) CSS. This is the perceived cost to a consumer of making a visit to a competitive store in order to find a missing SKU. The cost will include the physical cost of the trip, the psychological cost of not making the purchase immediately, and the psychological cost of not making the purchase at this store.

(1) Physical Cost

Shopping behaviour will clearly have a significant impact on the physical cost of switching store. For a repertoire shopper, who regularly visits more than one supermarket (73% in the survey quoted above), the physical cost of visiting an alternative store will be very small. Such a shopper may know that one store never stocks one desired item, and so habitually, and without inconvenience, buys it from another store.

Other types of shopper put greater value on time and convenience and gravitate to 'one-stop-shopping'. For shoppers who aim to reduce shopping to one trip a fortnight to their preferred store, the perceived physical cost of an extra trip to an alternative store might be significant.

Lastly, there is always a group of shoppers who are limited in their choice of stores through their own lack of mobility. If a shopper's means of transport is limited to feet or public transport or a lift, the cost of getting to an alternative outlet even a kilometre away may be insurmountable.

Obviously, a critical issue for physical cost is the physical presence of retail competition in relation to the bases (e.g. work, their child's school or home) of the shopper. At least this factor may be moving in favour of manufacturers as supermarket saturation increases.

(2) Psychological Costs of Not Making Purchase Immediately
Many packaged products keep fresh for a long time: tins of meat for years, coffee for months. UHT versions of milk products, nitrogen packing and vacuum sealing have made many purchases, even of fresh food, less urgent than they used to be. Most shoppers are now equipped with fridge and freezer. This all allows the shopper to maintain a considerable inventory of products at home. Beyond this, stocking-up at home enables the prudent shopper to benefit from promotions and negate the inconvenience of out-of-stock items. A promotion can increase home inventories; a stock-out may be allowed to deplete them.

In a main shopping trip, many purchases would be of this 'stocking up' category, with the shopper deciding purchases according to the products available, the offers on those products and the stock at home. However, a proportion of purchases are not made in this leisured and ponderous manner.

Some items are difficult for the consumer to stock for more than a day or two. If in addition they are consumed every day their purchase can be classed as 'urgent'. Depending on the household's food habits, bread, milk, fruit, salad, vegetables, fish and meat may demand purchase several times a week.

In addition, urgent needs arise for idiosyncratic reasons—missing ingredients for a planned meal, a bottle of wine, a pair of tights, a cheap away-from-home lunch, stain removing or insect killing products. Households also come up with idiosyncratic urgent shopping items because the home inventory has failed. Salt, disposable nappies or washing-up liquid are easy to stock, but a shortage lasting one day can be unacceptable. One study found 'fill-in' shoppers most likely to buy bread, milk, tobacco products, soft drinks and paper products[9] but a study would naturally miss the idiosyncratic class, as it has no pattern.

Urgent and impulsive wants can prompt extra 'fill in' shopping trips or be part of the main trip. Clearly they will affect the shopper's attitude. Urgency, inherent or accidental, puts the consumer under more pressure to satisfy the buying need on that shopping occasion. Hence urgency adds to the cost of store switching, CSS.

(3) Psychological Costs

The psychological costs of seeking the preferred SKU in another shop automatically include some frustration and inconvenience (e.g. extra effort in remembering). In addition a shopper may be loyal to a store, for rational or emotional reasons, and this hold over the shopper will increase the psychological cost of buying elsewhere. For example, a warehouse club may be able to push people to substitute items because shoppers might be highly motivated to maximise their purchases from that store.

For one-stop shoppers, a high level of own-label purchases can have a strongly positive effect on the CSS. If a shopper is in the habit of making many own-label purchases in one store, switching shops will mean facing (in effect) multiple out-of-stocks in the own-label brands. Now, it might be that the own labels purchased gave virtually zero marginal satisfaction. For example, many shoppers do not care which brand (or own brand) they buy for salt, olive oil or flour. On the other hand, whenever the cost of switching the own label brands is not negligible, it will be part of the CSS. For a shop like Sainsbury's, it will often be the case that over 60% of a shopper's purchases (many of them not commodities) are own brand. This implies that the cost of switching store (at least for a regular stocking up trip) will be large: over 60% of the usual brands bought are 'out of stock' in the other store.

At the other extreme, the *psychological cost* of going to another store may not even be positive. Dissatisfactions with the store (for example, a problem parking, repeatedly finding products out of stock, or feeling that there is more choice elsewhere) can in fact lead to a *negative emotional appeal*, working against the physical cost of switching stores. This means the shopper will enjoy an emotional benefit (rather than cost) in going elsewhere. Since location plays such a dominant role in store choice, it is likely that a proportion of shoppers shop in a given store despite a marginal or negative emotional appeal. These shoppers are just waiting to be pushed to make the physical effort to go to another store, where they will gain the emotional satisfaction of going to a 'better' shop.

9.2 WHAT WILL HAPPEN?

As stated above, basically four possible outcomes can be imagined. The shopper can in the immediate:

(1) Switch brand: substitute an alternative SKU (brand, flavour or size).
(2) Switch store: resolve to seek the SKU at another store.
(3) Defer: defer purchase until the current store restocks.
(4) Drop: not bother with the purchase.

Each of these outcomes will itself have a dynamic effect: for example, being forced to switch brand might cause frustration with the store (leading to a reduction in CSS in the future) or might weaken brand loyalty as an alternative SKU is found to be satisfactory.

We will argue now that the initial choice between these four outcomes depends on the brand loyalty (CSB) and store loyalty (CSS, including the urgency of the need).

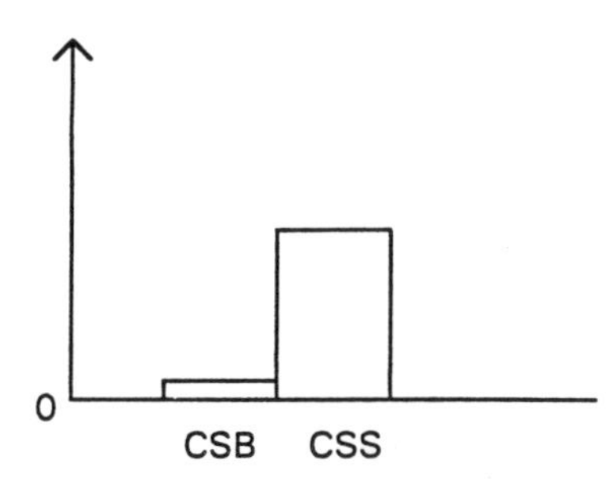

Figure 9.1 *Often marginal satisfaction for brands is pretty near to zero, cost of switching stores is unlikely to be zero*

(1) Retailer Power CSB<CSS (see Fig. 9.1)
If a shopper has gone into a shop and wishes to buy a product, it seems automatic that there will be some perceived costs to switching stores or deferring purchase. Thus, in cases where the marginal satisfaction for the SKU is negligible (or is brought down to zero by actions of the retailer such as in-store promotions) it is clear that the outcome of being out of stock will be to substitute another item. Thus the retailer holds on to the shopper, and in addition the forced trial of an alternative SKU poses a threat to any habit and preference which remains to the missing brand.

In this situation the power lies almost exclusively with the retailer, and applies particularly in areas with little added value and little differentiation between brands.

(2) Betting the Store 0<CSB<CSS (see Fig. 9.2)
If a consciously preferred item is not available and the cost of switching stores is relatively high, the shopper will be best off deferring the purchase until the preferred store restocks. In a sense the outcome is a stand-off between retailer and manufacturer, with consumers paying for loyalty to both parties with patience. A cautious store would be best off restocking without delay: continued out of stock might mean tempting the shopper to reconsider shopping trips to include a stocking store.

Deferral is no longer an option if the store does not restock, or if the shopper's need is urgent. Since the cost of switching

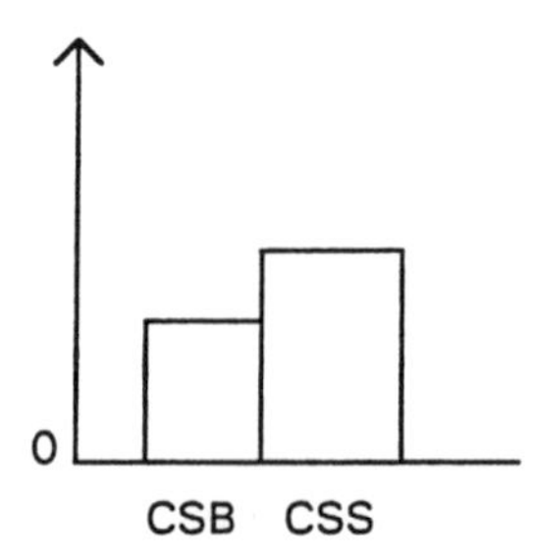

Figure 9.2 *The cost of switching brands is not negligible, but the cost of switching store is even higher*

store outweighs the cost of switching brand, the shopper is best off, in this situation, accepting the loss of satisfaction and buying the best alternative SKU available. The retailer has 'won', but not without some cost in terms of customer dissatisfaction. In this instance, the retailer has 'forced' the shopper to swap brands, and the shopper consciously feels 'the pain and dilemma of out-of-stock products'.

The long-term outcome is uncertain. To reduce irritation, shoppers must either modify their brand preference or modify their shopping habits so that they can easily visit a store stocking their preferred brand. This is a crunch point, with the store pitting its appeal and loyalty against that created by the manufacturer. By taking this uncompromising line ('betting the store') a retailer may be able to destroy a brand's CSB by forcing trial of substitutes which are found to be acceptable. The store may, equally, lose customers.

(3) Retail Nightmare CSB > CSS (see Fig. 9.3)
If the shopper feels the CSB quite strongly, or on the other hand, perceives little cost in switching stores, seeking the desired SKU from another shop becomes appealing. This is the retailer's nightmare, where a whole basket of shopping may be lost through a failure to deliver the range the shopper seeks.

If the cost of switching stores is relatively small but not negligible, and the need is non-urgent, the shopper may yet defer: deferring the purchase and avoiding an extra visit to

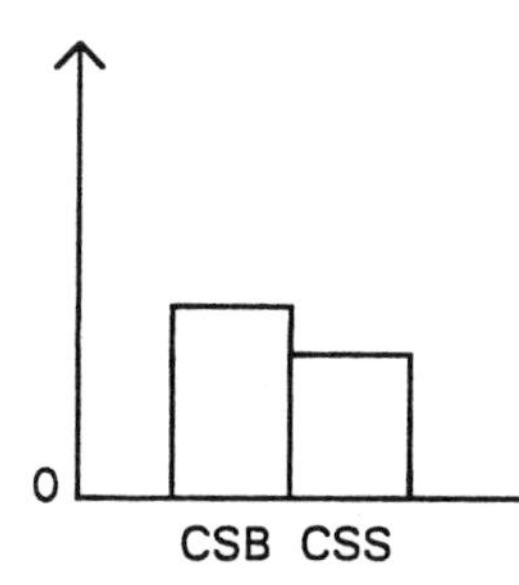

Figure 9.3 *Cost of switching store is normally not negligible, but cost of switching brand may be greater.*

another store. The willingness to defer depends on the perceived costs of switching store compared to the urgency of the need. The retailer should rush to re-stock before the shopper loses patience.

An urgent need ups the ante. If the urgency outweighs the difference between CSB and CSS, consumers are forced, quite against their preferences, to buy some alternative. This is a Pyrrhic victory for the store. On this occasion they have twisted the consumer's arm successfully, but the shopper is quite likely to modify shopping preferences as a result.

(4) Ephemeral Needs—Outcome Drop

There are shopping items which have a high 'presence elasticity'—that is, if the need is not satisfied, it disappears. For example, if a household drinks Diet Coke by the gallon and finds it out of stock on the regular Saturday shopping trip, they may be unable or unwilling to schedule an immediate trip to an alternative store. Thus they may (reluctantly) drink water all over the weekend. When restocking takes place the following week, potential consumption (over the previous weekend) will have been lost forever, to the cost of both the brand and the store. Coke believes that the more Coke a shopper buys, the more that person will consume.

A similar situation exists for impulse products, which are only considered for purchase if the consumer notices them in-store. This will often be the case for treats such as soft fruit or cut flowers. Often it will apply to new products seeking trial for the first time, both grocery and, for example, magazines or partworks, gadgets and children's novelties. This elasticity can be increased with advertising which explains or adds interest to the products.

For products with a high presence elasticity, bought if and only if they are there, sales will permanently be lost if they are not there. If the CSB is zero, the consumer is unaware of 'dropping' the purchase. This will be the case with impulse purchases of treats and novelties.

There are also purchases for which the CSB is not zero, but which are not essential and can be dropped. If a consumer is firmly settled on one brand, its absence may cause them to do without until they can restock. A typical example (aside from

Coke, mentioned above) would be a non-essential such as bath additive. Although the brand will be bought again in the future (the consumer may think they are 'postponing' purchase) it is 'dropped' in the sense that renewed purchases will not make up the lost sales. Potential consumption will have been lost forever, to the loss of both retailer and manufacturer.

A dropped sale of a brand with a positive CSB will also mean conscious dissatisfaction with the shop. The frustration felt will strike against the store's emotional appeal.

A new product will have a positive CSB normally only if it has been advertised. Even if the consumer does not miss a new product, the retailer none the less loses a potential sale and has perhaps an opportunity for increasing the consumer's satisfaction. Clearly this is also a lost opportunity for both store and manufacturer. For the manufacturer, presence is clearly crucial to every sale, but the interest and satisfaction generated by the new product will be given to those who are willing to grant it a good presence. Thus, both presence elasticity because of trial and the novelty value are arguments frequently given for getting a retailer to stock new products, and launch advertising is particularly valuable for exciting some dissatisfaction if not stocked.

9.3 BALANCE OF POWER

The discussion above seems to suggest that the retailer has great power to force brand switching: in how many cases can a manufacturer expect to generate a CSB greater than the store's CSS? This, however, underestimates the effect that frustration and disappointment will be having on the CSS. The CSB on one brand may not be sufficient to prompt store switching, but the CSBs will cumulate over brands for any individual shopper. Each unwilling brand switch will erode the emotional cost of switching stores: in the end this accumulating emotional disbenefit can significantly reduce the CSS. Once the shopper has been frustrated by three or four out-of-stock products, store loyalty may be insufficient to inhibit a trip to an alternative supermarket. Similarly, CSB will accumulate over time.

The greatest ally for brands is the uncertainty. The costs to retailers are often less visible than those to manufacturers: the cost is the risk they take in lowering the satisfaction of their shoppers. The cost of losing a sale to a retailer is not the potential loss from that one item. It is the fear that either being out of stock of one key item might lead the shopper to make a whole basket of purchases elsewhere, or that the accumulation of being out of stock of several brands will lead to a level of dissatisfaction which will bring into question the customer's long-term shopping pattern.

This is parallel to the situation for prices. The risk of a high price on one item is that for some group of consumers this item might be key in their price perception of the store. Losing the sale of that item matters little, but damaging the overall price perception might lose the whole basket, perhaps for a number of weeks. This risk keeps the retailer competitive on a whole raft of prices; the uncertainty in the impact of out-of-stocks can similarly force the listing of most of the most popular brands.

Because the issue is so complex, the retailer is wary of possible mistakes, either overestimating a store's power to influence brand choice or, conversely, overestimating the shopper's loyalty to brands. Conscious of these risks the retailer is open to advice and arguments from those who, steeped in knowledge of their product field, are best placed to understand the mechanisms of loyalty and substitution.

> Thus conscience doth make cowards of us all
> And thus the native hue of resolution
> Is sicklied o'er with the pale cast of thought,
> And enterprises of great pith and moment
> With this regard their currents turn awry
> And lose the name of action.

9.4 SOME EMPIRICAL RESULTS

Measuring a consumer's willingness to switch brand, compared to their willingness to switch shop is clearly a delicate operation. It will vary by consumer, by shop, and by urgency of shopping occasion.

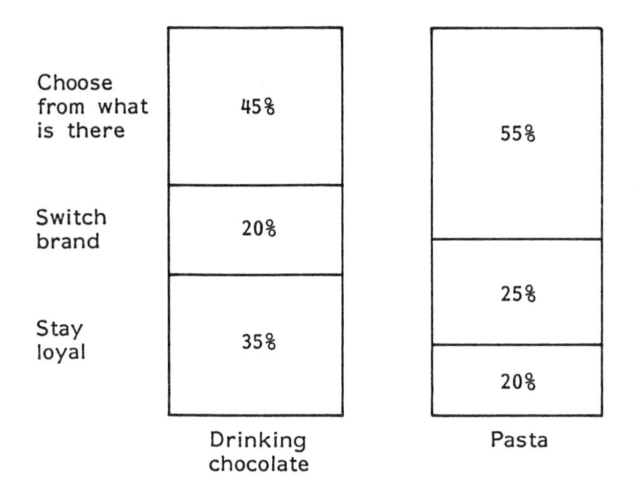

Figure 9.4 *Comparing the brand loyalty in two markets.*
Source: George Chetochin, Marketing Strategique de la Distribution, *Editions Liaisons, Paris, 1992, p. 177*

In France a researcher has published a study which aims to measure the willingness to stick out for a preferred brand. The results refer to two markets, pasta and instant drinking chocolate. First the study split pasta and drinking chocolate shoppers into three categories. Those who were sufficiently brand loyal that they would not buy a substitute if their brand was out of stock, those who would switch brands in such a situation, and those who selected on the basis of what is there, and are often looking for promotions and offers. The results are shown in Fig. 9.4.

The results presented in Fig. 9.4 indicate straight off that (for these shoppers) the retailer has more control over pasta purchases and has to be a bit more wary about mishandling shoppers buying drinking chocolate. However, for 45% of the pasta market and 55% of the chocolate market, consumers do feel some brand loyalty. Destocking the preferred brands will threaten the retailer's sales or image among these shoppers.

The study goes on to break down these classes of shopper by brand. Fig. 9.5 shows how 50% of Nesquick purchasers, about 21% of all buyers, are sufficiently loyal to switch shops or defer if Nesquick is not stocked. This high figure explains Nesquick's almost universal distribution in French supermarkets. Cadbury's Super Poulain scores about 1.5% in comparison.

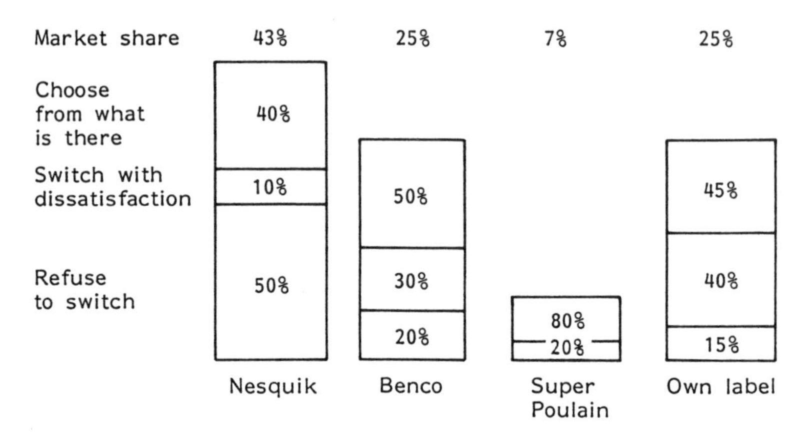

Figure 9.5 *Degrees of loyalty by brand among drinking chocolate buyers. Source: 'Customers' behaviour when confronted with a product stockout at a supermarket',* Progressive Grocer, *October 1968*

An American study carried out in the late 1960s (but still interesting as an example) looked at the choice of behaviour between 'switch brands', 'switch store' and 'defer' across a large number of product fields (see Table 9.3). Cigarettes and shampoo came out tops for beating the store switching cost; the retailer usually overpowered marginal brand satisfaction in facial tissues and canned green beans. Washing powder and margarine are things many shoppers are willing to wait for (their dogs are more impatient). Cereals do not push shoppers to switch stores that much, despite the importance of brands in this area, perhaps because of repertoire buying.

Table 9.3 *Consumer behaviour when confronted with a brand stockout at a supermarket, compared across product fields*

	Switch store	Switch brand	Defer (same store)
Cigarettes	80	11	11
Shampoo	61	26	17
Toothpaste	48	37	17
Dog food	46	44	16
Laundry detergent	47	33	25
Margarine	23	50	30
Cereal	26	53	24
Salad oil	24	55	25
Facial tissue	16	57	30
Canned green beans	19	63	22

Source: 'Customers' behaviour when confronted with a product stockout at a supermarket', *Progressive Grocer*, October 1968.

Of course, for market-oriented retailers Table 9.3 reads a little differently. Retailers who want to develop brands will see that product fields such as cigarettes, which motivate consumers strongly to seek the same brand each time, are the ones to go for (even if the brand sells at a loss). The above study shows a retailer that a consumer/shopper who smokes a retail brand is extremely likely to come back to the same store each week.

The totals in Table 9.3 add up to slightly over 100, because some respondents marked 'switch store' and 'defer', i.e. they were determined to buy a particular brand, but at the time it was unknown to them how they would resolve their purchasing challenge. From the retailer's point of view, these are shoppers wandering around with an unsatisfied need and at any moment they could be attracted into a competitive store to buy the missing SKU and, no doubt, several other items.

Another interesting aspect of this survey was that it showed how the decision was influenced not only by product field but also by the type of *neighbourhood* in which the store was located. For example, in high-income areas shoppers were more inclined to switch brands and generally much less likely to defer purchase. Black neighbourhoods were most likely to display 'double loyalty' (brand and store) indicated by a generally higher propensity to defer (see Table 9.4).

This survey was carried out in a particular market, at a particular time, and cannot be taken as a general result on reaction to out-of-stock. However, it is interesting because it demonstrates how CSB and CSS interact over a range of products and stores. It is this sort of data that both stores and

Table 9.4 *Typical consumer behaviour when confronted with a brand stock-out, compared across stores in different types of neighbourhoods in an American survey*

	Switch store	Switch brands	Defer, same store
Young married	30	54	16
Blue collar	25	44	32
High income	32	58	10
Black	29	36	46
Small town	29	51	21
Overall average	29	49	25

Source: 'Customers' behaviour when confronted with a product stockout at a supermarket', *Progressive Grocer*, October 1968.

manufacturers should be collecting and discussing with each other. In many situations *loyalty* dictates what will happen if the store is out of stock and is thus more important than *brand preference*. In our experience, the latter is more frequently measured.

9.5 FIGHTING FOR SHELFSPACE

During the crucial stocking negotiation between manufacturer and retailer, the likely outcomes of destocking are weighed by the two parties. Thinking about CSB and CSS helps both parties in their two major challenges. The first task is to understand the balance of power. Understanding the balance of power implies knowing how much satisfaction is given up on switching brand compared to how easy it is for a consumer to switch store. To whom will the cost fall? How strong is the consumer's attachment to the brand? How does the cost of switching brands differ for largely impulse purchase items such as confectionery? How much out-of-stock will the consumer tolerate from this particular store?

The second task is to influence the CSB and CSS: retailers and manufacturers are both free to alter the balance in their favour. The most cogent reason for becoming analytical about the balance of power is that this will suggest ways of influencing it. What strategies would influence the outcome in the favour of manufacturers and what in favour of the retailers? For example, being flippant, TV advertising will usually increase the CSB for a brand, but providing free buses between stores might have a similar net effect on the balance of power.

More seriously, there are six thought-provoking implications that drop out of this analysis.

(1) It is clear that manufacturers, collectively, should give incentives to consumers to shop around and, wherever possible, oppose retailer efforts to push shoppers towards one-stop shopping. It is interesting to note that most marketing investment goes on increasing the cost of brand switching, rather than decreasing the cost of store switching. The analysis suggests to manufacturers that they should reflect deeply on the effect of promotions. It is generally accepted that promotions encourage brand switching. The stakes are higher than presumed if, from

the 'battle for shelfspace' viewpoint, all this brand switching hands the consumer to the retailer on a plate. If (price) promotions encourage the shopper to switch brands, would it be possible for manufacturers to use price promotions to encourage store switching? This would be done, for example, by rotating powerful promotions around large stores in such a way that they do not overlap in time. Consumers would learn to follow these 'carousel' promotions.

Manufacturers could encourage or commission studies which show the benefits of shopping around. Most price comparisons between stores use a basket of comparable goods, and most indicate that the differences between stores are small. The difference would be much more pronounced if an extra basket belonging to the 'cherry picking' shopper could be added into the analysis.

(2) In general, retailers have every reason to encourage brand switching, breaking the loyalty of consumers to manufacturers. However, CSB is something that can add or detract from a store's CSS. It may be that certain brands or categories (e.g. foreign foods) are increasing the appeal of the store, because their CSB is adding to the store's CSS, because shoppers know that they are not stocked elsewhere. In particular, retailers who create CSB for their own brands, add this CSB to their CSS. This is, of course, a familiar theme of this book, reached by slightly different reasoning.

(3) A retailer seriously contemplating a delisting should do everything possible to reduce the loss of satisfaction to zero. When retailers present shoppers with out-of-stock items they should make conscious efforts to minimise the marginal satisfaction (CSB) lost by the consumer who accepts the alternative offered. The CSB is a marginal satisfaction depending not only on the brand itself, but also on the available substitutes. It is important for retailers to examine marginal satisfaction and substitution patterns. Shoppers may be happy to swap across brands from one reduced calorie mayonnaise to another, but not to swap to a full-fat mayonnaise of any make. Whenever a store goes out of stock on some SKU, it should know what substitute it expects its shoppers to take and the alternative SKUs have to be made as attractive as possible. This means stocking other SKUs which are likely to minimise the marginal satisfaction, and

then planning promotions, merchandising, layout, pricing to compensate any disappointed shopper. In addition, duration of stock-outs may be important for encouraging the defer option, over switching store, and then actualising the deferred purchase. For example, it would be possible to put up signs apologising for any inconvenience and promising resumed supplies within, say, two days. Since CSB accumulates both across brands and through time, retailers should plan delisting systematically, both across the store and through time.

(4) The analysis of this chapter shows the vital importance of information on shopping habits and in-store decision behaviour. Shopping habits are as crucial to negotiations as brand loyalties. A retailer whose shoppers are repertoire shoppers has to be more sensitive to consumer preferences than a competitor who through location or marketing effort has greater shopper loyalty. Modern retailers should find out about the loyalty of their shoppers and should compare their store loyalty to their brand loyalties. If a retailer accounts for, say, 15% of a brand's sales, what percentage of the 15% is lost if the retailer does delist it? How do shoppers break down with respect to brand loyalty: which shoppers are most determined to stick to their favourite brands, by age, economic group, time of shopping trip. Would it be interesting, for example, to 'run out' of some major brands on Friday night and Saturday morning? Can some branches in the chain afford a more cavalier attitude to out-of-stocks than others, as is the case with prices?

(5) Urgent purchases are something special. Urgent needs play into the hands of the retailer if the shopper is not brand loyal. This gives retailers more power over fresh produce. The tables are turned on brand loyal purchases, where urgent need can initiate a special trip to a competitor store, resulting in the loss of a basket of sales, or cause considerable resentment. A store specialising in fresh non-stockable items will generate more frequent visits and stores will always have much power to force purchase in the non-stockable lines. This is possibly another reason why manufacturers find it hard to create fresh 'brands': loyalty would be continually compromised by the inability of the shopper to stock-up.

(6) There are certain product fields where the retailer is destined to have considerable control, i.e. where choice is made

strictly from stocked brands. However, these are likely to be the 'dead' categories where the retailer also has little chance of differentiating itself from local retail competition (except on price). Canned green beans, from the survey mentioned above, being a good example. These products are most efficiently marketed under the retailer's umbrella brand, and from the manufacturers' point of view are industrial products. In these markets it is no longer viable to rely on consumer preference to create a successful brand. This is a another familiar theme of this book. The theatre of battle for mindspace and shelfspace are those added-value areas (such as cigarettes and shampoo) where it *is* possible to create loyalty, which can be owned either by manufacturer or by store.

The battle for shelfspace is an area where both manufacturers and retailers are rapidly developing their understanding. It is an area which lags behind consumer marketing in its sophistication, and in particular in data collection. This is bound to change, since the area is becoming so crucial for both parties.

Notes

(1) Quote from Mr Everaert, ex-chairman of Aholt.
(2) Olivier Géradon de Véra, Directeur general adjoint de la Secodip, taken from *Vive la Marque*, Eric Maillard, Institut du Commerce et de la Consommation, June 1991, p. 35.
(3) Peter Wilsher, 'Whose hands on the housekeeping', *Management Today*, December 1993, p. 38.
(4) Statement by Olivier Géradon de Véra, Directeur general adjoint de la Secodip, taken from *Vive la Marque*, Eric Maillard, Institut de Commerce et de la Consommation, June 1991, p. 35. This would not be true in the USA, where choice has long been considerably greater.
(5) Michael Sansolo, 'Rethinking the shopper', reporting on Coca-Cola Retailing Research Council Survey, 'Merchandising in the 1990s', *Progressive Grocer*, May 1989, pp. 63–6.
(6) Terry Leahy, Tesco, 'The retailers' viewpoint', in *Branding, A Key Marketing Tool*, Editor John M. Murphy, Macmillan, 1992, p. 116.
(7) Table 9.2 was created using figures published in 'The 60th Annual Report of the Grocery Industry' by *Progressive Grocer*, April 1993.

(8) Judith Passingham, Director of AGB's Superpanel, 'Own label and the store wars', *Admap*, March 1994.
(9) 'Marsh super study', presentation to the First Annual Marketing and Merchandising Forum, Nice, France, October 1991.

10
Trade Marketing

It is possible to find brand manufacturers who subscribe to three different attitudes to 'the trade', and to three different approaches to managing trade relations:

(1) There are those who believe that the retail trade still needs them badly—but for them consumer markets would not exist, and retailers should be suitably grateful. They resent the increasing 'bolshiness' of the trade, find it outrageous that their brands are not given their 'market' share of shelfspace and reject out of hand the possibility of making own label.
(2) Others are impressed with the retailers' tough stance in negotiations. They believe that this ability to negotiate hard is a phenomenon in its own right. The answer, for them, is to learn how to negotiate more effectively and to teach the retailer to seek co-operation by acting tough when necessary.
(3) A growing number of manufacturers recognise that a fundamental shift in power has taken and is taking place. They see that the concentration of the retail industry has left the survivors with permanently increased, and perhaps increasing, power. Their response is to adapt their organisations and business approach to concentrate more resources and effort on 'trade marketing'.

This book must be tough reading for members of the first group. If they have managed to keep their heads under the sand so far, the realisation of the new order must be hard upon them now. To be fair, ostrich manufacturers such as these are already largely extinct.

Members of the second group, those who focus on negotiations, are more numerous but equally deluded. Negotiations are not the real fight, and 'co-operation' (or 'partnership', in current jargon) is not a solution. Negotiations are the tip of the iceberg in the competition between manufacturer and retailer. The outcome of the negotiations depends to a small degree on the negotiating skills of the parties and to a large degree to the balance of power between them. Once negotiations begin, nine-tenths of the battle is over. The balance of power is dictated by brand loyalty, store loyalty, shopping habits and retail structure, and the extent to which the two parties understand these parameters.

Co-operation can be part of the equation, where there are efficiencies to be derived from it, but manufacturers and retailers are inevitably competing with each other. The increasingly market-oriented approach of the biggest retailers can only intensify the competition. 'Co-operation' and 'partnership' can only be won from retailers by answering their needs better than the competition. It is not cynical to define 'co-operation' as the outcome of two parties valuing what the other has, and each anticipating a long-term relationship with the other. Co-operation is not a means in itself, much less a solution to a weak position: it is the outcome of particular circumstances.

Those in the third group recognise the terms 'co-operation' and 'partnership' as mere codes and ciphers, the velvet glove concealing the iron fist. Their mantra is to consider the retail industry as a market of professional buyers: a market of crucial importance, whose needs must be analysed and satisfied competitively. Procter & Gamble have, famously, allocated a team of executives to work exclusively on the needs of Wal-Mart. This team moved physically to Bentonville, Arkansas to be in constant contact with the head office of Wal-Mart. In general, more and more manufacturers are becoming devotees of *trade marketing* and this activity attracts an increasing amount of manufacturer attention and investment.

Most consumer goods companies now have some sort of trade marketing arm, often developed from and within sales or account management. The function has in most cases grown up parallel to and independent from the consumer marketing side. We will argue that these functions are nowadays frequently in conflict and that a special effort has to be made to harmonise and integrate the two.

10.1 FROM SELLING TO TRADE MARKETING

For a long time, in both the USA and Europe, retailing was a rather controlled market with various 'price maintenance' laws and 'right to sell' legislation. Now suppliers face a free-trade market, similar to that with the consumer.

Industrial strategies fall on to the same war spectrum that applies to mature industries in general. Manufacturers can use strategies which hustle the retailer. They depend on giving the retailer money (discounts, subsidies, advertising moneys, etc.)—they *buy* shelfspace. A competitor who hustles more will be able to buy back the advantages. Funnily enough, these hustle strategies can be quite effective for large manufacturers.

Hustle strategies cost some money, but they help manufacturers stay in control. If the incentives are tied to quantity discounts and in-store marketing mix variables, hustle strategies inhibit the retailer from manipulating sales mix and in-store variables to its own ends. Conversely, though many retailers feel powerful when they are bribed and hustled by their suppliers, such strategies do not serve the best interests of their own businesses. The retailers are led to operate their stores in a way which satisfies the manufacturers' consumer marketing objectives (which are often in head-on conflict with those of market-oriented retailers). By encouraging a price orientation among retailers, consumers can be made more price sensitive in their choice of store, they switch stores by cherry picking promotions. Selling-oriented retailers need brands to make convincing price claims. Thus retailers' selling orientation towards consumers, jeopardises loyalty more at the store level than the brand level.

However, in certain markets, retailers are bravely rejecting the blandishments of manufacturers' hustle strategies. Retailers who once sold their assets for money, now are only willing to grant them to manufacturers who have something unique to offer them, or who show a willingness to help them satisfy their own objectives.

Shelfspace, number of facings, position, space in folders, local promotion, advertising, information (scanners), choice of new products are all key decisions for retailers. Selling them off to manufacturers is the simplest way of dealing with them. On the other hand, allocating these resources optimally from a retail business perspective might increase sales volumes, margins, the satisfaction and comfort of their shoppers, their store image and ultimately store loyalty. These retailers do not want to be hustled. Manufacturers who succeed with these modern retailers are those who have learnt to court and empathise, rather than pull out a wad of notes.

In countries where retailers are waking up to marketing-oriented strategies, there is less scope for hustling and more scope for marketing to them. To entice the new, independently minded retailers, manufacturers need to refocus on the retailers' needs and objectives and create value for them in a broader sense, other than just hustling with variously named incentives.

10.2 THE STRATEGIC TRIANGLE OF TRADE MARKETING

Trade marketing is industrial marketing—business-to-business marketing. Marketing to business is different from marketing to consumers. In essence, trade marketing is a balancing act involving three issues.

First, maximising the value offered to retailers. Business customers are buying with the objective of re-selling the product, and making a profit on it. The buying decision is assessed as closely as possible in terms of economic criteria. This does not mean that price is therefore the most important variable, but rather that the buying decision depends on the overall *value* provided, value being a trade-off between benefits and costs. A company wishing to sell to another business needs to become expert in analysing and manipulating the *value* delivered to their clients.

Second, ensuring the profitability of individual accounts. Offering greater value has cost implications and these costs vary between clients. Successful trade marketing implies managing the balance between giving value and making profits. In turn this means that the trade marketer must be able to work out how profitable each account is, and how that profitability is affected by different value-creating actions. In consumer marketing, costs (such as marketing support or R&D) are often brand specific and it makes sense to treat brands as profit centres. In industrial markets, the brand is only a part of what is supplied, and the terms for selling the brand (including price) vary between customers. For this reason, in industrial marketing, the client, or 'account', is often the most logical unit of analysis for costs and profits. Sales personnel have traditionally focused on volume rather than profit, and the accountancy systems used by companies often make it difficult for the trade marketers to assess the real profit implications of their efforts to provide value. Trade marketers need to be able to assess profit by account and by distribution channel.

Third, since the client base is much more concentrated in industrial markets, the danger of dependence is much more dramatic. One or two large customers may represent make-or-break contracts for the company. Having gained this fortunate position, an astute customer will exploit it in future negotiations. The supplier must divide and rule, or not divide and be ruled. Similarly, when large companies go down, they usually take some of their suppliers with them, the most vulnerable being those with the best relationships. The retail industry is relatively volatile, with frequent mergers and not infrequent bankruptcies. Thus when a retailer is a very profitable account, the supplier has to take into account risk and dependence, in a way that is unfamiliar to consumer marketers.

In a nutshell, these three elements constitute trade marketing. The company has to maximise the value offered, while earning acceptable profits and guarding against over-dependence on any one client (See Fig. 10.1).

10.2.1 Customer Value

The first objective of trade marketing is to create superior value for customers, compared to competitive suppliers. Since professional buyers will assess an offer as far as possible on its economic worth, the seller should try to assess value in the same

Figure 10.1 *The Trade Marketer's turn in the FMCG circus*

way, and in comparison to other suppliers. (Many retailers are sharpening up their assessment of the value offered by different lines: direct product profitability (DPP) is precisely focused on this issue.) To win sales a supplier must aim to offer relatively more value, *in the eyes of retail clients,* than competitor suppliers. In industrial marketing *analysing value* points out ways to compete, comparable to the role of *segmentation* in consumer markets.

'Superior value is key, not that it costs less.' The manufacturer looks at the aspects of its product and service that provide value to the professional buyer, and wins sales by creating greater value than competitive suppliers. To be able to measure value in a diagnostic and actionable way, it is necessary to break down value into its component parts. The value of an offer is a function of the total benefits derived from purchase of a product, compared with the total cost in acquiring it and selling it on to the end consumer:

$$\text{Value} = \frac{\text{Total benefits}}{\text{Total costs}}$$

A supplier can create greater value by increasing the total benefits without increasing costs or by providing equal benefits at lower cost.

In general, part of the benefits are related to the product itself, and part to the services and conditions that go with its sale. Similarly, the total cost is the sum of the price agreed and the costs associated with acquiring and handling the product.

$$\text{Value} = \frac{\text{Product benefits} + \text{Non product benefits}}{\text{Price} + \text{associated costs}}$$

The more benefits and costs can be broken down into their components, the more detailed is the assessment of the impact of separate aspects on overall value. Defining the components means identifying all the independent aspects which influence customers when making their choice.

10.2.1.1 Total Benefits

Theories of negotiation always stress the importance of increasing the number of dimensions covered by the negotiations, the logic being that if more benefits are put on the table there is more scope for finding win–win deals. Win–win deals happen when the parties find that they have asymmetric utility for an aspect. That is, it costs one party less to compromise on something than the benefit gained by the other party from that same compromise. A simple example would be terms of payment. A delay in receiving payment may cost less to the supplier than the benefit of the delay to buyer, due to differences in the cost of capital relevant to each. One of the primary objectives in any attempt to create value is to stimulate thinking on the variety of benefits that a retailer can derive from an offer.

Generally, it is useful to consider product-related and non-product benefits separately. Typical product-related benefits would include:

- *Profitability.* Businesses buy products to make money on them, not because the products wash whiter or smell nicer. The primary product benefit to a retailer buying some FMCG is the product's profitability on being re-sold. This translates into a certain gross margin, on a certain volume moved. Thus in a list of benefits, margin and rotation are likely to figure prominently.

- *Consumer pull (CSB).* In the chapter on mindspace we went into great detail about the cost to a shopper of switching brands, and how this compared to the cost of switching stores. Demonstrating convincingly that delisting will hurt consumer satisfaction and possibly lead to store switching will usually be second only in importance to direct profits as a benefit to retailers. Many premium products can also show that their consumers are more affluent and higher spending than average, which aims to underline the value of their presence—the retailer does not wish to upset its richest customers.
- *Marketing support.* Marketing activity targeted at the consumer is likely to improve rotation, and may affect margin. More critically, it is designed to increase consumer pull and thus the brand's CSB (see above), and thus the cost to the store of delisting. Thus promotional support directed at the consumer can be counted as an incentive (if not exactly a benefit) to the retailer.
- *Exclusivity.* The brand's CSB will add directly to the store's CSS. In addition, a product which is sold exclusively to one retailer will be likely to give higher margins.
- *Category considerations.* Category management is jargon that started appearing with the increased importance of trade marketing. Since retailers focus on categories rather than single brands, manufacturers need to take a wider view of the whole category. Retailers try to present shoppers with a complete but streamlined range of products. The ideal range would offer satisfactory alternatives in all major segments, cover a range of price points, and optimise impulse buying. The ideas of category management will be looked at in greater detail in Chapter 11. Suffice it to say for now that manufacturers should aim to create (or invest in) brands which have a category-strategic, rather than simply brand-strategic, role.
- *Marketing aims/image.* A retailer which has positioning aims (for example, trying to improve its image with respect to healthy or up-market food or trying to upstage wholesaler clubs with

huge packs), will value products which further those positioning aims. Similarly, a market-oriented retailer will have a strategy with respect to price structure, promotions, range and own label. By understanding the retailer's own objectives the right type or mix of products can be presented.

Non-product benefits are those which the supplying company attaches to its offer, but which are not tied to the product itself. Typical examples would be:

- *Administration, ECR and EDI.* It is widely recognised that the period between production and consumer purchase can be reduced, with savings in holding, inventory and labour costs. The buzz phrase for this greater efficiency is 'efficient consumer response', or ECR (see Table 10.1). The supply chain has to respond efficiently to the consumer's behaviour. The key to efficiency is a paper-free flow of information: information stored in a PC can replace inventory stored in a warehouse.

  The information is used to predict what will be sold where, and the prediction is continually adjusted once consumers actually reveal what they are going to do. Information has to flow smoothly around the system so that the right physical goods can arrive at their rendezvous with the consumer without dilly-dallying on the way.

  Two companies with compatible electronic data handling systems can link them to share data. This goes under the

Table 10.1 *Time taken by dry grocery product in the supply chain, with estimates of potential saving*

	Current situation	Efficient consumer response
Supplier's warehouse	38 days	27 days
Distributor's warehouse	40 days (Forward buy: 9 days, Turn inventory: 31 days)	12 days
Retail store	26 days	22 days
Total	104 days	61 days

Reproduced, with permission, from Henderson Crosthwaite, *Consumer Brief*, Vol. 16, No. 10, p. 14, 9 November 1993.

abbreviation EDI (electronic data interchange). This is used, for example, for automatic reordering between stores, depots and manufacturers and leads to economies not just through lower levels of inventory, but also in administration, and in a reduced rate of errors in orders and deliveries.

- *'Advice and help.'* Many manufacturers offer 'shelfspace allocation models', or 'category management advice'. Manufacturers specialising in a category may be able to advise the retailer on optimising sales of the whole category, through their specialist knowledge of the consumer, and their experience with other retailers. Unfortunately, such 'advice' is often a thinly disguised sales pitch which retailers treat with scepticism. Retailers' scepticism may go as far as charging manufacturers money for the time taken to listen to their arguments.[1] For smaller chains and independent retailers, space allocation is a serious concern, and help may gratefully be accepted. Retailers with their own marketing objectives will have their own space allocation models wired up for different ends. Category management can be useful, but it has to be a sincere commitment, based on data not available to the retailer. It has to influence the *content* of the manufacturer's offer as well as its presentation (see Chapter 11).

- *Special displays.* Similarly, smaller retailers often welcome a special display which 'adds excitement to the store experience', for example tie-ins which involve posters of Disney characters or major sporting events. Sophisticated retailers will design their own display materials to support their own special purchases or to the latest culinary tour de force of their own-label brands. Such retailers will, like as not, charge for a display inclined to increase the mindspace owned by a supplier.

10.2.1.2 Total Costs

The total cost to the retailer of selling the product on to the consumer, must be broken down into its component parts in a parallel way to benefits.

Price will usually come first in a list of costs, followed by terms of payment; beyond this the retailer faces a number of non-price costs. Retailers all value their precious shelfspace: even the most primitive assessment of retail profitability includes some notion of profit per linear foot. The retailer is conscious of many different handling costs which add to its enormous labour bill. All the tiny actions from loading on and off lorries, unpacking from outers, to mixing the right assortment of SKUs, putting on prices and arranging in a display, add up to form a significant part of the overall cost of a good. Choices made by the supplier will affect these costs. Separating out the elements which create costs helps pinpoint the most efficient way of reducing the overall cost. A typical list of costs might be:

- *Price.* The price, taking into account quantity discounts and various direct subsidies or allowances, clearly forms the first and most visible component of cost.
- *Terms of payment.* The terms of payment are an element of cost and the assessment of relative worth will vary between different retailers. The supplier wants to discover how heavily each cost weighs in the buying decision. This type of information will reveal how value can be increased most cheaply for the supplier.
- *Shelfspace.* Shelfspace demands may well vary from one competitive product to another, depending on the product form and its packaging. Compactness or efficient forms of display can impact on the total cost of selling a product.
- *Transportation.* By investing to understand how a particular retailer organises distribution, warehousing, transport, etc., a supplier can offer more suitable delivery arrangements perhaps direct to store, day or night, weekday or weekends, and so on. Again, this is a benefit more pertinent to less sophisticated channels. Major retailers may simply dictate their transportation needs.
- *Handling costs.* The design of the product, its packaging and outer packaging can be economical to transport in terms of size/weight, withstand rough treatment and be easy to unpack. The packaging may have particular qualities allowing it to stack, or be presented directly to the consumer. The store's prices, or store specific information such as category code, can be printed on in advance. The combination of SKUs in a delivery can be more or less suited to the assortment

needed on the shelf. Since labour forms such a large part of retail costs, the idea of saving two minutes per case is pretty exciting.
- *Inventory costs.* A retailer holding inventory suffers financial risks, financial costs, physical risks and physical costs. In inflationary times, the costs of holding goods are concealed. The value of the goods appreciate in nominal terms and the retailer may show a profit on the act of holding. In deflationary times, the opposite can happen. An untimely price cut can mean a warehouse manager wakes up on Monday morning with a warehouse full of goods worth less than on the previous Friday. The retailer also has the physical responsibility of looking after products. This will mean warehouse space, and may involve keeping it warm or cold. There are also the risks. Flood, fire, frost, mice, insects and bacteria damage products; employees and burglars steal them. Clearly there are many potential savings in cutting inventory to a minimum.
- *Obsolete goods.* Longer-lasting fresh produce, greater shelf stability or, where relevant, greater consistency, can reduce the cost of obsolete or returned goods.

Deciding which aspects of value count as benefits and which count as costs can become somewhat arbitrary. For example, is a more efficient pack form a benefit or a reduction in costs? Are terms of payment a benefit or a cost saving? The best answer is how they are perceived and considered by the client. But, in fact, counting something as an additional benefit rather than a reduction in cost will usually not affect the outcome of the analysis significantly. The important point is that all the different influences on benefits and costs are included. The objective of thinking in terms of product, non-product, benefits and costs is to try and stretch thought beyond product and price.

Assessing the various benefits and costs to the customer is an essential part of trade marketing, performed by every account person in every presentation to the retail buyer. There is a technique (called 'value analysis') which aggregates information on value in a more formal and explicit way. Value analysis is conceptually quite simple, but involves laborious calculations. There are user-friendly computer aids (such as 'FMCG Value')

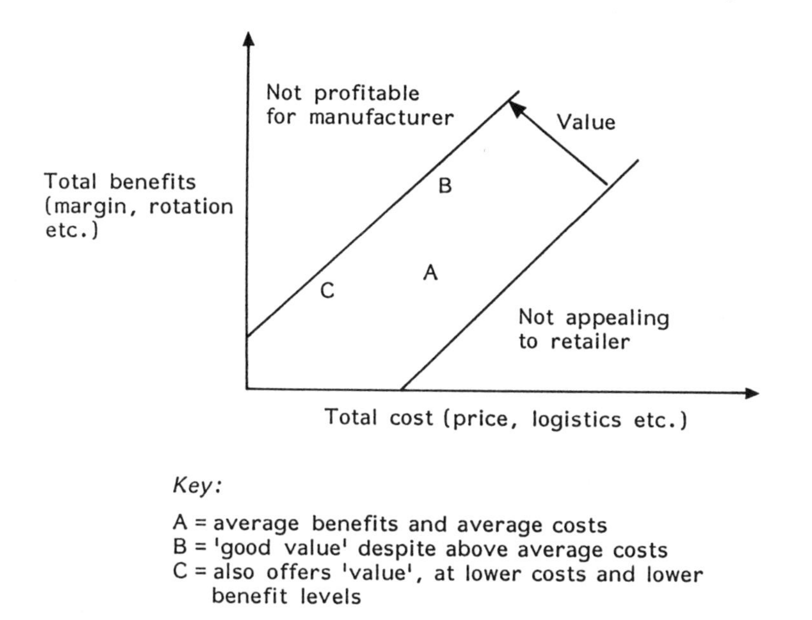

Figure 10.2 *Plotting competitors in terms of the value they offer to a certain group of customers*

which demand simply the inputs and will then plot various competitive position graphics, for defined segments etc., and allow rapid treatment of 'What if' questions.

Using such a computer package it is particularly revealing to calculate the benefit and cost indices for a number of competitors, and visualise the results by plotting them on a graph as shown at Fig. 10.2.

Value analysis creates a model of the value provided by a brand to a customer. By comparing estimated improvements in value with the estimated cost of investments needed to bring them about, the analyses suggest the most cost-efficient route to creating value for this customer.

Providing value, in the end, will usually depend to some extent on co-operation. The client (retailer) may have to share some information, or join in operations which end up making the supply chain more efficient. Value analysis may provide the impetus and forum for such co-operative discussions.

10.2.1.3 Value Analysis Compared to Direct Product Profitability

On their side, retailers are becoming more sophisticated in the way they assess the economic value of a product. Ushered in by the vast improvements in information technology (IT), many retailers operate some type of direct product profitability (DPP) analysis. The objective is to make a truer analysis of a product's contribution to the store's overall profits. To do this it is necessary to allocate costs, as exactly as possible, directly to the products that cause them. These costs include all those listed above: shelfspace, unpacking and stacking costs, inventory holding costs (financial and physical), handling costs, going right back to transportation and ordering costs.

DPP was pioneered by large manufacturers (for example Procter & Gamble) in their efforts to demonstrate to retailers the real value of their products. Many large retailers have now adopted some form of DPP, at least for part of their range, and usually acknowledge that it gives significantly different readings on 'value' or 'worth' from those obtained by looking just at gross profit. This information on the real profits created by a product is used as the basis for stocking, promoting and pricing decisions.

DPP is easier to describe in theory than it is to apply in all the complexity and commotion of the logistics chain from factory warehouse to supermarket check-out. In practice many arbitrary decisions have to be made about what costs should be allocated, and how they should be calculated. These arbitrary elements mean that different systems come up with different answers. The objectives of the parties making the arbitrary decisions naturally impacts on how those decisions are made. Retailers are often unwilling to reveal the details of their calculations to their suppliers, who may come up with rather different estimates themselves.

Value analysis is a more strategic exercise than DPP, with a broader definition of value. DPP is an exercise in accountancy which aims to optimise the short-term profitability. DPP usually makes no attempt to encompass qualitative or strategic reasons for offering a product, and does not integrate the notion of category considerations. By contrast, value analysis aims to include all the strategic aspects which should form part of the broader stocking decision.

10.2.2 Customer Profitability

Customer profitability is the second element of trade marketing. When considering whether the value offered to each customer can or should be improved, it is essential to appreciate the profitability of each customer. For many FMCG manufacturers, analysing customer profitability is a new demand.

Direct customer profitability has a similar logic to that of the retailer's direct product profitability. The logic is that costs should be allocated as nearly as possible to the activities (i.e. selling to a certain customer) that generate those costs. Direct customer profitability can share the same drawback as DPP: that it tends to focus on the short term, and ignores strategic issues. We come back to the strategic considerations below.

A manufacturer wants to maximise both the value offered to customers, and the profits earnt through satisfying those customers. Any activity which increases one without diminishing the other is a good thing. Manufacturers who become serious about trade marketing become more rigorous and systematic in the analysis of both components, to maximise the sum of customer satisfaction and customer profitability.

Under brand management brands are not allowed to subsidise one another, except for specific, strategic reasons. Under customer management, customers should not be allowed to cross subsidise, again unless there are explicit strategic reasons for doing so.

The costs of running an account are influenced by much more than the product provided and the price: volumes (ordered and per delivery), discounts, bonuses, salesforce attention, storage, merchandising support, promotions, returns, order processing and disputes all affect net profit.

A brand may be profitable despite being sold unprofitably to some clients. There might be a good reason for servicing less profitable clients, but this should be done knowingly. Conventional accounting practices often make it awkward to allocate costs accurately to the account that incurred them. When companies are organised into function-based departments, the associated costs are difficult to allocate by customer account. As a result, the most basic information such as which accounts generate highest profit and which are operating at a loss may be inaccessible.

Customer profitability analysis implies finding out the cost of customer servicing. For example, what is the cost of supplying different product mixes, delays in payment, discounts related to size of order, unique products/packaging for specific customers or different delivery requirements? Centralising this sort of information with the people, often the trade marketers, who decide how to allocate these resources, is a significant change in accounting practices for many companies. The salesforce is not used to having this type of profit responsibility. In many companies the responsibility for, say, delays of payment deals, is actually kept away from the sales department, because they are not felt competent to deal with such important financial commitments.

Once the information becomes available and centralised with the people responsible for account profitability they will become more sensitive to which accounts are less profitable, and be able to work out why this is so. This knowledge will influence how future trade marketing investments are allocated across accounts. What new accounts should be sought? It can lead to a more precise discount policy, more effective use of salesforce time and more effective use of marketing investment.

Understanding the profitability of individual accounts can suggest new bases for negotiation. If an account *is* unprofitable, what minimum changes are needed to make it profitable? Account-based profitability should also reveal the precise impact of losing the account. In negotiations, it is helpful to know the cost of not reaching an agreement.

Client profitability analysis has one clear weakness. Seeking only the most profitable activities or accounts might lead to an unacceptable degree of dependence. Using simply the criteria of profitability might point to an optimal solution of one low-cost customer. Anyone who has had the experience of losing a major client or of a partner exploiting their dominant position, hears alarm bells at this point. The simple quantitative analysis of profits has to be augmented by a qualitative sense of the stability of this source of income.

10.2.3 Dependence

Dependence is a permanent threat in industrial markets. If a supplier deals with, say, only 20 large clients, it is inevitable that a few will account for significant proportions of its output. To some extent, dependence is a natural part of trade marketing, which has to be accepted. On the other hand it makes sense to undertake a permanent effort to minimise dependence and the risk it poses. The following six suggestions illustrate industrial-type thinking where a small number of clients is the reality, but handling the relationships with those clients can minimise the risks of sudden changes in demand. The first three are directly concerned with avoiding dependence, the latter three are based on the idea of transforming dependence into interdependence.

(1) Balancing the 'consumer' portfolio with the 'industrial' one. As shown above, value can be created in different ways. From a value-creating perspective 'advertising to enhance brand loyalty' and 'terms of payment concessions' might have equally beneficial effects, for an equal investment. When dependence is thrown into the equation, increasing consumer pull is more attractive because it also helps decrease dependence. The trade marketer is stronger with a portfolio containing some 'power' brands and some tactical brands, and thus should resist any demotions from the first category to the second, despite pressure from clients pushing in the opposite direction.
(2) Dependence can be counterbalanced by developing close relations with several retailers, and in particular, a spread across different countries. An international producer has greater reserves in a power struggle with a national retailer. It follows that the development of close transnational links between retailers should be discouraged. Similarly, developing alternative 'routes to market' has a strategic value, beyond the immediate sales and profits derived from these alternate channels.
(3) Trade marketing sometimes involves selecting and thus deselecting sets of retailers, forming greater alliances with certain clients and allocating less resources to some others. This will link the supplier's growth to certain chains within the total trade market. Thus trade marketers need to be attentive to developments in the retail market. They must be able to predict the success of retailers, and aim to invest

strategically to build the best relations with retailers who are going to survive and grow, or be of special importance in their field in the future.

Moving from dependence into interdependence:

(4) The closer the relations in terms of logistics, joint initiatives to minimise inventory, sharing data, etc., the greater the value that a supplier can give. Other suppliers will be left behind in the race to deliver the retailer with value. Interdependence is achieved when co-operating more with a different supplier represents switching costs to the client. Whenever retailers' freedom to switch around their source of supply is to some degree restricted, the supplier's position is correspondingly stronger. Conversely, many retailers want to control more of the logistics chain, because this leaves them freer to swap supplier.

(5) Suppliers can similarly make themselves more secure if they provide goods based on patents, technology, or low costs that are hard to match. A retailer owning a brand has to guarantee the safety of its product and must guarantee a consistent quality. As a brand owner who does not own its own production facilities, it has a weakness in this regard. In some markets, such as prepared meals, where production standards, hygiene and safety are of paramount importance, a retailer and supplier can become mutually dependent. Similarly, if the consumer identifies a certain precise taste with a retailer chocolate bar or biscuit, the retailer cannot simply substitute a chocolate or biscuit 'of equal quality', disregarding the expectations of customers. As a protection, some industrial customers insist on dividing their orders 80/20 between two suppliers. This enables them to gain economies of scale from the bigger supplier, but gives them a permanent alternative source as a guarantee against (their) dependence. In industrial marketing, a supplying company is more secure the more they concentrate on products of a quality or specificity hard to replace exactly from another source of supply.

(6) Building relationships. FMCG manufacturers try to build relationships with their final consumers. Many have a

customer service department with a free telephone number, a PR department, and some even run clubs. In all communications and actions the company endeavours to present itself as a permanent and trustworthy entity. In trade marketing, building relationships with customers is, if anything, more crucial. Many industrial marketers (such as, say, pharmaceutical companies with prescribers, or travel companies with travel agents) spend huge amounts trying to make individual employees of their client companies feel positive towards them. Naturally, handled in a crass way this can create a negative impression. Handled thoughtfully and moderately it is a natural and positive part of business.

When trade marketing is selling oriented there is little to be gained by developing greater communication. When retailers are being offered sophisticated own labels, and once retailers are convinced of the necessity to squeeze efficiencies from the logistics chain, greater communication stands to benefit both parties. One of our manufacturer clients has employed us to run seminars using our STORWARS simulation for its executives and a mixture of invited executives, from retailers and selected (non-competing) manufacturing companies. More and more sophisticated products (such as fax machines and portable telephones) are being sold by mass retailers, and in these fields the joint benefits of training and information for store personnel is clear. If there are mutual gains to be made from understanding and co-operation, and mutual losses to be suffered from inflexibility and misunderstanding, then creating a forum in which each party can learn about the other and experiment with possible ways of working together reflects only the highest motives.

10.3 CONFLICTS BETWEEN TRADE MARKETING AND CONSUMER MARKETING

There is an inevitable tension between the marketing and sales functions in a company. For a long time marketing executives have been preaching to the rest of the organisation that success in the marketplace depends on the whole organisation becoming consumer driven. Just when final victory seems to be in sight, they find that the sales/trade marketing function has found its second wind.

The functions of trade and consumer marketing frequently overlap and potentially conflict. Both functions have an opinion on pricing, allocation of marketing budgets, packaging, product positioning, etc. When trade marketing and consumer marketing are in conflict, trade marketing will often 'win' (especially at the end of the year) simply because its effects are usually more immediate. Trade marketing puts more emphasis on negotiations (rather than balance of power) and achieving short-term sales volumes. Trade marketers propose price cuts and incentives to retailers with the objective of hitting volume targets set for the quarter. Consumer marketing is more often concerned with objectives which pay back on a longer-term timescale—building brand image, maintaining premium prices. As observed in connection with brand extensions (Chapter 4), many FMCG companies are hostage to their short-term profit figures, and top management is highly sensitive to the payback time on alternative investments.

Consumer marketing is not some sacred cow that should always be fed and protected. Our point is simply that, as trade marketing is of growing importance, and as there are areas where the two disciplines will lead the company in opposite directions, some mechanism has to be found to strike a harmonious balance between the two. Below we look at the areas for potential conflict.

10.3.1 Competition for Resources

In many companies, the marketing budget is set as a fixed amount which then has to be divided between trade marketing and consumer marketing. Thus the diversion of investments into marketing directed at the retailer reduces the resources available for brand-building investments towards the consumer. The trend and effect of promotional budgets 'going below the line' has been much ventilated in the press. Some figures are shown in Fig. 10.3.

Just as important but less visible than the out-of-pocket investments, is the investment of time and energy. More and

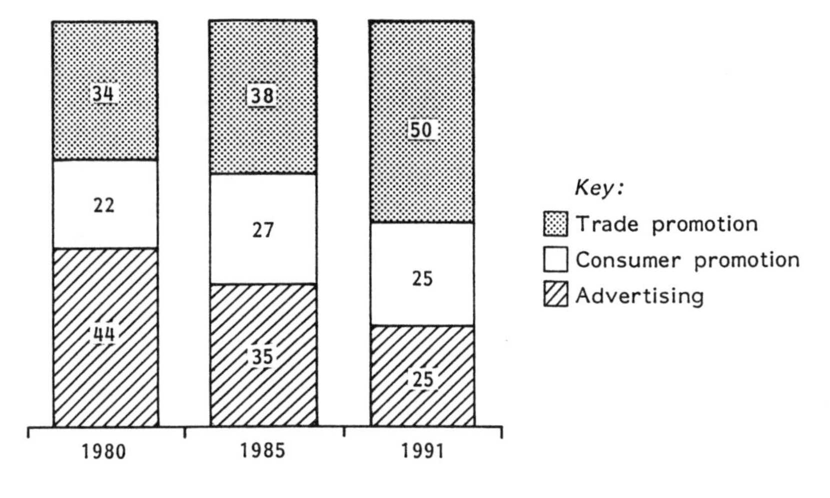

Figure 10.3 *Advertising versus promotional spending for US food companies* [2]

more brand management time is devoted to co-ordinating tailor-made promotions for different retailers and responding to numerous retailer requests for changes in the names, numbers or prices to be printed on packs.

10.3.2 Producing for Retailer Own Brands

Trade marketers see own label as something that the retail customer values and that the company can satisfy, often profitably. Trade marketing can have a point: the French coffee manufacturer Jaques Vabre built a strong position for its brands, via a complex trading arrangement with Carrefour. Jaques Vabre agreed to produce Carrefour's own-label coffee and in return Carrefour supported Jaques Vabre's range with premium shelfspace. This arrangement seems in the long term to have benefited both parties. The trade marketer, keen to offer clients the most competitive value that the company can provide, will have a view on the quality and technology that should be supplied. Trade marketers may be willing also to promise resources in terms of development facilities and time.

The consumer marketer views own label as a potentially deadly threat. Higher quality own label should be resisted at all costs.

Own label competes for resources with the marketing department's own-brand development projects. Even old-product development (reformulating, repackaging) presents the same dilemma: should the own label get the latest novelty?

Own label can become a very emotional issue, creating warring factions in a company. The separated functions of trade and consumer marketing need to be brought together to be able to assess the risks and opportunities own label presents.

10.3.3 Pricing

Trade marketers can always boost the value they give to retailers by dropping their prices, or adding various bonuses, and they have a reputation for longing to do so. This longing can lead the trade marketer to ignore needs and objectives of consumer marketing. For example, from the consumer point of view, the product should form a defined part of a range with the correct price relative to other products in the range. Consumer marketers spend their careers justifying higher prices for their brands. Price is not simply money received, but also perception, positioning and the possibility to invest in brand-building activities for a profitable future.

10.3.4 New Products and Category Management

There are both consumer marketing reasons and trade marketing reasons for wishing to launch new products and brand extensions; they will not necessarily point to the same new products/extensions. From a trade point of view, completing the range by launching me-toos against competitive products might be interesting, from a consumer point of view, servicing new segments might be more attractive. The trade marketing group will get their ideas for new products from the trade, consumer marketing direct from the shopper. Since a new product has to be accepted by both groups, a new product development group should represent both sides.

10.3.5 Packaging

Packaging is another marketing variable of great interest both to retail customers and to end consumers. Packaging affects the retailer's handling costs and the amount of space taken on the shelves. For the consumer, packaging is a strong element of communication and often important to product use. The two interests are sometimes happily aligned, as in the case of ultra compact disposable nappies: as attractive to store managers as small-hipped toddlers are to their Mums. In many cases the tastes of the two customers are unhappily contradictory. Perrier must owe a large part of its consumer appreciation to its elegant and unique glass bottle. On the other hand, this same glass bottle (a) can break, (b) is heavy, (c) has a fat waist that pushes the bottles apart on the pallet.

Indeed, every sensuous curve in every supermarket bottle, creates useless empty space inside the square outers stacked in the retailers' lorries and storage facilities. For handling and close packing a cylindrical, or, indeed, squarish plastic bottle, such as that of Vittel, is far better. For luxury goods such as foie gras or wrinkle removing eye contouring cream, a large pack is attractive to the consumer, greedy for more. For example, a cardboard box containing a glass jar of L'Oréal's Plénitude, takes up nearly ten times the volume of the net contents. Halving the width of the pack would increase its trade appeal, but bring home a hard truth to the consumer. Another potential conflict arises over strength of packaging. Retailers want to avoid spoilt and damaged products, and these days also avoid criminal tampering with the products on shelf; consumers often complain that packs are difficult to open.

Consumer appeal is an important element of the value that a product delivers to a retailer. Integrating this appeal into the trade marketing's strategic triangle is clearly a delicate challenge.

10.3.6 Targeting Retailers

Trade marketers will view the retail trade as a market with segments, and view some customers as more desirable than others. Desirability will be based on criteria such as size, and particularly volume, and the easiness of servicing. More sophisticated retailers, with modern logistics systems will be seen as 'excellent' customers. They re-order by EDI, they operate from their own centralised warehouses, they have a triple-A credit rating.

Looking at retailers as mindspace competitors, these top retailers are precisely the ones that pose the most threat. A consumer marketing executive might not choose to give this group most favoured trading partner status. Less sophisticated retailers might be given relatively greater priority, following a policy of developing alternative distribution channels.

10.4 MANAGING TWO LAYERS OF CUSTOMERS

Trade marketing is clearly essential for marketing companies which are to thrive in a climate where the distribution is winning greater and greater influence.

However, learning to straddle two very different approaches to business is hard. It is not sufficient for a company to have a trade marketing function and a consumer marketing function, each of which does its best for all the lines produced. Manufacturing companies have to integrate their marketing to retailers with their marketing to consumers.

It is necessary to assess the relative importance of the two markets for each brand. Some brands will fulfil different roles to others, some stay mostly consumer, some go mostly industrial, some have a strategic role, and some a merely tactical one. Brands are no longer automatically the centralising heart of the business. Some may be rented or sold to retailers, while those with strong consumer franchises will be sustained and strengthened to oppose the retailers' domination. The changed climate is complex.

Industrial marketing (balancing value, profitability and dependence) is itself a subtle and complex challenge. Good salesmen are often not trained, and perhaps not naturally inclined, to understand the logistics operations that have so much impact on both value and profit. Information technology is becoming more important to logistics, but those expert in information technology may be at sea in the practical and commercial aspects of selling and servicing clients. It is fair to say that, at the time of writing, few organisations and few individuals are experienced in each aspect and in combining them together. A new and extremely complex speciality is being created by the changing marketplace. This new speciality implies understanding and integrating both consumer and industrial marketing disciplines which manages to respond simultaneously to two layers of customers.

It took companies a generation to develop consumer marketing expertise to the level found today in FMCG companies. No doubt it will take another generation to develop the techniques and to train the managers who will eventually raise this 'integrated marketing management' to its highest levels.

Note

(1) Lois Therrien, 'Want shelf space at the supermarket? Ante up', *Business Week*, 7 August 1989, p. 46.

(2) This chart (Fig. 10.3) was created using figures published in Salomon Brothers Research Report (Food), June 1993; obtained from Donnelley Marketing.

11
The New Order and its Challenges

In more and more countries, the retail industry is becoming more concentrated and more sophisticated. This trend is based on social changes, technology and the managerial sophistication that has revolutionised the retail industry. Once large-volume, high-investment chains have used up the differential advantage provided by location, they slowly discover that the surest and most powerful way to create loyal, and thus profitable business, is to offer their customers uniquely appealing products that are uniquely available in their stores.

At one extreme, major chains develop their own quality brands and fresh products and their own self-conscious philosophy of consumer reassurance. At the other extreme, equally profitable chains, positioned at the opposite end of the price–quality spectrum, handle hardly more than a handful of well-known manufacturers' brands. Their stores, filled with pallets still bearing most of their outer wrapping, offer 'false' brands, unknown and unadvertised, or half-hearted mimics of brand leaders. The disturbing commonalty between these two extremes is their lack of dependence on traditional manufacturer brands. In between are other stores who still rely on their location and manufacturers' brands to attract shoppers, but the success of the own brands sets an example which no modern retailer can ignore. Whenever retailers have seriously attempted to implement strategies which involve ousting manufacturer brands, they have succeeded and profited. The process has led them to compete, very successfully, with the traditional providers of brands.

This new and powerful source of 'mindspace' competition has come at an unfortunate time for manufacturers. Manufacturers were already suffering something of a crisis in branding in Europe and the USA. After decades of profitable growth, FMCG markets are hitting middle age: minimal growth and minimal product differences have led to brand proliferation and hypersegmentation. Umbrella branding and brand extension have left many ranges vulnerable to the umbrella branding that retailers can do more cheaply than manufacturers.

Companies now have to work out how their brands can be exploited most efficiently in countries where retailers are competing to provide brand reassurance. Each brand needs to be re-assessed in the context of a mature market, eroded quality differences, blasé consumers, hypersegmentation and retail type-2 competition. Companies who have always operated under the traditional brand paradigm, for all their brands, now have to consider whether this paradigm will continue to hold, especially for their weaker brands. Brands have to be reviewed through the retailer's eyes as part of its 'category'.

The changed environment also demands that manufacturers take a more proactive stance towards retailing and shopping behaviour. Manufacturers must consider whether they can influence retailers' ability to build strong brands. Manufacturers may be able to influence the intensity or type of retail competition and thus improve their power balance. Manufacturers may be able to influence the way retailers position their own brands. Can a greater understanding of shopping behaviour lead to ways of influencing shopping habits? Manufacturers should certainly apply their experience in advanced retail markets to keep control of mindspace in countries where retailers are not yet strong.

Meeting these challenges has implications for the way manufacturers are organised. If powerful consumer brands are no longer the unique organisational goal, what type of organisation is appropriate for integrating trade and consumer needs? Should the company move to an organisation focused on categories rather than brands, in order to share more exactly the retailer's point of view? Should 'consumer' brands and 'industrial' brands be handled by the same organisation or separately?

The challenges of brand management (including NPD) in the new environment and proactive strategies towards the retail trade are the two main subjects of this last chapter.

11.1 BRAND MANAGEMENT IN THE CHANGED ENVIRONMENT

Brands are needed by all consumers, however cynical they like to imagine themselves. No shopper wants to make a hundred new choices at every weekly shop, and the huge choice available in a modern supermarket makes quick recognition and guarantees of consistent taste and quality essential for everybody. Whether the shopper prefers a retailer's branded proposition, or that of manufacturers, depends on personality and beliefs, but also, very significantly, on the product field.

Branding provides three services to the consumer: identification, quality assurance and associations. Retailers are perfectly able to provide the first of these services. The second branding service depends on: (a) being able to acquire high-quality products, and (b) being able to reassure. In product areas where the technology for making good products is widely diffused, and the assessment of the product is simple for the consumer, retailers reassure very well. Retailers have problems when the technology for making excellent products is held by a small number of large manufacturers, or where specific functions are sought and their assessment is rather difficult.

The third branding service, associations, poses a special set of problems for retailers. Retailers tend to have functional, good-value images, and where this fits with the branding need, they can provide satisfactory associations. When the associations required involve image or answer a need for identification or fun, retailers are held back by their down-to-earth images. In these areas the critical mass of the manufacturers allows them to create the desired images via advertising, and invest in understanding their markets to optimise their psychographic positionings and innovations.

In Chapter 8 we looked at the battle for mindspace, the advantages of the retailer and the advantages of the manufacturer in providing the branding service. They are summarised in Table 11.1.

Table 11.1 *Comparison of the advantages of manufacturers and retailers in their competition to provide the consumer with branding in FMCGs*

	Manufacturers	Retailers
Sources of power	Critical mass and specialisation: • Technology • Media advertising • Consumer understanding	Owning the stores: • Direct communication • Control of marketing mix variables • Information
Advantages	• Superior quality • Image • Variety, choice, novelty • Ubiquity	Efficiency in branding for product areas where the advantages listed to the left are not dominant
Product fields where advantages dominate	• Costly and rapidly evolving technology • Specific function and hard to assess (e.g. toothpaste) • Image important: brand name visible after purchase • Variety, sense of choice important (e.g. hair care) • Fun, novelty important • Sold through variety of distribution channels	• Real product differences small and easily assessed • Spare capacity exists at manufacturer level • Product is chosen and used without need for prestige/communication value, e.g. spaghetti, toothpaste • Low-interest purchases, habitual • Sold largely through mass merchandisers

Consumers will 'buy' branding from the organisation which can provide it most cost efficiently. Consumers are willing, to a variable degree, to trade-off some and any of their three branding needs for a lower price.

Hard-discount retailers provide branding at the most minimal level, and most quality manufacturers are not seriously threatened by their success. There always has been a price sector of the FMCG market, where quality is modest and margins are low. Hard discounters provide a good ratio of value, but they do not compete head-on with mainstream quality brands. The brand strategies long used by manufacturers are quite adequate to compete successfully with the hard discounter's own label.

The situation is completely different at the other extreme of the retail market where Sainsbury's, Safeway, Tesco, Carrefour, Albert Hein, Migros, Loblaws and Wal-Mart compete for the consumer's mind. Against their challenge, manufacturers can adopt three different strategies to develop their brands:

- *Premium strategy*. In product fields where technology, image or innovation are important, they can follow the value-adding tactics that have served well for years. They can justify higher branding costs with higher brand satisfaction, functional and emotional. They should resist sharing the premium brand technology with retailers.
- *Value strategy*. Manufacturers can compete directly with retailers on overall value. They can aim to provide the product, with its necessary branding, at a price which the retailer cannot match via industrial suppliers and store branding.
- *Industrial strategy*. Manufacturers can accept that for certain products (even high-quality ones) the most efficient route to market is via the retailer. The retailer will provide some or all of the branding services (name, reassurance, packaging, merchandising), and manufacturer and retailer will share the profits (which may be considerable) in proportion to their contribution to the overall added value.

In this list of three options, there may be no viable choice for certain 'second-tier' brands. Manufacturers have to take a long, hard look at their brand portfolios and assess which brands cannot survive the squeeze between the premium brands, the value brands and the industrial (i.e. tertiary and retailer controlled type-1 and type-2) brands. These second-tier brands can still be of value to the company, but not under the classic brand paradigm.

At the moment, most companies treat major brands and minor brands in much the same way. A minor brand is treated as a scaled-down version of a major brand, with smaller budgets but with the same objectives and similar marketing actions: advertising, promotions, etc. The brand manager of a less successful brand is less senior than the brand manager of a power brand, but has the same job.

Each brand must be competitive in the value it delivers to retail customers. FMCG manufacturers are expert at creating consumer value: the challenge now is to understand, in addition, what is the most efficient way to create retail value for each of their brands. The value of premium brands is dependent on their consumer mindspace, and for these brands the traditional 'brand paradigm' still holds, with perhaps some small modifications. For these brands the most efficient way to motivate retailers is by winning the battle for mindspace. For second-tier brands, consumer pull falls below the threshold which retailers believe they can afford to ignore. In markets where consumers are hardly able to discern any differences in quality or value, money spent directly with the consumer may simply be thrown away.

Resources have to be allocated between consumer and trade for each brand. There is a risk of falling between two stools: both consumer and trade objectives demand investment, and it is possible to spend in both areas without beating competitors in either.

Reassessing the brand portfolio is an urgent task in the current climate. Brands should not all be managed in the same way, with the same objectives. For each brand it is necessary to define an achievable and useful role, with respect to the consumer and with respect to the trade. Appropriate management must then be given to each type of brand.

11.1.1 Premium Brands

Premium brands have a strong enough consumer differential advantage for this to create an argument for the trade to value the brand, i.e. the perceived cost to the consumer of switching brand is such that non-stocking will reduce the appeal of the store. At the extreme, there are brands (often called 'power' brands) which have such strong consumer loyalty that they become virtually unavoidable to the trade (Fig. 9.5, page 212, which suggested that 21% of chocolate drink purchasers would object to the absence of Nesquick).

Premium brands have some qualities which retailers cannot match. For example, instant coffee is a weak area for retailers because the only people with the technical know-how to match the big brand owners are the big brand owners. Similarly powerful are consumer brands which depend so much on image or personality that brand advertising is an essential part of the appeal, and retail image a turn off. In some markets variety and choice are provided by the specialists, and these carefully

Table 11.2 *Market share rank compared to net margins for UK grocery brands*

Market share rank	Net margin %
1	17.9
2	2.8
3	−0.9
4	−5.9

Reproduced, with permission, from P. Doyle, 'Building successful brands: The strategic option', *Journal of Consumer Marketing*, Vol. 7, No. 2, Spring 1990.

differentiated brands are necessary to the retailer to satisfy this need for choice among its customers. In some markets (such as toys, chilled desserts) there is a significant 'novelty sector' which depends for its existence on innovation and paid-for communication.

However, it is more possible to sustain a premium brand if it is the leader rather than follower in its market. A brand leader is more able to hold its consumers through investing in brand-building actions. The second, third and fourth brands will be squeezed both by the branded competition and the retailer-controlled brands. In other words, traditional premium brands can still do well, but in the changed environment there is space for fewer of them (see Table 11.2).

Premium brands have to take note of the changing climate. The fact that some companies (or parts of companies) are following purely industrial strategies, using cheaply created retail mindspace to sell quality products, puts enormous pressure on the other players. If a retailer procures an own brand of a quality comparable to the brand leader, but sells it at a lower price, it can set a new standard of price-quality for the market. If the ratio of quality to price offered to the consumer improves, even brands which clearly offer extra qualities, have to reduce their price or improve their quality (or both) to stay on the 'iso-value line' of consumer expectations. (See Fig. 11.1.)

Over time there is a trend for the value ratio to improve from the consumers' point of view (see Fig. 11.1). This is productivity and progress. All brands have to keep in line or suffer sales declines. In the past, the iso-value line was defined at the top right by the big manufacturers and the brand leaders, at the

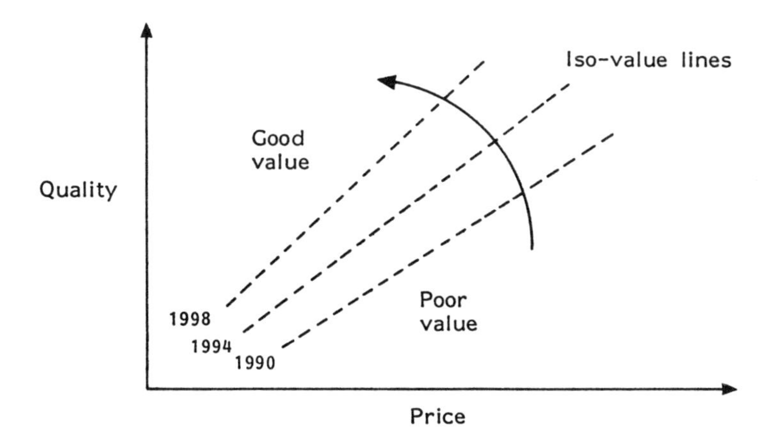

Figure 11.1 *Brands are forced to offer comparable ratios of benefits to price 'you get what you pay for'. This ratio improves over time, now often pushed by retailer brands, particularly in recent years at the top right (see arrow)*

bottom left by smaller producers and own label. Nowadays, the top half of the line is being rotated over to the left by retailer-controlled brands. Retailers can offer exceptionally good value because they have hiked a lift down the learning curve by exploiting manufacturers' excess capacity, and speeded their rise up the mindspace curve by umbrella branding.

In 1993, there were a series of incidents where the stock market capitalisation value of blue chip FMCG companies dropped precipitately following price cuts forced on the companies. Two of these events were dubbed 'Marlboro Friday', and 'BSN Tuesday', though Philip Morris and BSN were not actually the worst-affected companies. The message of these stock market re-evaluations is that even managers of power brands can no longer afford to overestimate their brands' ability to justify a premium. The price margin between premium brands and their quality own label competition needs to be held down to a level which does not become too taxing to brand users. The trade-off between volume sales and price premium is more critical because the perceived quality differences are eroded. Innovation is often bounded: cost efficiency and exploiting the economies of scale and internationalisation are the only ways out.

In addition to more circumspect premiums, brand management must work through the retail trade to hold on to control of the marketing mix variables, which day in day out create usage, habit and mindspace for FMCGs, including premium brands. As the trade has become more powerful, companies have tended to channel more of their marketing budgets towards the trade, and this has happened across the board. In general, given an increase in retail power, more marketing investment should be allocated to the retailer. However, this process is not equal across all brands: the balance will vary for each of the brands in the portfolio. For premium brands, there is a risk that they are weakened by moving too much of the budget below the line.

The only good argument for investing some of the marketing budget with the trade is with the objective of controlling mindspace: motivating retailers to put their in-store push behind the brands. Marketing investment allocated to retailers should always be 'earmarked' towards shelf position, merchandising, in-store media support, etc., rather than being given with no strings attached. Incentives which encourage the retailer to buy and sell-on greater quantities are equally desirable, because these too will engage retailers to use their in-store variables to push the brand.

Premium brands may not deliver the retailer the best DPP. These brands motivate the retailer by creating and expanding the market and by being what consumers want and expect to find in their store whenever they go shopping.

11.1.2 Value Brands

The idea of moving to a philosophy of exceptional value, to coalesce consumer preference segments, was discussed in Chapter 4, as a way of reacting to hypersegmentation. Instead of trying to add value by targeting specific groups of consumers with more and more tailored products, the value company offers consumers the chance to compromise their preferences, to some degree, in favour of noticeably lower prices. Hard discounting retailers follow this reasoning, and attract a significant proportion of shoppers. Manufacturing companies can also re-engineer their operations and products to provide an exceptional value ratio.

A value strategy can provide an effective platform for competing both against premium brands, and against the value proposition of retailers. Retailers are efficient in procuring their products from low-cost producers and efficient in the way they provide branding, but manufacturers have greater critical mass, which is also important to efficiency. If the manufacturing company can really obtain the most efficient cost structures, as a result of its scale and commitment, it may be able to beat retailers at their own game. In countries where retailers have no own labels, or only type-1 own labels, a major manufacturer occupying the value position may be the best way to inhibit further own-label growth.

In a market-oriented company, production follows from the information provided by market research. In a value-oriented company, the marketing people have to become more sensitive to the needs of their colleagues in production. The marketing department of Mars confectionery does not brief the R&D department for luxury or novelty brands. Marketing at Mars means developing high-volume brands which capitalise on Mars's production strengths. A 'Power' brand according to Mars is one which will stack up so much technical learning and experience that Mars will be able to bring it to the market at a quality and price that no other company in the world can match.

The marketing department in a value company must look for large segments, find the common denominator and isolate the product functions which are essential to giving satisfaction, i.e. concentrate on features which create value at an efficient cost to the consumer. Consumer research efforts can be devoted to finding new uses, new usage occasions, or new target groups for a given product, rather than to finding niches for new products or brand extensions.

Another important role of value marketing is to iron out seasonal or other fluctuations in demand so that production capacity is always optimally used. Promotions and quantity discounts can themselves cause big fluctuations in demand, and thus production inefficiencies. Marketing for value brands has to plan pricing and promotional strategies that are efficient to implement and smooth rather than upset delivery patterns. As with EDLP for retailers, simplified pricing strategies are part of a manufacturer's value cost structure and therefore appropriate to a manufacturer obsessed with occupying the lowest cost position.

Marketing and R&D savings are made because relatively less of each are needed—it is easier to sell products offering exceptional value, and a technological benefit for the consumer is not needed. Value will move the product off the shelf. The company needs to be at the frontier in terms of production technology, but its products do not need to be the most sophisticated in the market. Mars, Amstrad and Aldi do not provide technologically advanced products or services to the consumer.

R&D is not directed to anticipating consumer wants, but to serving existing wants more efficiently. The challenge is to provide the familiar and known cheaper than anyone else. R&D's task is to produce a quality acceptable to the market, at unmatchable prices, by cutting out more esoteric functions and designing for efficient production. Amstrad owed its years of phenomenal growth and profits to designs which cut production costs, e.g. using only one power source for all the elements in hi-fi, or simplifying the architecture in computers. Value-oriented companies eliminate non-essentials, design products which share components, and transfer some of the costs (such as delivery, assembly) to the consumer. Value-oriented companies streamline their product range, and are willing to drop last year's lines in favour of new, confident that they can make the best choice for the consumer. Procter & Gamble, who now espouse a value strategy, claim they have reduced or are reducing their product range by 25% in many categories. The same search for value has to be applied to all areas of operation: management, distribution, pricing (simpler and more uniform: deals and promotions cost management time and effort to run).

In international markets, faced with poorer consumers, the value-oriented company will choose a quality and price at a lower level than in a high-income country, but still representing the same value ratio. Thus Procter & Gamble launched Pampers 'Uni' in Brazil, where Ultra Pampers would have been too costly for the average family.[1]

Profit margins are not necessarily lower on value-oriented brands. A value-driven company that gets its costs down does not have to accept a tight margin to ensure its leading price position. Kwik Save, Ratner's (made-to-a-price jewellery) and

Amstrad all enjoyed years of relatively high profitability and return on shareholders' equity while following uncompromisingly low price strategies. The low profits go to the companies that pussy-foot around in the no-man's land between the differentiated, premium brands and the cost-based, excellent-value brands.

11.1.3 Second-tier Brands

Great brand manufacturers, such as Unilever, Procter & Gamble, Danone, Allied Lyon, Nestlé and Reckitt & Colman, all own fistfuls of premium brands which derive their power from their consumer franchises. However, even these great brand machines all inevitably own a suitcase-full of lesser brands, picked up from acquisitions, at the end of their life cycle or brands that simply never made it. Some smaller companies are being forced to recognise that they have no true premium brands, capable of motivating the distribution according to the old brand paradigm. In many companies, big and small, managers in charge of third and fourth brands, are finding that the added value they can create for their lesser brands is insufficient to hold on to share.

The defining characteristic of a second-tier brand is that it cannot justify sufficient investment to gain momentum. Marketing budgets have already been trimmed, compared to previous years, and the share of voice achieved compared to the brand leaders is insufficient to hold share. This leads to a downward spiral. Traditional brand management feels demoralised because they are fighting against a trend that they cannot turn around with the resources available to them. When brands do not earn a high margin they cannot support their identity with marketing inputs and have to cut their quality to reduce costs. Quality guarantee is a foundation stone of most long-successful brands, and disappointing quality flattens consumer perceptions of the market so that all products are perceived as being similar, equal and commodity. This perception makes it increasingly difficult for brands to differentiate themselves and they are sucked into further cost trimming and price cuts.

The changing environment for FMCGs means that some brands are simply unable to compete as traditional premium brands. They are squeezed of all profit or even margin by the category's power brands, retailer-controlled quality brands and tertiary brands (i.e. brands sold on a price platform, without consumer promotion or retail reassurance—also called 'cheapies' and 'false brands'). For these 'squeezed-out' brands the time is nigh to make an objective appraisal of their future. Lumping brand budgets together to sponsor corporate or umbrella campaigns does not deal with retail competition. Spending more and more on promotions until brand equity is totally used up means being slowly boiled alive.

Hopefully, even if the company's brands are too weak to thrive under the brand paradigm, the company still has resources that will have continuing relevance to a future which is already quite visible. There are ways to make an attractive proposition to retailers without having premium brands. Consumer differential advantage is just one part of the value equation, developing new retailer benefits is a new horizon of opportunity for exhausted or diminutive consumer brands.

For second-tier brands, the most effective marketing may be a hybrid of industrial and consumer marketing. This means most marketing moneys spent are spent behind tactical promotions and trade incentives. In certain retail climates, third, fourth and fifth national brands can have a role (see below). In markets where retailers compete strongly for mindspace, the best management for second-tier brands may be something radically different. Below we explore (in no particular order) eight options for re-deploying weaker brands such that they have a continuing value into the next century.

(1) Re-cycle name with NPD

If a name has some consumer awareness, liking and respect, but is currently attached to a product which needs little branding, it may be possible to exploit the name by transferring it to a new product with a more distinctive consumer benefit. This is similar to a brand extension (obviously, the name has to 'fit') except that in this case all the communication and promotion would concentrate on the new version. For example, not so long ago Lux soap (as used by movie stars) was a power brand. In the

USA and the UK, particularly, where the brand once marked its greatest successes, soap has become a commodity. The face- and body-care market has gone through a technical revolution: it is beyond credibility that a modern film star would attack her facial skin with soap. Unilever has recognised the hopelessness of consumer promotion of the soap, and has reused the name and rose motif on 'modern bath aids'.

(2) Offer exclusivity to one retail chain

Exclusivity is almost equivalent to selling the brand to a retail chain, except that the brand rights and production remain with the manufacturer. Once a retailer has exclusive rights it has the same interest in nourishing the brand's mindspace as it does with its own type-2 own brands. Cadbury's Waverly Mint Leaves thus retired from the hectic life of a premium brand to become exclusive to Woolworth's (a large confectionery outlet) in the UK. The brand is now enjoying a relaxed and profitable old age. In their competition against large brands, retailers can find common cause with small manufacturers, and small brands who are also struggling against the power of dominant brands. In fact retailers have an interest in supporting and encouraging weaker manufacturers. If smaller manufacturers are willing to seize the opportunity and accept retailers as their primary target market, this can provide them with a viable position against their traditional competition: large manufacturers.

This type of proposition is recognised explicitly in the following quotation from the annual report of Ahold (the dominant grocery retailer in Holland):

> Far-reaching co-operation will be particularly feasible with medium-size suppliers who are strongly marketing oriented. . . . Co-operation with major international suppliers will take place at a different level, chiefly because retailers cannot differentiate themselves with the products of these manufacturers.[2]

If a brand is willing to forgo some distribution it can consider becoming exclusive or semi-exclusive with a large retailer. Both parties have potential gains to make. The brand can ask for a stocking policy which favours it, or marketing mix effects in its favour, for example, that its competitor be out of stock, or priced high. The store, by having the brand exclusively can add the brand's CSB to its own CSS, and so increase its loyalty among buyers of that brand. This mechanism is, of course, exactly that of type-2 retail own brands. The manufacturer is stepping halfway to being an own brand while still keeping some autonomy and independence. This is a way of selling brand equity to a retailer without becoming totally dependent or subsumed. In some cases retailers have completely bought such brands.

(3) Sell brand

Some second-tier brands can be sold to another company with the muscle to make them viable as part of a range. Names with a classy history can often be more valuable if owned by a company with the muscle and technology to leverage them. Unilever has been highly successful in revitalising the old-fashioned name of Chesebrough Pond's Cold Cream, which would probably have faded away under its old ownership. The acquiring company could equally be a retailer: MFI furniture bought the names Hygena and Schreiber to put on its kitchen units. MFI had the muscle and distribution to exploit the high awareness of the brands.

Later in this chapter we look at category management and the goal of being 'category captain' as a way of increasing a manufacturer's weight in negotiations with the trade. As companies try to complete their offering in a category, buying small complementary brands is a quick route to augmenting their range. The value and profitability of a small brand can be restored if it is given a range role by the category captain. For example, United Biscuits has sold its UK chocolate business to Kraft (part of Philip Morris). UB wants to concentrate on biscuits and snacks, while Philip Morris is focusing on confectionery.[3]

(4) Target-selected channels

In some situations, where brands are distributed through different channels, there is scope for a brand which specialises in one of the channels. Smaller channels—for example, hair dressers, beauty salons, boutiques, chemists and pharmacies—respond positively to a range which is exclusive to them and denied to the more price-oriented competition. Targeting a specific channel can mean significant reduction in costs, and can also mean the opportunity to serve the channel needs more precisely. For example, a medium-priced national brand may still be welcome in independent supermarkets which do not have own labels, and who are relatively less courted by the larger manufacturers. Similarly, if sales are still moving well through vending machines or canteens and cafés but not supermarkets, it is better to cut costs by not trying to sell so widely, and concentrate on sizes or packs that are ideally suited to the needs of the selected channels.

(5) Tertiary (price) brand

In many product fields, a pattern of prices is emerging along the lines of that shown in Fig. 11.2.

Retailers price their type-2 own label at an index of 80 to 90 compared to the leading national brand, with premium and niche brands priced 10–20% above. A tertiary brand is then priced at 50–70% of the national brand, to answer to the hard-discounter competition and satisfy the price-oriented segment of the consumer market. If a company has the production costs to make it feasible, it may find a viable positioning by taking the second-tier brand's price (and quality) down to compete at type-1

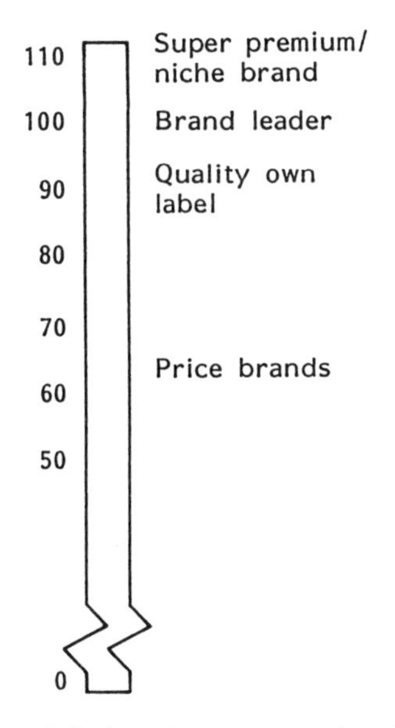

Figure 11.2 *Many retailers satisfy the price spectrum by offering brands priced in a pattern similar to that shown*

own label levels. Using a no longer competitive consumer brand as a tertiary brand with a price differential advantage may be an effective exploitation: mindspace hangs around so long that many consumers perceive the cheapie as being a real (advertised) brand at a false brand price. Princes' tinned tomatoes have taken this route, with great success. Coca-Cola Schweppes Beverages (UK) follows this strategy for a soft drink brand called Cresta. They have production and bottling efficiencies which mean they can sell their Cresta soft drink at exceptional value, a level own-label producers find hard to match. Cresta was an advertised brand (recall a polar bear observing 'It's frothy, man!') 20 years ago, but still finds its mindspace can be rekindled by shelfspace and an interesting price. Obviously this option is closed if the brand happens also to carry the company name (such as Cadbury's Bar Six). Most consumers do not associate Cresta with Schweppes or Coca-Cola.

Retailers have shown that shelfspace is the most economical way to gain mindspace for low-tech, good-value, low-image products. Retailers are interested in this proposition because price is a *sine qua non* of their image. They welcome tertiary brands to cover the price points in their ranges.

(6) Fighter brand

A small brand can sometimes justify its existence by being a strategic aid to a power brand, rather than being acceptably profitable in its own right. Power brands are constantly attacked by competitors wanting to take some segment of their consumers. This is often done by introducing some new attribute into the consumer's frame of reference. For example, detergents have been launched which destroy odours, or which do not pollute rivers. The power brand can be tempted to parry such attacks either by modifying its positioning in some way, say by adding these dimensions to its claims, or in some cases, by dropping its price. These are both risky and expensive tactics for a successful brand. In some cases it is possible instead to reposition a second-tier brand to put pressure on the attacker. Thus the 'fighter' brand could position itself on the main proposition of the attacking brand and at the same time offer a price differential. This will reduce the profit of the attacker and distract it from its assault on the power brand, leaving the power brand free to maintain its original positioning and pricing.

A fighter brand will often take a price positioning, to protect a major brand. This is different from a tertiary brand because the objective is not to earn money directly, but to protect a power brand by making life difficult for competitors. Normally the financial objective of a fighter brand will be only to break even. In their native Holland, Van den Berg market a fighter margarine called Zeeuws Meisje. This brand has a financial target of break even, and pays its way by absorbing volume from competitors. Without its presence, competitors would be stronger and freer in their competition against Van den Berg's premium brands.

(7) Managing for cash

Trying to manage a second-tier brand as a premium brand is pushing water uphill. It is a drain on company resources, and a continual source of disappointment to the executives involved. False hope may be derived from the continuing loyalty of some users, who recognise distinct qualities and benefits in this brand.

The solution in such cases may be to give up the struggle for share and manage the brand for profit. This will mean withdrawing investment which does not provide immediate payback and reducing to a minimum management time devoted to the brand. The cash generated by the brand will be redirected to new product development and building premium brands for the company.

This treatment will eventually run the brand to such a low level that it must be divested (though the tenacity and profitability of brands with a small group of loyal users can be surprising). In the time between taking this brutal decision and divesting, the brand will be fulfilling a useful financial role and helping to secure the long-term future of the company. If the brutal decision is fudged, the same brand may stagger on for years, holding off decline but at the same time costing the company resources.

(8) Niching

It is more profitable to be number one in a small market, than to be number five in a big market (see Table 11.3). Smaller brands can be profitable if they dominate some defensible segment of the market.

Table 11.3 *Profitable niches: size of market related to average profitability*

Size of market (million dollars)	Business performance %
0–50	28.1
50–100	26.8
100–250	24.2
250–500	22.4
500–1000	20.6
over 1000	10.9

Reproduced, with permission, from D. Clifford and R. Cavanagh, *The Winning Performance: How America's High Growth, Midsized Companies Succeed*, Sidgwick & Jackson, London, 1985, p. 54.

The idea of niching is that a small brand or small competitor can pick off a distinct part of a market. All its efforts, for example in product reformulation, packaging and advertising, are focused on serving the one segment (niche) uniquely well. Its aim is to create a little pocket of profitability that is either difficult or uneconomic for competitors to usurp. Schweppes holds its own in the global soft drinks market, by dominating a sophisticated niche with its bitter tonic and up-market mixers (though it suffers from retail imitators).

Niching is only possible under certain, quite restrictive, conditions. In all cases survival depends on being able to charge a premium over the mainstream alternative, and on the size of the niche remaining small.

Thus the most sustainable niche strategy is usually at the premium end of the market, where image plays a part, and a (relatively) high price tag can be seen as a positive reinforcement of preference. In many FMCG areas the unit price of goods (such as jam, honey, or mustard) is so trivial that a proportion of affluent shoppers can afford to pay even double for a premium offer. In other product fields (such as beer, health foods, and beauty aids) some consumers like to feel they have discovered a smaller and less 'commercial' product. Thus the value of the product is linked to being small and less well known. In such situations, relatively small companies or brands can hold out in markets where economies of scale are important in the mainstream sector. A niche strategy confers on the company the status of that niche, which is an asset that a large competitor has trouble imitating. Equally important, it is hardly worth while to do so, given the size of the niche. The best solution for the mass producer is to buy the niche player.

For niche players, profit must be pursued rather than share. If share starts to dominate and prices are dropped, the niche player finds themselves back in the mainstream market where it is difficult for them to compete.

A ninth strategy, not to be ignored, is to drop the brand without further ado. Simplifying ranges, focusing management effort, and reducing the number of brands to force onto the supermarket shelfspace are some of the advantages of fewer lines. Brands can be dropped in countries where own label is strong and still promoted in countries where they have more of a role.

Managing second-tier brands demands a flexibility, imagination and entrepreneurial spirit that is rather different from the diligent, efficient management that has been developed to support premium brands. For second-tier brands the brand paradigm no longer holds, and there are no formulae or rules for their management. In one case it might mean looking for corporate buyers, in another it might mean creating an exclusive package for a single large retail client. Eight suggestions were listed above, but there are no doubt further possibilities. The essence is to look for opportunities that fit with the resources of the brand.

11.1.4 Private Label, Industrial Strategies

In certain countries retailers are determined to increase the quality of their own label to improve profits and customer loyalty. In the UK about a third of groceries are sold under own labels and this proportion (after sometimes faltering) is still increasing. The rest of Europe is heading in the same direction—own-label sales in Europe grew by an average of 11% per year between 1987 and 1993.[4]

This means that own-label competition is pressing painfully on brand leaders as well as on more marginal national brands. At the same time, there is correspondingly greater potential to sell high-quality goods to retailers, and to gain better margins than in the past. Quality retailers are seeking brands which will make their customers loyal, and do not price their own labels at the bottom of the market. The producer saves money on consumer marketing, and thus goods which take this route to market can often be priced competitively for their quality and still earn good margins.

For successful premium brand manufacturers with spare capacity or highly efficient production, this industrial market offers increased volume and extra revenue. For some squeezed-out manufacturers who can no longer create sufficient consumer-pull to sell their brands, selling on the industrial market directly to retailers is the only viable option. Competing for mindspace against larger competitors involves enormous investment and expertise, and with the rise of market-oriented retailers, a more efficient source of consumer reassurance and mindspace has become available. As we saw in Chapter 4, going industrial is a way of coping with hypersegmentation: team up with a retailer who can provide low-cost umbrella branding. It is equally a way of avoiding competing directly against the efficient retailers. Smaller manufacturers, crushed in their fight with the premium-brand owners, may have no alternative.

Own label has developed to a level where every producer has to make an objective strategic assessment of the private label opportunity. Too often providing own label becomes a highly charged emotional issue within brand-oriented companies. The first necessity in developing a rational approach to producing for retailer controlled brands is to de-emotionalise the debate.

11.1.4.1 Dilemmas and Downside Risks

Providing own label has often been seen as a dilemma: the choice between doing or letting a competitor do. Some manufacturers feel that all would be better off if nobody provided own label, and thus doing so is a betrayal. Own-label contracts have been opposed on the grounds that providing products to retailers could demoralise employees, be picked up by the media and eventually upset brand users. This dilemma is now generally dead—brand manufacturers have already lost their cartel in FMCGs. Indeed, most FMCG companies already provide own-label to some degree. There is only a dilemma if the manufacturer will itself make a noticeable contribution to improving the quality of own label. Thus P&G, Mars, Kellogg's, Gillette and Coca-Cola all refuse own label contracts, while Unilever, Pepsico, Nestlé, Heinz, Playtex, Ralston Purina, Hershey, RJR Nabisco and McCain are among the majority who do.[5] The question now is the degree and approach.

In the past, own label was often approached in an opportunistic way, mainly as a chance to increase volume. This can lead to difficulties, for example, if the branded business picks up and the spare capacity is no longer spare. Own label can then end up competing with brands for production capacity or necessitate unbudgeted extra shifts. In addition, costing of opportunistic own label is usually lax and may not take into account subsequent demands of the retail client, for example for formula modifications, new pack forms and so on.

A company aiming to operate profitably in the growing industrial/own-label market, has to approach it as rigorously and strategically as the consumer market. A decision to service the industrial FMCG market is a decision to make major, irrevocable, investments. To give value (which is the only way to succeed) implies developing low-cost production (capital investment) and a most efficient supply chain. It means being able to innovate to retailers' requirements. Lead times have to be fast: in some cases six weeks between the retailer request for a new line and its arrival on shelf, complete with tailor-made packaging, and launch display. Previous success in brand marketing does not guarantee that a company will be able to make a success in this new discipline.

Own-label strategy is a different ball game from consumer marketing. Many companies (Danone, Unilever, UB) feel that the own-label market should be dealt with by a separate organisation. Brands and own label should be separate profit centres to avoid conflicts over allocating overheads. Even production may be best separated. Common production facilities can lead retailers to question the costs of producing the branded version, based on their knowledge of the costs of production of the own label.

Separate management for the industrial business helps to avoid conflicts between the brands and the private-label business. These can arise over use of production capacity or use of technology—should the own label get new developments, and when (retailers can be very demanding of R&D).

For companies with successful premium brands, the greatest risk is that they end up competing with themselves. They need to ensure that they will be able to retain a superior technical quality for their brands. If their excellent industrial product ends up cannibalising their excellent brand, their brands will lose their mindspace—the company's true raison d'être. This note may be diffused by setting up a separate own-label organisation.

In addition, successful private label and brand strategies need very different core competencies. A manager who excels in the low-cost, efficient execution of retail demands, may not be the best at mindspace management and all the rest of consumer marketing. Management needs to specialise in different skills, and not have to share time between the two. This reinforces the idea that the two activities should be managed separately.

11.1.4.2 Levels within Own Label

A purely industrial company (or division of a consumer company) can focus solely on efficient production and logistics and become a low-cost producer for retailer controlled brands (type-1 or type-2). Such companies aim only to understand trade marketing, and the needs of their retail customers. They leave the consumer marketing to their retail partners.

In countries or distribution channels where retailers are less sophisticated, there is also room for industrial manufacturers who can provide consumer understanding and brand management skills in addition to efficient production. Teaming up with a retailer who can provide umbrella branding, shelfspace and in-store support, but who needs help in product innovation and managing these assets optimally is an opportunity for some 'squeezed-out' manufacturers. Cott Corporation, mentioned in Chapter 8, has expanded impressively by providing quality own label, with brand management support, for retail clients. In 1991, Cott had four customers; by 1994 they were supplying 44 US supermarkets and mass merchandisers (including Wal-Mart, Safeway, Fleming, 7–11, Lucky Stores) and starting to supply supermarkets in Europe. Revenues rose from C$43m in 1990 to around C$1 billion in 1993.[6] These sales have been largely taken from brands, and more will be taken. Cott found a gap in the FMCG market, left by manufacturers' slow adaptation to the changed market situation. Cott's success indicates that retailers find brand procurement and management (i.e. developing type-2s) sufficiently arduous and labour intensive, that they are willing to buy it in.

11.1.4.3 Conclusion

Own label is a necessary strategic issue to face. It is not an easy market, compared to the branded one, and is different. For a company with the right resources and philosophy, own label can be an opportunity. On the other hand, the commitment and investment to make a success of industrial marketing might drain and destroy a consumer-oriented company currently just able to subsist from its brands. For companies which are exceptionally strong in their technological delivery or which operate in markets where manufacturers have many mindspace advantages over retailers, the right decision may still be to concentrate single-mindedly on building their consumer franchise.

11.1.5 New Product Development

The most frequently repeated conventional wisdom about new products is that the failure rate is huge. The second most frequently quoted piece of conventional wisdom is that new products are vital for a company's long-term success. According to one authority, companies which lead their industries in profitability and growth get 49% of their profits from products developed in the previous five years, compared to 11% for the least successful.[7] Innovative new product development also keeps down retail competition (recall Fig. 8.2 page 183).

Thus finding and sifting new product winners is both risky and essential—a company has to do it and has to do it well. Consumer companies might improve their new product development success rate if they put more effort into creating retailer value as well as consumer differential advantage.

In Chapter 8 we looked at the areas where retailers could provide branding efficiently and the areas which they found more difficult. It follows that developing new brands in some areas (prestige, novelty) is going to be relatively more viable and profitable than others (crispbreads, spaghetti sauce).

It is only sensible to steer clear of areas where retailers have the advantage. For example, Campbell's Soup Co. launched a line of fresh salads and soups, under the brand name 'Fresh Chef'. The products were shelf stable for only one week, which meant that Campbell's had to predict the consumer off-take of each line very exactly. This proved impossible.[8] Retailers are in a better position to react quickly to shopping information and are therefore the natural managers of fresh brands such as this.

If the technology for a new product is protected (through patent, investment cost or secret) a new consumer brand in the old tradition is still the most effective approach. For example, L'Oréal's launch in 1992–93 of a new hair colorant called 'Casting'. The product was based on an innovation which creates a much longer-lasting colour than any other non-bleaching, one-step colorants. This is a communicable benefit, that consumers desired: a halfway house between permanently dying hair, and tints which rinse out with a couple of washes. Advertising, and the reassurance of the L'Oréal umbrella brand, backed up Casting's technical superiority to win a loyal clientèle. Such a new product has every chance of success based on consumer demand.

A genuine innovation, these days, is one that a retailer (i.e. industrial supplier) cannot copy—such as that of Casting. If a new product has no uncopiable consumer benefit, the traditional branding approach will no longer work. Branding used to allow pioneers to gain some protection even if their innovation could be copied. Me-toos from manufacturers would find it less easy to gain mindspace or shelfspace. In a situation where retailers are also competing, branding no longer provides the same degree of protection. If the me-too is provided by a retailer (as a type-2 own label) then retailers will throw the weight of their shelfspace, their shelf layout, their pricing structure and their merchandising behind the me-too in favour of the original.

New products have to be presented to the retailer to gain shelfspace: retailers are increasingly demanding to see projects at a more precocious stage. At the same times, the same retailer is looking for innovative new products for its own brand. A football team might as well take their opponent's reserve to act as their goalkeeper. The retailer does not see its double role as unfair, arguing that a genuine innovation is one which a retailer cannot rip off.

In some FMCG areas it may be that the only people able to introduce new brands in the future will be the retailers who don't have to pay for shelf space up front. Since retailers demand such high margins and/or payment for introducing new products, they are already often the only ones to profit from a manufacturer's launch.

Johnson Wax launched medium-priced bath additive Tahiti in the UK. The brand was aimed at the 'gap' Johnson Wax had measured between expensive brands such as Badedas and Fa, and own label. It turned out that the trade were quite happy for such a gap to exist, as this gap was to the advantage of their own brands. Tahiti was eventually withdrawn. Unigate developed a range of dairy products targeted at children. In consumer tests the concept and name—Safari—got the thumbs up. Retailers gave the idea of a whole new range entering their crowded chilled cabinets a definite thumbs down. These concepts are too easy to copy: if retailers want them they will procure them for their own brands (surprisingly quickly). Against this Häagen Dazs and Müller have managed to launch successfully into the premium ends of ice-creams and yoghurt. Retailers may welcome manufacturers who stake out and maintain a high-price brand as a reference point. Indulgence and luxury are also areas where retail image has yet to reach, and against which retailers can contrast their good-value position.

Manufacturers have to develop new strategies for getting a fair price for their not-so-innovative innovations. Developing a new product in the pre-1980s mould, doting it with a launch budget and slotting allowances only to see it being copied by retailers and other manufacturers does not achieve this; a better use of innovations might be to incorporate them into existing brands.

When a manufacturer launches a new product these days, it should be as confident and knowledgeable about the likely trade reaction as it is about the likely consumer one. New products have to be successful not just in consumer appeal, but in trade appeal. Does the new product have a positive category effect?

Is it physically easier to handle? Or does it take up less space in store than an existing product? New product development must be a joint effort between 'trade marketing' and 'consumer marketing'.

It is amazing that books on brand marketing, and new product development agencies, do not yet (as of 1994) seem to have adjusted to the importance of retailers. For example, Novaction ('World Leaders in Brand Engineering Experience') base their models for predicting new product success exclusively on measures of consumer acceptance.

A double filter may seem to imply that testing will knock out a greater proportion of new brands—even fewer will get through the whole process. But this takes too narrow a view of the manufacturer's potential sources of business. Retailers such as Sainsbury's have dramatic new product development ambitions but even Sainsbury's cannot maintain the resources or experience of specialist manufacturers. Marks & Spencer are famous for their new product development partnerships with suppliers. What we are seeing is the marketing part of manufacturing organisations being partially duplicated within retailers. In a manufacturing company the marketing department liaises with R&D to create new products. Now it is the marketing department of retailers, armed with considerable knowledge of consumer wants, who are seeking to match the demands with products.

Precociously sharing a new product concept with retail partners may feel a little like placing one's head in a tiger's mouth. If the retailer likes the new concept it may swap its hat from retail partner to competitive brand marketer, and come out with a similar new product itself. The point is that it would have done it three months later anyway.

A manufacturer with an idea for a new product should go to the trade with an answer to the question: 'Why shouldn't we launch that ourselves?' The answer might be:

(1) because we are the only manufacturers who can make it, or market it (in the next, say, three years)
(2) we are already working on your own label version, somewhat different, to be launched three months later
(3) you can have it as an exclusive own label on these terms.

One way of providing branding is via retail reassurance. If the new product is of a type where retail reassurance is the most cost effective, manufacturers should seriously consider marketing the brand via a quality retailer, or selling the idea to a retailer for him to develop as a new brand. Some large manufacturers already sell off NPD projects that do not reach their own benchmarks to retailers or industrial suppliers. The same logic applies to potential me-toos: the own-label route may be the most economical. The manufacturer still has to ensure payment for its technical skills, but approaching the market in partnership with a powerful retailer may be a surer route than the risks of a traditional launch.

An example of this strategy working is given by Heinz. Heinz, a world force in soup, never managed to prise the US soup consumer from Campbell's. After a valiant attempt to do so, Heinz decided to take the own-label route to market in the USA. Given their technical quality, Heinz found market-oriented retailers ready to market their soups at prices reflecting both the quality of the product and the cheaper route to market.[9] (Heinz takes a much harder line to own label in the UK.)

Manufacturers are finding that retailers can create mindspace more efficiently in some product fields. New product development is simply a particular case of this general rule. Retailers can launch certain new products more cheaply, and with lower cost for failure. This means that manufacturers should concentrate on areas where they have advantages over retailers for creating branding. The output of mundane product reformulation, may best be brought to market via retailer-controlled brands.

Manufacturers hold, and will continue to hold, unique reserves of consumer and product understanding. Both retailer and consumer wish to benefit. New product development is about finding the best way to make them pay for these skills.

11.2 MANAGING RETAILERS

In the first half of this chapter we have argued that manufacturers' brand marketing strategies must be influenced by the business strategies of the retailers through whom they are marketing, and with whom they are competing.

We talked above about managing brands: it also makes sense to ask whether the manufacturer can, in various ways, manage the retailer. We look now at three ways of doing this. The first avenue we explore is the potential for reducing retailers' ability to take over mindspace. The second is the scope to reduce concentration, or at least to reduce the effects of concentration: the divide and rule principle. The third is category management: making an effort to become more sensitive to the retailer's perception and choice of brands to stock, and so to produce and promote brands which the retailer will really want to sell.

11.2.1 Mindspace and Concentration

Essentially there are two threats posed by retailers to manufacturers. These are mindspace and concentration. Mindspace matters because, at the end of the day, this is the resource that makes manufacturers' brands non-substitutable and 'unavoidable' to the trade. Concentration matters because it makes the threat of delisting so dramatic for the supplier, that it becomes hard to call the retailer's bluff, even on the most powerful consumer brands. Concentration makes certain retailers 'unavoidable' for manufacturers.

11.2.1.1 Mindspace Control

Suppliers of premium brands can thrive alongside a retail trade that provides type-1 own label, including hard discounters. Low-quality retail brands compete primarily with tertiary brands, and operate in the low margin sector of the FMCG market. The pain starts when own label increases in quality. When the quality of retailer brands matches or surpasses that of premium brands, and retailers use advertising and quality packaging to support their type-2 own label, premium brands find it difficult to justify their premiums, and even their existence.

As retailers compete for consumer trust, some manufacturer brand positions become untenable. Quality national brands with weak consumer differential advantages can be viable as me-toos to leading competitor brands or accepted by selling-oriented retailers as a mechanism for controlling power brands, or simply because the manufacturer pays for shelfspace. Such a brand can end up with no raison d'être in the eyes of a marketing-oriented retailer. The quality manufacturer then has to look at new strategies for marketing these 'pushed out' brands (see above).

Wouldn't it be nice to distract these quality retailers sufficiently that they gave up their brand-building efforts?

Retail competition

Retail competition, which retailers seem doomed to be unable to control, is a great ally of manufacturers.

The orderly market created by a type-2 own label (including fresh products) approach is attractive to the leading chains, seeking a profitable way to compete with each other. However, if the leading chains move too far upmarket, with their loyalty-creating high-quality own brands, they can sow the seeds of their own destruction. While a selling orientation tends to weed out the weakest competition, orderly competition with its high margins tends to foster expansionist ambitions and attract new entrants.

Retailers are natural hostages to the 'grow or die' business mentality. More and bigger outlets means having the critical mass to develop successful type-2 own label; it means a national presence for advertising and is the main tool in the location game. In the UK, between 1985 and 1992 Sainsbury's and Tesco expanded their selling space by over 40%. Both project this expansion to continue into the next century.[10] The expansionist dreams of several companies in a static market must eventually lead to a reality of head-on collision. The overcapacity beast is out of its cage ready to chase its makers into selling strategies once more.

High margins are also dangerous because they attract new entrants. If the leading stores become preoccupied with higher quality and competing with manufacturers for mindspace, they leave the bottom end of their market open for hard discounters. Many top retailers spend huge media budgets behind the proposition that their own labels are better value because they cut out all the marketing machinery (including advertising). The hard discounter's story 'we cut out all inessentials to give you extreme value for money' works as well against quality retailers as the quality retailers' own-label claim does against brands.

These new lean, mean players may be independent start-ups or international arrivistes (such as Aldi, Netto, Norma and Lidl) or current players looking for market niches for a second string (Food Giant, Pioneer). The effect of a hard discounter placed within the catchment area of a profitable superstore can have an extensive impact, a 'chain' reaction, one might say. The store near to the discounter is likely to lose a proportion of its sales. Some shoppers will switch completely while others modify their shopping habits to include occasional trips to the discounter. Losing, say, 10% of volume poses such a threat to the quality store that it feels compelled to react on basic items by reducing its prices. This creates an imbalance in price between the quality store and other (quality) competition within its catchment area. Thus, other stores, placed further from the original hard discounter, are in turn forced to react, and a spiral towards lower prices has begun.

However, it is an ill wind that turns none to good, and retail overcapacity and price competition has the potential to help manufacturers. Overcapacity implies that on average consumers have more options when choosing a store and a poorer retail industry is less able to carry out the brand-building, mindspace-accumulating activities which endanger quality manufacturer brands.

Why price wars help manufacturers

Forced to fight on price (and we have shown this can happen to any mass retailer), retailers become too distracted by operational concerns, and too poor, to cultivate a high added-value marketing approach. If they reduce the prices and quality of their own label to fight the price war this plays into the manufacturers' hands; if they use big brands to fight the price war this too plays into the manufacturers' hands. It is only the quality retailer brand approach that really threatens the power base of suppliers.

A good example of this is Tesco's reaction to price competition in 1993. In August, Tesco launched a range of own label called 'Value Lines' at a quality below that of their type-2 own label, but, above all, at extremely competitive prices. From the perspective of retail competition the initiative succeeded, more than turning around Tesco's slight market share loss of the early summer. On the mindspace front Tesco probably dropped back five years.

Comparing June to December 1993, share of own label increased from around 40% to 50% by packs, but only from 43% to 45% by value.[11] This implies that the own label being sold in June 1993, was on average, sold at a price index of 108%, a premium of 8% compared to the average product. In December, it was sold at a discount: at 90% of the price of the average product. If Tesco could play that manufacturer trick of dissociating itself from its brands (see Coca-Cola/Schweppes and Cresta, p. 260) this would be less important. In fact, most shoppers will identify Value Lines as Tesco's own label, and their experience will influence their perceptions of the umbrella brand 'Tesco'. Cheap own label will take sales primarily from quality own label (brand extensions target primarily their own users) and from cheaper brands, because they target the price-sensitive shopper. In this situation, premium brand owners should sigh with relief and plan new advertising campaigns focusing on all those qualities and specific functional claims that they do so well.

When retailers make an effort to promote quality brands, they take share and, in the longer run, mindspace from premium manufacturer brands. This effort costs money, particularly in the number and quality of employees devoted to product development, procurement and brand management. This is a heavy investment in a market as competitive and price sensitive as retailing.

In a situation where retailers are forced to neglect their brand-building activities and to make price comparisons with their competitors, their mindspace building activities are likely to suffer. Cheaper own-label strategies are likely to make smaller and cheaper (tertiary) brands suffer, but at the same time, will hurt premium brands less. In the battle for mindspace manufacturers can hope for, and perhaps encourage, periods where the trade becomes distracted by price wars and cut-throat retail competition.

11.2.1.2 Divide and Rule

(1) Shopping habits

The more retailers succeed in concentrating shopping, the more power they have. A shopper converted to less frequent, one-stop shopping forfeits the right to choose favourite brands.

One-stop shopping is the ideal for the retailer: 100% of the shopper's expenditure, and the shopper cannot compare prices. The only actions a one-stop shopper can take against the non-stocking of a preferred band is to switch brand or defer purchase. The retailer is in a strong position to switch the sale to an alternative brand, which suits it better. This gives it more power in negotiations with manufacturers. Conversely, shoppers who distribute their expenditure across several shops, and who make more shopping trips, increase the competitive pressure between stores and increase the manufacturer's power in negotiations.

Much of the marketing effort of retailers is designed to create store loyalty. It is the fear that their shoppers will switch shop which makes retailers stock larger ranges of brands, and stock popular brands.

Given these simple observations, it seems surprising that, to date, manufacturers have paid relatively little attention to the shopping habits of their consumers. Even if such information does not lead to action to change the trend, it helps to anticipate the increasing power of certain chains, and to be aware of the relative strength of different stores, in different countries, among different social groups.

(2) Information on shopping behaviour

The starting point for brand marketers when asking how to promote their brand is the brand decision made by the consumer. For example, is it rational or emotional, is it sole or joint, is it lengthy or impulsive, what is the influence of price. These are the questions to ask to understand the competitive struggle between manufacturers.

The competitive struggle between the manufacturer and its distribution often implies understanding shopping behaviour. Both need to be aware of the determinants of store choice and shopping frequency and in-store behaviour. There may be segments of shoppers who visit a greater variety of outlets: what attitudes encourage one-stop shopping and what encourages shopping around? For different segments of shoppers and different product categories: what is the level of planned purchases and what is the level of planning (brand, product category)? How do consumers choose in front of the shelf, what is the value of different shelf positions, and the position within the store? Most importantly, what happens when the brand is out of stock. Who are shoppers? How do young shoppers differ from older ones, richer from poorer, men from women? The Marsh Super Study identified three types of shopper: stock up (more than 35 items), routine (cherry picking, 11 to 34 items) and fill-in (fewer than 10 items), and showed that their needs, shopping habits (e.g. time of day, number of stores visited regularly) and demographic profile all varied.[12] They spent an average of, respectively, 39, 23 and 11 minutes in the store. Pretty snappy decision makers.

(3) Retail structure

As retail structure went from high street to large out-of-town stores, retailers' power to railroad consumer choice increased. However, as superstore coverage reaches saturation point, the quasi-monopoly power of some units will come under attack. Repertoire shopping across retailers or the availability of products through alternative channels of distribution, represents a major constraint on retailer power.

One-stop, infrequent shopping is encouraged by large out-of-town stores. This mode of retailing has grown at the expense of others, but this new form of retail outlet must have a limit. Certain items (bread, vegetables) have to be bought regularly, and don't merit a trip out of town. Items will be forgotten on the major trip, and be needed urgently. In addition, the size of shopping trolley and car boot put some limits on the bulk-buying logic. This means that in the stable state, out-of-town superstores will not have the whole retail market to themselves. The old-style town centre supermarkets are not complementary competition to superstores, some new concepts in retailing seem likely to arise.

This something new can already be seen in convenience chains such as 7–11. Mail order, direct mail and telephone shopping are other forms of retailing which both fit in with modern life (time flexible, convenient) and can benefit from information technology. Their appeal to date has tended to focus on high value and fashion, but is also being developed for heavy or bulky goods. Milk, beer and soft drinks, pet food, potatoes and disposable nappies are currently hauled back from out-of town supermarkets often by tired women after a day's work. There is clear potential for services which deliver bulky commodities to the home, or direct to the car boot, say, on the way home from work. Manufacturers should encourage all types of outlets to spread their ranges, e.g. groceries in drugstores and pharmacies or in mail-order catalogues.

It is quite possible that these alternative methods of delivery (convenience stores, home deliveries) will be developed by large supermarket chains. However, it would be in the interests of manufacturers either to secure alternative distribution channels themselves, or to encourage third parties interested in developing them.

Often these third parties will be other retailers, or distributors who already have access to many consumers: petrol stations, mail order or credit card companies, DIY shops, video libraries. Their differential advantage will be location and convenience, and they will need brands to reassure on quality.

A retail structure which results in high competition will mean both small margins on power brands, and greater fear of the effect of stock-outs. Just as competition among manufacturers works for the retailer, competition among retailers works in favour of manufacturers.

(4) Promotions

Promotions, and especially price promotions, lead to brand switching. Continual promotions teach consumers to look for bargains and are often thought to reduce brand loyalties. As brand loyalty gives power to manufacturers, control over promotions may be a way for retailers to reduce manufacturer power.

Promotions may be perceived as coming from the retailer or from the manufacturer. Thinking about building loyalty, the retailer should prefer the consumer to feel that bargains are offered thanks to the store and are less available in other stores. A manufacturer planning promotions should favour those likely to build longer-term loyalty to its brand. For example, a common type of promotion asks consumers to collect coupons printed on the boxes of the product. Such a promotion might demand that the consumer buys six promotional packs within a limited period. This is a brand-oriented promotion which demands brand loyalty (over six purchases). Conversely, another common form of promotion is free product 'three for the price of two', etc. This is likely to rake sales from other brands, but leave the consumer looking for a new offer the next week. In addition, this promotion is more likely to be presented to the consumer as an effort made by the store, rather than by the manufacturer. The store may go so far as to calculate and display the delivered 'price per unit' to be compared to the regular price in stores without the promotion.

(5) Support weak retailers

The development of efficient retailers was for many years welcomed by manufacturers. The efficient stores were the best customers, shifting greater volumes per location, and using the most up-to-date logistics and re-ordering systems. With hindsight, it is even possible to say that large manufacturers helped and encouraged the development of retailers capable of competing for mindspace, and accounting for such large proportions of sales that they become 'unavoidable' to the manufacturer.

In sophisticated markets it is not unusual for 20% of retail accounts take 80% of a manufacturer's business. Manufacturers are inclined to see these large retailers as their 'best' clients, as well as being their worst competition. Using a cost-based pricing approach these clients are sold products at the lowest prices. This enables them to offer lower prices and work towards being in the 10% of retailers who account for 90% of business in the near future.

The larger shops offering the lowest prices move consumers towards one-stop shopping. Within the bounds of financial prudence, manufacturers have an interest in combating this trend and encouraging promiscuous shopping behaviour.

There has to be a balance between encouraging the concentration in retailing which offers manufacturers economies in logistics, and accepting some cost inefficiencies in order to strengthen their strategic position. For strategic reasons, retailers who are losing money and customers should in fact be encouraged and supported by manufacturers, helped with their marketing, and helped to become more efficient.

Manufacturers should be hesitant in actions which encourage greater and greater concentration in retailing, even though they may help overall logistics and administration costs. This is especially important in a time when short-term cost reductions are important. Manufacturers sometimes have to accept some cost inefficiencies to further their long-term power position versus the trade.

(6) Favour brand sellers

Independent discount chains can develop their credibility with well-known brands (as Colryt do in Belgium, Dia did until 1993 in Spain and Kwik Save did until 1992 in the UK). Similarly, for their own reasons certain large chains (such as Auchan in France and Asda in the UK) have, at certain periods, adopted strategies of stocking a wide-range of national brands. In a competitive retail marketplace, such a store is at a natural disadvantage: consumers can compare all their prices across stores. Thus if all stores are treated equally (and not strategically) by manufacturers, these stores will have a tough time. It makes sense in the long run for manufacturers to support such store propositions, rewarding their loyalty to brands. The availability of competitively priced national brands and wide choice may influence the consumer's demand for national brands in other parts of the retail trade. In sophisticated markets the large 'mindspace' chains may take a strategic stand of their own against the manufacturers who favour the 'brand' stores. Manufacturers should begin their strategic action before the mindspace retailers are strong enough to counter-attack.

(7) Consumer advice

'Basket' prices which show all the retailers to be close together on price encourage shoppers to go one-stop. Most price comparison research tends to concentrate on a 'basket' of goods. It would be interesting to the consumer to see not just this aggregate figure, but how much money could be saved by constructing this basket from the lowest prices offered in two or three stores. Consumer promotions should be alternated through time with different retailers, to teach consumers the benefits of shopping around. Similarly, it would be in the manufacturers' interests to vary prices for different brands across retailers.

11.2.1.3 Managing Retailers Internationally and for the Future

The stance of retailers varies by channel within national markets, and varies markedly between geographical regions. Across Europe, an international producer will face the full range of retail postures, from type-2 mindspace retailers, through huge selling-oriented retailers to small chains and 'Mom and Pop' stores. In most of Asia, the retail developments seen in the West have not yet happened, and own label is virtually unknown. For the foreseeable future there will remain significant portions of the retail trade whose business objectives are to promote manufacturers' brands to consumers in various competitive and convenient ways.

Since manufacturers are so much more international than retailers, they have the opportunity to learn in some of their national markets and apply their experience in the less sophisticated countries.

Faced with the rise of the retailer in the USA and north-western Europe, manufacturers have tended to be reactive and even slow. With this experience, manufacturers are equipped to take a much more proactive stance with retailers developing in southern Europe and the rest of the world.

Manufacturers are unlikely to be able to organise collective action. Individual action might be easier if the general principles involved were widely appreciated by all large manufacturers, and, for example, publicised and promoted by manufacturer associations. The general principles are to:

(1) keep the 'value' gap small or filled
(2) develop alternative channels, and smaller chains
(3) favour channels who concentrate on promoting brands.

In markets where 'mindspace' retailers are already strong, manufacturers can hope for a swing back to price orientation and can try to influence shopping behaviour to reduce the effect of retail concentration. Apart from this they are left to redeploy weaker brands as best they can and concentrate on areas where they have not lost control of mindspace. In areas and channels where mindspace still lies with the manufacturer, they should be able to manage the value balance, slow down retail concentration and encourage the retailers who promote brands, sufficiently never to get into a battle for the consumers' mindspace.

11.2.1.4 Internationalisation of Retailers

If large international manufacturers intend to manage retail development throughout the world, they need to be aware of how their sophisticated retail partners are developing their international interests.

Faced with saturation in their local markets, a number of major western European retailers are seriously pursuing international expansion. Internationalisation would allow these retailers to grow and to diversify their risk, to counterbalance the power of large multi-national manufacturers, and to leverage their competencies (logistics, merchandising, store concepts, and own label) into less sophisticated markets.

As with manufacturers, there are three routes: organic growth, acquisition and alliances.

A number of retailers have tried to cross borders with their existing formulas, with varying degrees of success. Carrefour is an interesting example. Their attempt to introduce their hypermarket concept into the USA, UK, Belgium, Holland and Germany were severe flops. The same strategy took off well in southern Europe (Spain, Portugal), South America (Brazil, Argentina) and the Far East (Taiwan, Vietnam). Promodes, another large French retailer has also met success with organic expansion in southern Europe and south-east Asia. It is reasonable to conclude that taking a more sophisticated retail model to a less sophisticated retail market starkly improves the chances of success.

Hard discounters have expanded even across sophisticated markets. The formula seems to have wide enough appeal to take a viable share in all markets, and having an established culture and expertise in cost cutting, plus relations with efficient industrial suppliers, can give enough leverage to compete against local competition. Even so, a master hard discounter such as Aldi, has struggled to establish itself in Denmark, and expanded less quickly than initially projected in the UK.

A faster route, and one which overcomes some of challenges of adjusting to the local situation and managing from a distance is to acquire an existing chain. In the USA for example, Sainsbury's has bought Shaws, Delhaize, A&P, Food Lion and Tenglemann. Ahold, the number one retailer in Holland, has developed a retail network through the north-east and east coast of the USA by purchasing a whole series of retail companies: Tops (New York); Finast (Ohio); Edwards (New England); Giant Food (Pennsylvania, Maryland, W. Virginia, Virginia); Bi-Lo (Carolinas, Georgia); Red Food Stores (Tennessee). In 1993, Ahold's US sales were 94% of those in Holland, with profits in the US greater than those of the parent company.

Most acquirers prefer to leave the existing management in place, unless there are significant problems. The synergy comes from sharing with the incumbent management the techniques and philosophy of the acquirer.

The third channel for spreading retail sophistication and concentration around the world is through alliances (see Table 11.4).

Table 11.4 *Examples of major European buying groups operating in 1994*

Name	Companies	Countries
Eurogroup	GIB	Belgium
	Vendex	Holland
	FoodRewe	Germany
	Coop Schweitz	Switzerland
Associated Marketing Services (AMS)	Ahold	Holland
	Argyll	UK
	Casino	France
	Migros	Switzerland
	Dansk Supermarket	Denmark
	La Rinascente	Italy
	ICA	Spain
	Kesko	Finland
	Mercadonna	Spain
	Hagen	Norway
European Marketing Distribution (EMD)	Markant	Germany
	Markant	Holland
	Socadip	France
	Zev	Austria
	Selex Iberia	Spain
	Selex Gruppo	Italy
	Uniarme	Portugal

Compiled from information taken from Patrick Molle, *Le Commerce et le distribution en Europe*, Editions Liaisons, Paris, 1992.

Ahold, Argyll and Casino (all members of AMS), have gone so far as to swap financial participation in each other (an action similar to those sometimes taken by manufacturers in different national markets). They concede that their integration into one transnational group could be a long-term goal.

Buying groups exist to share technology, know-how and information on manufacturers' conditions, to exploit opportunities for parallel importing of and joint negotiations on major international brands, and to co-operate in own-label development.

Compared to the international presence of major manufacturers, most buying groups are loose coalitions, with limited scope for concerted action. In some ways, implicitly or explicitly, they reduce the potential for their members to expand internationally organically or via acquisition.

In the race to globalise, and the aim to manage the FMCG industry globally, manufacturers are many steps ahead. On the other hand, retailers have come a long way in 50 years, and clearly intend to keep up the pace through the next 50. The challenge for manufacturers will be to stay ahead and to avoid financing the retailers' international expansion as they financed their expansion in national markets.

11.2.2 Efficient Consumer Response

Manufacturers must view retailers as mindspace competitors, and thus efforts to manage and limit retail power are crucial. However, of at least as great interest is the possibility of co-operation and joint gains.

Efficient Consumer Response (ECR) is a range of initiatives directed at making the whole supply chain, up to consumer purchase, optimally efficient. One pan-European study[13] estimated the overall potential benefits to be 2.3–3.4% of retail sales. A similar study in the US put potential joint gains at around 11 percentage points of retail sales, achievable within 2–3 years.[14]

One of the most visible and topical aspects of ECR is optimising the efficiency of the logistics chain. The ECR ideal is a smooth paperless flow of information from the consumer, back through the store to the supplier, and a smooth, rapid, flow of product through a minimum of warehousing, back to the consumer. EDI (electronic data interchange) is an essential part of the system, both for efficiency and speed, and progress in the technology available makes this currently an exciting and promising activity. However, this is only one half of the ECR concept. In particular, it is the part that is likely to diffuse to all manufacturers and retailers over time. That is to say, it will provide limited sustainable competitive advantage in the long term.

The other half of ECR, with considerable competitive interest in the long term, is to provide every shopper, on every buying occasion, with the optimal assortment, the optimal products, the optimal range of prices and the optimal promotional and marketing activities.

The optimal range varies by type of outlet, and will clearly evolve over time. As new products continually inflate the store's and shopper's choice: optimising means paring the range down for retail efficiency, while maximising the consumer's satisfaction and potential purchasing.

New product development sensitive to retail needs was discussed above. ECR would aim to take this a step further with the possibility of joint development. The costs and disadvantages of classic test marketing (retail co-operation, media and advertising production costs, the lack of secrecy or speed) are growing. A significantly more efficient and faster way of testing is available through a retail partner.

ECR also means maximising demand through co-ordinated promotions by retailers and manufacturers. It means optimal efficiency in pricing, couponing, merchandising, sampling. For example, information available to retailers can make sampling operations more tightly targeted, and thus save waste. Figure 7.4, page 161, showed the tiny proportion of distributed coupons actually redeemed; 97% are wasted paper and wasted distribution, much of which should be cut out. Direct marketing efforts would benefit from being jointly planned by manufacturers and retailer. Manufacturers have experience to share, retailers have more detailed information on shoppers, and access.

Many of these initiatives are more strategic than co-operating over logistics. In many cases, retailers will not be able to co-operate to the same degree with more than one supplier per category. Thus the 'marketing' half of ECR is of great interest to manufacturers in their competitive struggle with one another. Since initiatives often need to be undertaken at the category level (the retailer views FMCG market in categories), we now look at category management, a subject of growing importance in most FMCG companies.

11.2.2.1 Category Understanding

Category *management* is the buzz word, but category understanding might be a better goal. Category management seems to assume that the manufacturer can still walk into the store and arrange *its* category in the way that *it* believes will give the greatest benefit to the company and to the retail partner. As such, category management is getting itself a bad name among retailers. 'Preserve us', they plead, 'from producers preaching predictable prescriptions: present our products preponderantly and proliferate your profits! . . . Preposterous prejudiced propaganda.'

Category understanding should be undertaken as an effort to see the market from the retail point of view, and thus to offer brands which retailers will wish to stock. There is a clear analogy with consumer marketing. The idea is not to sell (to retailers) what you can produce, but to produce what you can sell to retailers. From a retail point of view each brand must have a logic with respect to the category.

A manufacturer taking a category-based view of the market understands the role of the category within different chains and different store formats. Different retailers will have widely different category objectives. The objectives of Sainsbury's in the UK, will be different from a hard discounter and different from a major chain in Italy. The role of own label, the retailer's technical sophistication, the retailer's size and the size of its stores will affect category objectives. Retailers' marketing aims—price positioning, quality positioning, growth objectives, margin objectives will affect its 'ideal' category.

(1) Retailers Objectives

The retailer has three objectives when selecting categories, and the products to create the category: First, to provide a satisfactory shopping experience for shoppers. An interesting analogy for this is how the developer of a shopping centre tries to attract the right mix of stores to the centre.[15] The developer will want a big-name supermarket, a major chain store, say, some upmarket boutiques, and services such as shoe repairs, a newsagent and a popular fast-service restaurant. It won't just be the outlets with the highest profit per square metre that will be selected; units will be chosen to create a good shopping mall, and arranged for the shoppers' convenience. Within this overall plan, each outlet has to optimise its own return.

Similarly, a store must offer the right categories, in the right place in store. It must define its categories in a way that seems natural and helpful to the shopper. A category (such as a staffed delicatessen) could be less than normally profitable on a margin per square metre basis, but justify its space on shopper satisfaction and store ambience.

The retailer's second priority is to maximise satisfaction, revenue and profits from each category. A well-planned category will satisfy the largest possible proportion of shoppers, actualise every potential sale, and prompt unplanned purchases. Profits will be affected by the mix of sales: the range should price discriminate, satisfying price-sensitive customers while earning higher margins from quality-sensitive shoppers. For many retailers, category planning involves promoting their own label brands, both for strategic and margin reasons.

Thirdly, all retailers seek to maximise efficiency by limiting and simplifying the range of products handled. This objective usually works directly against the other objectives, but limiting customers to a smaller range sharply reduces a retailer's costs in handling, inventory and shelfspace. Profits per square foot will usually be increased by reducing the space taken by a category.

Achieving these three objectives will depend intimately on the situation of each individual store. Even within a chain, stores can vary enormously in size, and by type of area (poor/affluent, old/young, retail competition). The category has to vary accordingly—there can be no catch-all solution to the question of category planning.

Category planning implies understanding the role of the category within the store, and the brands within the category. At the store level, for example, the importance of the category in forming store image: how range sensitive are shoppers with respect to this category, and how price sensitive? How can the category as a whole be managed to improve store revenues and profits, the effects of greater shelfspace, position in store, promotions, merchandising?

Within the category, what is the optimal combination of brands to cover the maximum of buying intentions, the optimal price structure for price discriminating without losing sales. Retailers want to know the most efficient way to reduce SKUs to the amount of space available, and to reduce inventory to a minimum. At the brand level, what is the most common price reference point for the category? How price-sensitive are consumers within the category? What is the overall category effect of destocking various brands, and how can the impact of scaling down the range be minimised?

(2) Manufacturer's advantage: specialisation

Clearly, category management is a priority for retailers themselves, and manufacturers have to recognise both the retailer's expertise, and its right to organise its store in accordance with its understanding of its shoppers' desires. Shoppers' desires may easily differ from the natural layout imagined by manufacturers. Producers are organised by product area, whereas consumers may shop, for example, by meal. A retailer may have trouble putting fresh steak, frozen chips, prepacked salad and salad dressing next to each other, but it is worth thinking about. Consumers are used to the product category layout initially set up by product manufacturers, but retailers should be free to experiment with layouts influenced by the patterns of purchases made together, or by certain segments of shoppers. A market-oriented store should ask what layout is ideal for its shoppers, ignoring which supplier it gets its products from.

Within categories stores will have their own general category plan, which will become familiar to their consumers. For example, a store may always place own labels at eye level, premium brands above, tertiary brands below. They cannot then welcome 50 manufacturers each recommending an independent 'ideal' format for 'their' three square metres.

Manufacturers do, however, have a role to play in category planning, because they have particular advantages. They can synthesise their experiences across the different stores they serve, both nationally and internationally. They have the critical mass to make it worth while to carry out consumer research both on the segments which must be covered and on buying behaviour in store. In particular it is worth while for a manufacturer to analyse the retailer's scanner data for the category, even when it is not economic for the retailer to do so in each of its many categories.

The retailer is interested in the consumers' behaviour in each of the two or three hundred categories offered by a large retailer. Quite clearly it is never going to be worth while for each store, or even each chain, to look at all the interesting analyses possible in each category. For a manufacturer, concentrating on a small set of product categories, it is worth while to carry out the detailed analyses on the retailer's data, if the retailer is willing to supply the data. The manufacturer can relate in-store data with the information collected from consumer research: how consumers choose in this category, which consumers choose what, which brands compete most closely with each other, and which command the greatest brand loyalty. This data is valuable to the category managers at the retailer, but due to their lack of critical mass in each category, they do not have budgets or the personnel to discover the information for themselves. It is cheaper to run the same analysis for ten different stores, than for one store to devise and carry out ten different analyses. Since the retailers have this data, and since both could benefit from its analysis, but only the manufacturer has the specialisation to make it worth while, some form of co-operation is on the cards.

(3) Differential advantage through category management

Category management will no doubt spread to all FMCG companies, in the same way that consumer marketing has done. Even so it will be an ongoing source of advantage for manufacturers who understand it particularly well.

The 'ideal' category will evolve with new retail objectives and formats, with new products, with consumer tastes and behaviour. Manufacturers have the opportunity to develop a competitive understanding of category mechanics, in the same way that developing a competitive understanding of consumer brand preference gives a sustainable lead in consumer marketing. (Indeed, the two are related.)

Being the *first* to initiate a category management approach can be particularly useful. The advantages of the pioneer are in terms of category definition and in sharing data.

If retailers can be encouraged to view the category in a certain way, they may be unwilling to change their definition of the category subsequently. It is a natural advantage for a manufacturer to be able to define the category to fit with the areas in which it is present and strong. For example, many products are to do with cleaning the house. These range from polishes, cleaners for wood, floors, glass, baths, carpets, oven and kitchen, through to bleach, and household chemicals (distilled water, dry-cleaning fluid, hydrochloric acid) toilet cleaners, stain removers, air fresheners, sponges and cloths, rubber gloves: the first manufacturer to discover and plan the most efficient organisation of this area will have some scope in making the necessarily arbitrary decisions about what to include.

The advantages of category management are especially noticeable for manufacturers who have the good fortune to dominate small categories (such as air fresheners or shoes care) as retailers are likely to concentrate their limited category management resources towards large areas such as, say, soft drinks and hot beverages. Johnson's Wax claim to have created advantages for themselves over competitor Reckitt & Colman, by becoming the recognised expert in category management in their area.

Category management has to aim at the ideal of sharing data with retailers (within the bounds of common sense). This again is a reason for being the first rather than the last manufacturer to implement category management. Retailers are more likely to be persuaded to co-operate on data sharing with the first offer which demonstrates clear advantages to both parties, and be less interested by subsequent proposals. A combined retailer–supplier initiative within a category could test and develop different displays for different types of stores, relating category composition to store characteristics such as size, profile of catchment area, local competition etc., and could work out the impact of each brand on category sales, with advantages to both parties. The advantage to the manufacturer in being able to see which brands are most attractive on a category basis is that it will manage its brands from a category strategic point of view. A category perspective might suggest new products to the manufacturer, new forms of display, pinpoint areas where competitors are weak or suggest alliances with other manufacturers, or brands to buy to strengthen its category position. Above all, it will want this information before its competitors.

(4) Category management and smaller manufacturers
'Category captains' are recognised by retailers as having the greatest knowledge of consumer behaviour and category mechanics in the area, and usually will have the most comprehensive range. Retailers believe that stocking this company's range, backed with their consumer understanding for positioning, merchandising, pricing, shelf allocation etc., should optimise category sales. This opportunity goes by default to the dominant manufacturers, e.g. Gillette in shaving, Kellogg's in cereals, L'Oréal in hair colorants (in Europe).

Smaller players, who recognise that they cannot call themselves category captains, have to take a different tack. It is still essential to take a view of the category, to see how their brands fit in the retailer's assortment. There is much talk of preferred supplier status. This usually means selecting a particular retailer or group of retailers in which to invest disproportionately, and thus provide them with support (e.g. promotional) or services that increase the value of the brands to them. However, this also implies to some extent de-selecting some other retailers, which could reduce overall distribution.

Another approach might be called category lieutenant, where a smaller supplier looks to complement the category captain by providing niche brands in areas where the captain is weak, and perhaps offering me-toos to the retailer who wishes to reduce the dominance of the category captain. An alternative view of the category, and alternative brands which put pressure on the category leader are welcome. No retailer wants to be dependent on its largest supplier.

11.2.3 Organisational Implications

If structure is driven by strategy, and strategy is driven by the market situation, then the dramatically new 'matrix market' must have some impact on the organisation of FMCG companies.

The exact impact will depend on how the company plans to respond to the new challenges, and also on the existing organisation and company approach. Changes in organisational structure, and in the power vested in different parts of the organisation, will generally come about gradually, as an evolution towards more effective management. It is clearly fatuous to try to recommend some ideal organisational structure, or a plan for bringing it into being. We shall limit ourselves to a few observations.

11.2.3.1 Route to Market and Category Management

Company organisation has for a long time juggled with the dimensions of brand and country. Most large companies have some sort of matrix organisation which aims to harmonise brand management and international management, while giving enough autonomy to countries or regions to adapt to their consumers' desires. Now these organisations are being asked to adapt to cope with a third dimension.

This third dimension is the vastly complex area of retail customers. Somehow another priority, developing and serving the companies' 'routes to market', has to be integrated with brand and country management. The trade perspective must become embedded into the company's decision processes, as the consumer and international perspective already have been.

Developing a trade marketing capacity alongside consumer marketing skills is only a halfway solution. If a trade marketing function is simply bolted on to a consumer marketing organisation, the assumptions of 'consumer is king' and 'brand-centred marketing' are not questioned or altered to deal with the changed situation.

The 'route to market' function cannot be left to consider the trade in isolation from the consumer. A more integrated decision process is required. Planning the company's product categories to satisfy the various distribution channels, will impact on brand management. Managing premium brands and developing mindspace among consumers clearly will remain a primary goal for most FMCG companies, but the changed market demands an outlook and organisation that harmonises the trade and consumer approaches.

Integrating the trade marketing view and the consumer marketing view will affect many elements of the marketing mix.

Packaging has to be designed for supermarket handling as well as consumer appeal and in home use. Merchandising has to appeal to the shopper passing quickly by and to the store manager assessing it in the context of marketing, objectives, store, EPOS (electronic point of sale, i.e. scanner) system. Pricing has to be planned in terms of a trade price objective and a retail price objective. The organisational structure must foster communication and harmony between the executives dealing with trade and consumer demands.

Retailers and consumers do not always want the same things, and sometimes they want conflicting things. The challenge is to integrate trade marketing with consumer marketing without throwing out the baby (usually a brand) with the bath water.

11.2.3.2 The Route to Market Function

The sales and account management in the company is really in the centre of the changes which are taking place, and will certainly end up being the most affected. The relationship between sales and other parts of the organisation, the responsibility and skills of sales personnel, and the stature, weight, and scope of their discipline are all destined to change.

It may be that the route to market structure should become a parallel function to brand management, with both structures finally reporting to an overall authority, perhaps by category. Decisions balancing strategy towards the trade and brand strategies must be made at a level where both are integrated.

The company must have an overall category strategy. This means defining and implementing the chosen category role: captainship, lieutenant or preferred supplier and assessing and planning the brand portfolio from the retail perspective.

The route to market function would ensure customer value (at retail level). Logically, this would imply having responsibility for all the functions involved in bringing the products to the customer (physical distribution, wholesale and retail trade, logistics, administration) for a particular product category, because these functions create value for retail customers. This makes the route to market function very broad and more sophisticated than that of current sales and national accounts managers. New skills and know-how are necessary to manage the strategic triangle (customer value, profitability and dependence), and to represent the needs of the trade within the company and to co-operate with the consumer franchise management. Profit responsibility, for example, is not usually part of the sales or account function at present.

The route to market function is the company's main contact with the trade. It should develop an expertise on its market comparable to that of brand management's understanding of consumers. It should be able to predict which retailers will last, which will provide profits in the long term, which are growing. If more favoured deals or exclusivity are to be given, what is the relative worth of each retailer. The function must balance the importance given to the 'non-large accounts' and alternative distribution channels. These routes might provide opportunities for future development and a strategic balance against the constantly increasing power of the largest accounts.

The 'route to market' function would have to connect up internationally, both to share information and to respond to retailers and retailing at an international level.

11.2.3.3 Geography

The need to market to distributors can be a countervailing force to globalisation or internationalisation. Consumers in two different countries may be more similar than trade. Retailers in the USA are generally less concentrated than in Europe. In some European countries retailers have become very serious marketers and brand controllers; in others, retailers are in a 'selling phase'. These differences have significant implications for manufacturers, and their approach to the trade. Retailers are national, or even regional, and so route to market strategies must often be national or regional. Consumer marketing has become very interested in looking for synergy, opportunity and economies of scale across borders. The company has to consider ways of integrating these two different geographical perspectives.

The different local tastes of consumers can actually help manufacturers deal with international buying groups of retailers. Buying groups and alliances can work for global brands, but fall apart once the retailers all want nationally differentiated products. Thus, globalising products makes the internationalisation of retail buying more possible and likely. Conversely, marketing to the different needs of retailers in different countries, is a way to counter international buying groups.

11.2.3.4 Brand Management

Keeping both eyes on the consumer is critical for FMCG companies. Understanding consumer needs and developing of consumer mindspace is still the core activity of management. The idea of separating out and emphasising the task of route to market, also has the purpose of leaving the more traditional role of consumer marketing to focus on the consumer.

Brand management has to become more flexible. A distinction should be made between premium brands, value brands, second-tier brand managements, and, if appropriate, private label. Each needs their specificity and culture. There should not be a brand paradigm that is applied willy-nilly, year-in year-out to any branded product owned by the company. Top brands have to be handled differently from second-tier brands and industrial brands (i.e. own label) because their market situation is fundamentally of a different nature. Companies should not just put junior people on smaller brands, and give them smaller budgets. The separation of power brand and second-tier brand management recognises the different approaches and competencies required for the two tasks. The role of second-tier brand managers often involves expertise in wider business, financial and cost control areas, and a greater emphasis on tactical and trade marketing.

In particular, some process of review defining realistic management for each brand, by country, is essential. Depending on the power of the brand, and the country, sometimes brand management should have more say, and sometimes category considerations should dominate. The reviewing committee should not be afraid to drop pushed-out brands in countries where the retail trade is a mindspace competitor.

The role of 'premium' brand managers is not only to build their brand but also to be involved with the international aspects, as these are the brands most likely to be looking for scope beyond national borders. Brand management also has to dovetail into the category strategy which uses the full potential of the company's brands.

11.2.3.5 Private Label

Fitting private-label management into a company's organisation raises difficult questions. There are good arguments for creating a separate function, with an independent director. This approach forces the private-label business to be totally accountable for its profitability. It ensures appropriate costing and overhead allocations for private label and that the competition for production and R&D resources are more explicit. This structure is also suggested because private label business needs very different core competencies than the brands' business. Management that is single-mindedly driven by low cost and efficient execution of retail demands may not be compatible with mindspace management and all the rest of consumer marketing.

However, private-label business has an impact on the company's consumer franchise, its route to market and its overall brand portfolio management. Therefore the views of these disciplines have to be represented in development of private label strategy.

11.2.3.6 Market Research

Current market research tends to focus on how consumers choose between brands, the importance of product attributes, the effects of advertising, promotion and price in swaying choice. This type of research is brand driven, and brand financed. As we saw above, trade management and brand management both need to learn all they can about the consumer as shopper. For route to market managers, shopping behaviour is a fundamental influence on their customers' business and market strategies. For brand managers, shopping and in-store behaviour intimately affects brand choice and brand loyalty.

Data should be collected on shopping habits, by account and by area to understand better the degree of distortion likely from the retailer, and the power of different stores and retailers to sway brand choice. Some shoppers prefer one-stop shopping, and are loyal to one store. Who are they? Are their numbers growing?

Which retailers have most of these shoppers? Or which geographical areas? Currently few manufacturers have a clear understanding of how shopping habits vary in the population, or which shoppers follow which patterns. More research needs to be done on in-store behaviour: the role of the category within the store, behaviour in front of the shelf. The decision process in front of the shelf is currently less well researched than the formation of absolute brand preferences. This suggests that much current research implicitly assumes that the consumer decides on a brand and then goes shopping. This may have been more nearly the case when shoppers read out their lists at a counter and the grocer packed up their bags. That hasn't happened for 30 years.

In-store consumer research has immediate application to trade marketing, but should be used in conjunction with trade research: how do retailers see the role of the category within their stores? How do they believe the shopper behaves in front of the shelf?

Nielsen-type data and consumer panel data needs to be analysed store by store and account by account. Aggregating across retail outlets is a brand-management-oriented habit.

These are all straightforward issues for which many manufacturers should get the same quality information as they currently have about consumer preferences and behaviour.

Notes

(1) Bill Saporito, 'Behind the tumult at P & G', *Fortune Magazine*, 7 March 1994, pp. 49–54.
(2) Royal Ahold, Annual Report, 1992.
(3) 'Food industry survey', *The Economist*, 4 December 1993.
(4) 'Euromonitor Strategy 2000 Report', Reported in *Marketing*, Haymarket Publications, 30 September 1993.
(5) *Supermarketing Magazine*, 29 April 1994, p. 28.
(6) Don Daniels, Robert Kaplan and Ray Goldberg, 'Cott Corporation: Private Label in the 1990s', Case history, Harvard Business School, 1993, and private communication with Cotts.
(7) Thomas P. Hustad, editor of *Journal of Product Innovation Management*, quoted by Christopher Power et al., 'Flops', cover story, *Business Week*, 16 August 1993, p. 34.
(8) VP in charge, Mr Baum, quoted by Christopher Power et al., 'Flops', cover story, *Business Week*, 16 August 1993, p. 34.

(9) Interview with Anthony O'Reilly, CEO Heinz, given to *Aim Magazine*, published by A.C. Nielsen, Vol. III, No. 1, 1991.
(10) Economist Intelligence Unit, *Retail Business Quarterly* trade review No. 20, December 1991. These plans have subsequently been modified downwards.
(11) Judith Passingham, quoting figures from AGB's TCA Superpanel, 'Own label and the store wars', *Admap*, March 1994.
(12) 'Marsh Super Study', presentation to the First Annual Marketing and Merchandising Forum, Nice, France, October 1991.
(13) 'Supplier-Retailer collaboration in Supply Chain Management', Project V, The Coca-Cola Retailing Research Group, Europe, May 1994. Research involved 127 major European companies.
(14) Efficient Consumer Response, FMI, Washington DC, January 1993.
(15) Glen A. Terbeek, 'Why category management will fail', *Progressive Grocer* special report, Part 2, September 1993, p. 11.

Index

Numbers in bold type indicate illustrations